Pleasure

...ure's in my car
...in the bars I'm searching.
...he love that's strong
...thing in the song I'm learning
...m learning.
...ure's in the sand
...m within the hand she's holding.
...asure's on the screen
...ventures at nineteen, I'm searching
...m searching in my heart.

mayhem s

bring drink

9.3.79

5.

23.1.86 PARIS To ...
La Tour Eiffel vue du Tracadéro
SALON INTERNATIONAL
DE L'AGRICULTURE
PARIS
de Versailles
18 Mars 1986
PARIS
Mr + Mrs KEMP
love Gary + Martin
XX
image in   editions   63, rue Fg St Martin, 60300 Senlis
Photo J.L. Staincq, agence Vloo Tél. 1 48 59 68 49

SPANDAU BALLET
BLITZ
24.1.8

True.

I know this time it's true.

And a pill on my tongue,
...if I have to write the next ...
...to be said?

...y heart.

...left him !

I KNOW
THIS MUCH

To Finlay, Milo and Kit

I KNOW THIS MUCH

From Soho to Spandau

GARY KEMP

FOURTH ESTATE · London

First published in 2009 by
Fourth Estate
An imprint of HarperCollins *Publishers*
77–85 Fulham Palace Road
London W6 8JB
www.4thestate.co.uk

Visist our authors' blog: www.fifthestate.co.uk
LOVE THIS BOOK? WWW.BOOKARMY.COM

10 9 8 7 6 5 4 3 2 1

A catalogue record for this book is available from the British Library

HB ISBN 978-0-00-732330-2
TPB ISBN 978-0-00-732943-4

Designed and typeset by seagulls.net

Printed in Great Britain by Clays Ltd, St Ives plc

Mixed Sources
Product group from well-managed
forests and other controlled sources
www.fsc.org Cert no. SW-COC-1806
© 1996 Forest Stewardship Council
FSC

FSC is a non-profit international organisation established to promote the responsible management of the world's forests. Products carrying the FSC label are independently certified to assure consumers that they come from forests that are managed to meet the social, economic and ecological needs of present and future generations.

Find out more about HarperCollins and the environment at
www.harpercollins.co.uk/green

Photographs not credited below have been supplied by the author. The author and publisher are grateful to the following for permission to reproduce their copyright material.

The Same Band – courtesy Ian Fox; first Blitz gig – Derek Ridgers; Steve Strange – David Johnson; Waldorf hotel – Herbie Knott/Rex Features; St. Tropez – Jean Aponte; HMS *Belfast* – Virginia Turbett; Botanical Gardens – David Johnson; Steve Dagger – Graham Smith; Casablanca club, Top Of The Pops backstage – Neil Mackenzie Matthews; at the Kemps' house – Martin Kemp; New York – Neil Mackenzie Matthews; Ibiza – alanolley.com; Kemp family, Liverpool Empire, True tour – David Johnson; Parade tour Gary, 'baroque 'n' roll' – Denis O'Regan; Barricades tour – Patrizia Savarese; Charlie Kray, 'being Ronnie' – Richard Blanshard/Miramax; Gary and Lauren – Nick Harvey; Jonathan Ross show – Brian J. Ritchie / Rex Features.

While every effort has been made to trace the owners of copyright material reproduced herein, the publishers would like to apologise for any omissions and will be pleased to incorporate missing acknowledgements in any future editions.

*'I have nothing to say, entirely, simply,
and with solidity of myself,
without confusion, disorder, blending, mingling.'*

Montaigne

*'The annoying thing is that critics in twenty years
time will probably write a great, nostalgic, dewy-eyed
retrospective on how good it was in these clubs in
London and how these innovators were doing this
that and the other.'*

Steve Dagger (*Sounds*, 1980)

*'Time, he flexes like a whore,
Falls wanking to the floor;
His trick is you and me, boy.'*

David Bowie

I stand opposite the house. I've come here for something – ghosts maybe – but what can I possibly expect? Others hold the key. I feel hurt by its silent disregard. The old step, shaped from children's play, looks deserted now, unattended, no longer the stage it once was, and sadly smaller. Looking up, I can just see through the first-floor window, the window nearest the pub, the pub now gutted and boarded, empty and silent. There's a shaft of light on the far wall of the room that reveals its size, and suddenly the geometry unfolds and begins to take shape: the two single beds pushed against each wall; the large walnut wardrobe; the Arsenal scarf hanging like a smile on the moon-landing wallpaper; and the square hole my father made in the wall to keep a caring eye on his sleeping babes. To the left, a small boy with a new guitar now sits on his bed. I should know him but he's hard to see, hard to define, so many years have distorted him. But now I can hear the lively piano coming from the pub, the pub that spills people, all noisy and lewd with Christmas beer, into the cold street. I try to ignore them, to experience the guitar, strange in my hands, but the celebrations outside disturb my concentration. Laying it down on the bed, I cross over to the window to see what it is.

And suddenly, there I am.

There are moments in life when your entire confidence depends on the coordination between you and an inanimate object. Symbolically, and actually, the problem was a noose around my neck. Every time I knotted my tie the pointy bit was either above or below my waistband – too long and I felt like an accountant, too short and I resembled a Soho bartender. I rip it off again, wipe the back of my hand across my forehead and try to steady myself before another attempt. I'd earlier decided to go for the pink Turnbull and Asser shirt, freshly depinned, but I'd changed my mind and broke sweat struggling to remove my cufflinks in order to change into the more sober, white one. Pink had looked too presumptuous; a little cocksure. I don't want to give that impression.

Unfortunately clothes had always been an obsession. As a boy there had been my snake belt and Trackers, with their compass-in-the-heel bonus, then tears spilt over desired Ben Shermans and Budgie jackets; two-tones; brogues; toppers; the thrill of my first Bowie loons; cheesecloth; plastic sandals; mohair jumpers; Smiths; straights; high-tops; GI chic; loafers; kilts; Annello & Davide ballet pumps, and all the madness that was the eighties dressing-up box. The event determines the clothes, but the execution of putting them on prepares you for it, and right now I'm suffering from nerves and in a bit of a state about the length of my tie.

I struggle with the knot in the mirror and wonder if any of this really matters. What the hell am I thinking about! My hair's freshly trimmed but my face looks tired and drawn from lack of sleep. Last night I'd woken again to play out potential moments from the trial in my head and had not slept since 4 a.m. God, this isn't working! A flush of insecurity pours into my chest and I feel sick down to my knees, but the doorbell rings (was that it earlier?) and I pull up the heart-shaped knot, throw on my jacket and coat and head downstairs. My tie will have to do. So, I hope, will my truth.

Ian Mill fills the room. Not just physically – he has a large, well-stocked frame, a picture of his own success – but also in terms of his character – a Pickwickian presence born of public-school confidence and class. 'Spy' should have drawn him for a Victorian issue of *Vanity Fair*. He picks up a handful of folders from his aching desk, buries them into his obediently open briefcase and, with a swipe of his hand, clears his barrister's wig from the table, places it on the top of the folders and closes his case with a snap.

'Gentlemen?'

I wonder if he'd put the tonal question mark after 'Gentlemen' for other, more suspicious reasons. Here, in the theatre of law, stands the last bastion of the class system. Accents are prepared and nurtured, polished and loaded, before being sent out to pronounce judgement upon the fools of the world. I gaze through the window on to the red-bricked Inns of Court, survivors of the Great Fire of London and the Blitz, serving as historic reminders of the eternity of order. I find a certain comfort in all of this, and a genetically encoded forelock is being pulled as Steve Dagger and I follow Ian and our team out of the chambers and into the cold bright day that lights the Inns with a nostalgic beauty. As we walk towards the court I feel myself locked into a crashing inevitability and envy the otherness of passing people, on their way to meetings, coffee, loved ones. But Ian bestrides the Strand and it's all I can do to keep up. We are about to enter his arena.

The Gothic, grey-stone edifice that is the Royal Courts of Justice could be the grand entrance to Oz, overdressed with multiple arches and varied ornate carvings, with a dark spire that points its righteous finger to heaven. But people don't come here to ask for a heart or courage, just judgement, and, of course, some money. Outside, a pack of media jostle for a statement and some pictures, and I submit myself to the hungry lenses, suddenly relieved that I hadn't gone for the pink.

We pass through security, and make our way to Court 59. I dread my first meeting with the others. Will it all seem ridiculous when it happens? Will they drop the whole thing on seeing me and realise how preposterous it all is? We arrive at a tiny anteroom and Ian vanishes, leaving Dagger and me, and my two young lawyers, feeling temporarily rudderless. He returns dressed for his performance: wig pressed snugly over his boyish blond waves; white barrister bands tight around his pink neck, and a flowing, long black gown. I feel sick again and wish I'd never read *Bleak House*.

He resettles his wig; it seems to be focusing his mind. 'Try to sit at the front. Good to be seen clearly by the judge.'

Our Queen's Counsel, Barbara Dohmann, arrives – a small, middle-aged German woman whom I'm glad to hear is referred to in the business as 'Doberman' – and we shuffle into the aesthetically neutered courtroom. I'm relieved to see that the others aren't here yet and, following Ian's thrusting finger, we slide on to the front bench. Dagger squashes up to my right. This is the man who'd helped to create Spandau Ballet; who has lived, breathed and dreamt it as much any one of us. The rejection he has suffered would have been just as painful, the accusations worse.

He prods me, and with a nod points out their barrister, our adversary, Andrew Sutcliffe. Sharp and feral, his thin nose hovers importantly over his opening statement and I wonder how much pleasure he anticipates from my destruction. Beyond him, in the public seats, I notice some familiar faces – long-term followers of the band: fans. They look excited as they settle into their spaces and arrange their bags between their legs. Next to them are members of the press, notebooks and pens appearing from mucky pockets, and I can feel them begin to scrutinise me and I wonder how you look when you're about to be sued out of your home.

The courtroom door opens; a sudden hush of voices from outside, and, turning, I catch my first sight of what they call the plaintiffs, the men who've brought me here, the same men that I'd known as boys, that I'd embraced a thousand times, that I'd lived a young man's dream with: John Keeble, Steve Norman, Tony Hadley – men who had been my friends. I want to say hello – it feels ridiculous not to, we've known each other since school – but they avoid my gaze as they sideways-step into the bench at the back of the room. I'm surprised by John's rock-'n'roll-flavoured peroxide hair, a recent statement of his commitment to the cause. I was probably closer to him than to any other throughout the whole extraordinary ride. I manage to catch his eye but he rejects it and sits between Steve and Tony. The press start to scribble. They can sense fear. To them, we must have the distressed look of people who've swum too far out to sea.

The fifth member of the band is missing – my brother. Only recently recovered from two brain operations to remove benign tumours, he is now – thankfully – forging a career as a successful TV star and has rightly chosen to avoid the court. But I have with me, in my heart, his blessing.

Two young clerks with over-gelled hair and oversized tie-knots arrive with trolleys teetering with box-files. Wheeling them to the front of the courtroom, they casually unload the fifteen or so numbered boxes across the long console table directly in front of me. I quickly understand what they contain. Within them lies my life: cuttings of articles, interviews and photographs; letters and faxes; contracts – a yellowing, fading potpourri of our history to be judged by bewigged, gowned men from another world. All had come to this. Inside those dull boxes lay the innocent faces of five young working-class lads from London, living the greatest story they could have wished for, a story that is about to be told in the many different ways they remember it.

I suddenly realise how familiar this all is and feel sure now that it will drag itself through to the bitter end. This, after all, is another show. We're finally back together again; and the music will be played, and hearts will race. Here, surrounded by a crew of helpers and advisers, with a stage to stand on and an audience to listen, Spandau Ballet is once more the headline act.

'All stand for the judge.'

A stooped-looking clerk, the judge's toadying roadie, makes the announcement from the dais and we noisily obey. The stenographer crooks her fingers over her keys as though she's about to start a concerto, and Mr Justice Park, middle aged, thin and grey, but with gown flowing dramatically behind him, enters stage left and takes his central seat.

As I watch this powdered pomp begin, it occurs to me that the court is pure theatre. With its cast of goodies and baddies, it is improvised, emotional, and although without a predetermined denouement, as sure as in any good Greek tragedy there'll be a grand judgement from above, a winner and a loser, and before then, an awful lot of dressing up.

CHAPTER ONE

WAKEY WAKEY!

It began with an unwanted Christmas present. The year previously I'd been given a lunar landing module – well, a six-inch one, but I could hover it over a grey plastic moonscape with such grace and stability that my ten-year-old mind felt the primal thrill of power rushing through it. You controlled the landing by aiming a fan-gun at the module's attached balloon while issuing orders in a croaky American accent with lots of 'beeps' thrown in between the commands. What the 'beeps' in space-talk were for I was never quite sure, but they had something to do with adventure, bravery and the future that we now lived in. American accents were a must if any boy were to cut the mustard in an Islington playground and have any level of cultural credibility among his peers. Whatever the asphalt fantasy, it usually demanded you being an American, be it a Thunderbird, a superhero, or one of the Rat Patrol. I even did James Bond in American.

Apollo, though, was everything. The Christmas before, my family had all sat spellbound in front of our small television as *Apollo 8* vanished into radio silence around the dark side of the moon, a phrase coined especially for a child's imagination, and we waited, gripped, for its return. Man had never been so far from home and those men had taken my imagination along with them. Sitting in awe, new presents suddenly ignored, we listened to Commander Jim Lovell, floating in a black sea of risk, reading to us across the void from the book of Genesis. The following summer I was woken early to see black-and-white ghosts walk upon the moon. My father cried. We watched it over and over until the morning came and the magical moon faded from outside our window.

My lunar module also needed a bit of space to be successfully manoeuvred and in our front room that wasn't easy. It would often catch its leg on the net curtains. But if I were careful with its flight I could edge it along the drinks cabinet, with its purely ornamental minia-tures and solitary bottle of Stone's Ginger Wine, over my father's *News of the World* as he read it, past the budgie, perched proprietorily on the paper's edge, and down over the floral-patterned settee towards the moon surface in front of my father's slippers, while trying not to go too near the heat of the glowing electric fire with its shadowy flame effect. The right side of the plastic coals had, sadly, broken, but the other side benefited hugely from the spinning device that created the 'flames' and added a greater sense of homeliness to our lives. One electric bar out of the two was always cold and ash grey whatever the weather, thus saving my parents the money to buy toys for their two boys, like Lunar Land-ing, or guns that shot ping-pong balls around corners.

But on this Christmas morning of 1970, no toys appeared for me. My younger brother Martin was rapidly tearing the wrapping off the presents that had been delivered soundlessly into the pillowcase he'd left at the foot of his bed. My pillowcase, on the other hand – and to my horror – was empty. My father winked knowingly at me and left the room while my mother helped Martin eagerly unwrap an endless procession of gifts. My toy was obviously so huge it couldn't fit into any pillowcase, but my heart sank as Dad sheepishly returned with something clutched awkwardly to his chest: a guitar. He looked as though he were about to dance with it.

'We thought you'd like this,' he said, turning it around in his hands. I found it hard to hide my displeasure. It wasn't even wrapped.

'We saw you playing with your cousin's toy guitar and thought you'd like a proper one.' He could see he had some convincing to do and held it out gingerly towards me.

My childhood felt over. Was this to presage a future of socks and underpants for Christmas? I accepted my fate, took the guitar and sat it in my lap. It smelt of polish. Furniture smelt of polish, not Christmas presents; this was something adult, belonging to a world I wasn't sure I wanted to enter yet. My arms clumsily wrapped themselves around its curvaceous body with its two 'F' holes like mournful, drooping eyes. Scratches on its tobacco-brown skin revealed that I wasn't the first. It had its own story and I immediately felt pity for the thing – it was made to play beautiful music, but it had found itself in the hands of a disappointed child.

Nobody in the known history of the Kemps or Greens – my mother's family – had ever played a musical instrument. I had attempted the descant recorder for one term, until I found myself at a junior school concert standing in a pool of my own drool while playing 'Sloop John B'. A dripping recorder does not do much for a young boy's standing among giggling schoolgirls.

But we were the proud owners of a radiogram – an old-style record player-cum-radio that fitted my mother's brief of looking like a piece of furniture. When this highly polished example of veneered technology was not in use, it became a plinth for chalk ornaments, frogs made from seashells, and a miniature glass lighthouse filled with coloured sands from the Isle of Wight, all placed strategically by my mother on lace doilies. Our record collection was sparse and mostly never played: a Frank Sinatra anthology that had lost its inner sleeve; a rollicking Billy

Cotton album of innuendo-filled music-hall standards called *Wakey Wakey!*, plus some random Matt Monro, Patsy Cline, and Dave Clark Five singles, some of which had lost their centrepieces. To play these, one would have to place the record as centrally as possible upon the deck, and then suffer the wow and flutter as it gradually ellipsed in ever-expanding orbits around the spindle. The radio part of this dual wonder was more often used, and appears quite vividly in one of my earliest memories.

October 22 1962 was six days after my third birthday. My memory starts with my father leaning into the radiogram and tuning into the one o'clock news. He'd come home from work on his 'dinner break' but was agitated and I must have felt this as I'd followed him across the room, attempting noisily to get his attention. I watched as, hushing me, he stared hard at the amber-lit panel, hungry for the information its warm, authoritative voice was delivering. And then Dad said, 'There might be a war.'

I can assume that his statement shocked me, even at that age, as why else should it be so deeply branded upon my memory? So real was the nearness of the last war that even as a three-year-old it was a concept I had already began to grasp – and fear. But I suppose what stunned me most of all was that first shocking experience of witnessing my father's vulnerability. My superman, the one whom I thought I could absolutely rely on for constant protection, was frightened. Something one day might slip through the protection of our perfect world and destroy it, and even he couldn't stop it.

It was the Cuban Missile Crisis and, of course, the man who could save the world had an American accent. Kennedy never joined the list of heroic characters that I tirelessly embodied in the playground, but his assassination the year after became another early memory, primarily because it stopped the TV and instead of *Top Cat*, *The Beverly Hillbillies* or *Supercar*, I was forced to stare at a photograph of him, silently being broadcast across the channels.

I was born at St Bartholomew's Hospital within earshot of St Mary-le-Bow's bells on 16 October 1959. No one seems to remember at what time, for like all things to do with childbirth or war it was never spoken about and eventually forgotten. I was brought home to a house in Islington that was more connected with a Victorian past than any nuclear present. It belonged to an era of austerity that was yet to taste the 'white heat', or even the white goods, of the technological revolution. It seems hard to imagine now, but this central-London dwelling would not have electricity until 1960, when my father and his brother finally connected us to the modern world, so I must picture myself entering 138 Rotherfield Street by the yellow shroud of gaslight.

My father, Frank, had lived in this early nineteenth-century terraced house since 1945, when, as a fourteen-year-old, he had moved there with his father and mother and his brother, Percy. His two sisters had already moved into their own marital homes, while his older brother, Bill, was away fighting in Burma, a war from which he would never fully recover, or mentally leave, until his death in 2008.

I have a picture of my paternal grandmother, the wonderfully named Eliza Ettie Ruth Crisp, taken in 1912 when she was aged sixteen. Her large, moon face looks slightly bewildered by the photographic situation she's been thrown into. She's dressed in the high white collar, lace apron and bonnet of a girl in service – a maid. She sits, her hand resting awkwardly on a book – undoubtedly under the direction of the studio photographer – giving her the look of being caught reading during a break in work. I can just see the book's title on the spine and I take a magnifying glass to discover what it might be. It leaves me a little saddened and with a feeling that she's been slightly humiliated as the title's two words enlarge into focus: *Stickphast Cement*. Of course, it would be a surprise if Eliza had ever read or owned a book other than the family Bible.

My paternal grandfather, Walter, wounded out of Flanders, had become disabled from his work at a veneering factory after a swinging tree trunk delivered itself into his shrapnel-softened leg. Jobless and desperate, he and Eliza created and ran a business from the kitchen of the rooms they rented above a mews garage in Islington. There, the two boys, Frank and Percy, along with Eliza's father, Granddad Crisp – a hansom cab driver and a man whose photos prove that braces always need a belt for extra security – would bag up nuts and sweets and help Eliza make toffee apples to sell to the queues outside the nearby Collins' Music Hall. It kept the Kemps fed and housed, but unfortunately, when the Second World War came, Eliza's little helpers were soon considered to be in danger from the new threat of German bombing raids. Equipped with gas masks, the two boys made their way through crowds of weeping mothers to Highbury and Islington station and a two-year stay away from home.

One evening, during the London Blitz, a Luftwaffe pilot caught in 'ack-ack' fire evacuated his payload of bombs. Below him was Walter, tall and lean, quickly making his way home through the empty streets, the sky above alight with tracer. Within seconds the eight bombs had landed around him, sucking him into the huge hole they'd created in the road. Luckily the bombs didn't detonate and, dazed, he crawled out and back to Eliza. But Walter's nerves were forever blown apart. Afterwards, he became wrecked and sleepless, and my father would often see the red glow of his cigarette as he lay smoking in bed through many a long night.

Unfortunately my father and mother were experiencing another hell. Both tell similar evacuation stories of beatings, accusations of stealing, and destroyed or censored letters home. Sadly for my mother it would end at the age of nine, in a breakdown of bed-wetting, fear of noise and inconsolable night-crying. While they were both away, two bombs fell silently through the London night sky and destroyed each of their family homes and any evidence of their younger lives.

Walter and Eliza were temporarily relocated to the relatively peaceful suburb of Finchley, and Frank was granted his wish to return from rural exile to his family. His war was not over, though, and as a Boy Scout he was drafted into the role of stretcher-bearer at Finchley Memorial Hospital. On 6 June 1944, D-Day, a heavy raid delivered itself in retaliation upon the city. Frank carried eight dead bodies, young and old, into the morgue that evening, at one point having to shuffle them around to fit them all in. Later that night he lay sleepless in his bed, listening to Allied planes making their way to France and the final act of the war.

With the war over, the Kemp family returned to Islington and new rooms in Rotherfield Street, rented from a local landlord. But the brothers would still have to replace the walls and ceilings themselves, as a doodlebug had dropped in the street and partially destroyed them. They took the top floor, their parents' brass bed set up in the living room creating a centrepiece reminiscent of Roald Dahl, but in reality it was nothing but cramped and stifling. On the floor below, even more Dahl-esque, lived two 'filthy old boys', as my father called them.

Sadly, the family didn't have the means to indulge Frank's aspirations or potential, and his desires to stay on at school beyond fourteen and become a journalist were impossible even to contemplate. So Frank was sent to work as a printer – ironically, printing ruled lines onto paper for others to write on. In 1952, after his two years in National Service, he returned to the print and a blind date with a shy, Irish-faced girl from the New North Road called Eileen Green. Their first evening together ended with what must have been a memorable visit to the London Palladium to see Little Richard perform. A few dates later and they were helping to shake its Grand Circle up and down while watching Bill Haley and the Comets. Somewhere between the rock and roll they fell in love.

On Eileen's first visit to her new boyfriend's house she was welcomed at the front door by one of the resident 'old boys'. Wrapped against the cold in ancient grey clothes and carrying an oil lamp in his greasy fingers, he beckoned her in, slowly guided her up the narrow stairs, and pointed her on past their own stinking rooms towards the top floor and the waiting Frank. The fragile Eileen swore she would never come again to this decrepit place, but eventually married Frank, and, as a proud virgin in white, moved into the house on their wedding night. Awkwardly undressing for bed, she broke the gas mantle, casting them both, gratefully, I'm sure, into darkness.

Eventually, they rented two rooms on the floor below and uncomfortably shared the kitchen with the elderly gents, now in their nineties, who infuriated Frank with their habit of keeping coal piled in a corner of the landing outside their door. Thankfully, the two nonagenarians soon shuffled off their shabby mortal coils, and with my arrival my father took over their space and turned it into a bedroom for me, giving his new family the whole floor.

Almost two years later my brother was born in my parents' bedroom. My father looked after me, banned, like all men of his time, from the proceedings, while two midwives and a doctor saw Martin into the world. My mother had chosen to have Martin at home, not for any holistic purpose or lack of NHS service, but because she couldn't leave me, as my father was unable to take time off work. Unfortunately, Martin was thought to be a 'blue' baby – meaning he might have a potentially fatal blood condition – and was immediately rushed to hospital. When cleared, he would return home to two murder attempts from his brother.

The first was more of an experiment. He was asleep in his cot and my fury at his satisfied, gurgling presence was unbounded. I must have realised his breathing was essential to life because first I poured the remains of a pot of Lyle's Golden Syrup on to his face, and then, pleased with my initial syrupy delivery, followed it with a bowl of sugar – a fine recipe for suffocation, I thought. He would at least enjoy it while it lasted. I watched little sweet bubbles form and pop around his mouth and nostrils and then suddenly there was a room full of screams, a crying baby, and a punished, whimpering child. I'd failed. This time.

A few weeks later I took my chance again. A sunny day meant a stroll to the New River Walk, a faux little brook that was actually designed to bring in fresh drinking water to thirsty Londoners but was now a favourite haunt of new mothers. Outside our house my old perambulator proudly stood with its new incumbent tucked tightly inside. My mother went back to shut the door and I took my chance. I grabbed the handlebar and shoved the huge beast of a pram into the road. A woman passing by screamed as it flew from the kerb, tipped backwards onto its canopied end and, wheels spinning helplessly in midair, came to a stop. But so swaddled was Martin that he never moved from the security of the covers, his head safely cushioned by the pillow, and within seconds my mother had him and the pram back on the pavement. With a stinging arse I saw that he was blessed, and probably worth keeping.

Below us, on the ground floor, the landlord had his rental office, and one day a week a line of people would snake through our 'passage' to pay their rent through a hole in the wall, a public encroachment which never seemed to bother us, although my mother would struggle to push her pram past the grumbling tenants. On a wet day they'd all cram into the narrow hall for protection, filling the house with the smell of damp clothes and the murmuring of local rumour. Under all of this, in the basement, lived an elderly woman, who eventually filled the house with a fetid stench of her own, alerting us to her lonely death.

The house contained no bathrooms, and the only toilet was outside in a small walled yard where my father had once kept chickens that he horrifically 'burst' by swelling their stomachs with an inappropriate diet of barley. On one side stood a brick air-raid shelter full of paint pots, rusting bicycles and hidden creatures. On the wall hung a tin bath that I never remember coming into the house – a 'good wash' was always had in the kitchen sink. I only remember this being once a week, unless my father took me to the local baths, where I'd lie tense and repulsed in one of their large cubicled tubs, with its flaking enamel and worryingly brown rust spots, timidly calling, 'More hot water, please' to the old geezer patrolling the corridor outside. Our outside toilet was a reeking, damp home for insects, and although torches were required in the evenings, it was beyond the call of nature to visit it at night. I also feared the empty basement that you had to pass to get to it, especially in the knowledge that the old woman had recently rotted there, not to mention our cat Ginger, who'd spent his last hours of life spewing on the dusty floorboards. To make things worse, in winter the pipes would freeze and the cistern would stop working altogether. Night-time relief was had in a bucket, and it was common in the morning to see Uncle Percy or Aunt Jean carrying theirs down to the loo. A stroke had taken Eliza before I was born and Walter just after, so my uncle, now married, lived upstairs with his wife and two children. We were joined in the house by my older cousin, her Turkish-Cypriot husband and their son, who all moved into the old ground-floor rent office when the council took over the property and turned the room into a dwelling.

It was now a house full of relatives (and, oddly, a monkey – my cousin's husband having bought one in Club Row market as a pet); and although the three families kept themselves separate, sequestered on their different floors, the children claimed the doorstep, the yard and the damp basement space for their adventures in imagination.

CHAPTER TWO

HOME-MADE

Rotherfield Primary stood at the end of the street; a typical redbrick Victorian state school, infused with the smell of sour milk and hot plimsolls. The rule for boys was to wear shorts until they were eleven, which gave the local long-trousered schools great ammunition to abuse us with. In June, shorts made sense, but in winter we were a swarm of goosebumps. Towards the end of my time there my mother thought it too extravagant to buy me a new pair, even though I'd reached a size where my hulking thighs were bursting out of my shorts like escaping sausage meat, and when I sat down they'd ride up and resemble a pair of worsted underpants.

My parents were constantly pushed to the limit of their purse just buying what was necessary, and so to give love and save cash my mother knitted jumpers for us. I particularly remember a rusty brown one that I wore proudly for school the day it was finished, although I was a little unsure about the jagged blue 'G' she'd sewn on its breast. Martin, of course, had a perfectly straight 'M'.

I was spotted – for rust can be a little lurid – as soon as I entered the school gates. I'd forgotten about the 'G'.

'That stands for Germ!' A playground nasty confronted me; even at eight, he already had the worn face of a man. 'Look! G for Germ!' He was now pointing out his witty discovery to his host of sycophants. The phrase became a ringing tune repeated endlessly for my benefit by more and more of his cronies. I never wore the jumper again without tears.

Even visiting barbershops seemed frivolous when my dad could easily do it himself. It was the era of the as-seen-on-TV gadget, and the kings of these domestic necessities were K-Tel. They'd sell you things that you never knew you needed, with chirpy, urgent voiceovers and slick demonstrations. Vegetable choppers, knitting machines, even hair trimmers arrived at our house. This last device was designed to trim the hair by just combing it through. In actual fact, it tore the hair in random places as it ripped its way down; a medieval torture instrument by any other name. My father would force us on to a chair and then begin his Sweeney Todd-like operation. You'd sit and pray for no pain, but then it would catch on a knot or a curl and successfully remove your hair whole from its follicle. It felt as if it had been yanked from the back of your eye and you jumped like a galvanised frog. To make things worse, the more haircuts my dad administered the blunter the 'trimmer' became. When it was over I'd sit in the chair, shoulders covered in broken pieces of hair, and wipe away tears. I'm not sure if these home-made haircuts were actually to save money or simply to satisfy my father's love for DIY.

He was creative with his hands, and apart from the usual shelves and decorating, if there was a fancy dress competition or an Easter hat parade then Martin and I would invariably be wearing something grand, often mechanical, and always of a winning formula. I felt his love for us through the time and effort he put in, and the Kemp boys stood out at school because of it; though not always in the way we would have chosen.

My brother had a fully working windmill bonnet made for him once, and I remember awkwardly walking to school dressed as a knave-of-hearts playing card – a large painted box hung on me from braces, while a hat and straw wig finished off my nursery-rhyme look. Embarrassingly, I won. As usual.

On one awful occasion, though, my mother cried over what I had to wear. I was crossing the street and must have been struggling to walk as my shoes were too tight. My poor mother was mortified – they had no money at the time to buy me a new pair. I didn't think we were any different – everyone we knew owned very little; houses were rented, and everything we sat on, slept on, drove in and watched was on HP. Constant saving through 'Christmas Boxes', coupons or Green Shield Stamps would pay for holidays, and bottles were always returned promptly for their thruppence deposit.

My parents needed to work hard for money, and at times our front room resembled a factory. My father not only worked Saturday mornings but also brought home work for some extra cash, and for a while we had a small printing press squeezed into a corner. The smell of ink soon became a familiar, homely one. My mother also worked from home as a machinist, stitching up 'golliwogs' among other things, and the rattle of the Singer sewing machine and Mum's frantically pedalling foot became our constant soundtrack.

To a child, things reveal themselves in symbols. Once, for a curious, forgotten reason, but probably to find money for sweets, I reached into my mother's coat pocket as it hung over a chair. Not only was I surprised to find the pockets empty, but also both of them had holes, and my hand reached down into the dusty lining. It shocked me and I snatched my hand away. It felt as though I'd discovered something hidden about my mother. And, possibly, about us.

Like Dad, Mum was the youngest of a family of five children. She knew very little about her father, Thomas Green, as he'd died from gangrene before she was born, and so hated was he that he was never mentioned thereafter. A drinker and a bully, this road-worker of Irish descent, proudly born on St Patrick's Day, would terrorise the home – when he chose to be there, as he often vanished for long periods of time. His background is unknown, his Catholic family having ostracised him when he married Elizabeth Bristow of Shoreditch, an Anglican with no previous pious convictions. 'Liz' – ten years his junior – worked in the local bathhouse and blamed her later debilitating rheumatoid arthritis on the dampness of her workplace. A woman in constant pain when I knew her, she rarely spoke to me, and because of her 'bad legs' played little with her grandchildren.

I picture her, grey hair, grey face, puffing billows of grey smoke around the room, as if her body were making grey at such a rate it needed to expel the surplus. Sitting toothless and pinnied in her twelfth-floor flat, bloated legs on a leatherette pouffe, mechanical ashtray perched on a metal stalk by her side, she would talk to my mother while Martin and I sat motionless on the sofa, letting her clouds slowly embrace us. When Nan's constant smoking had filled her faithful ashtray, I was allowed the privilege of operating it, and with a press of a button would watch its little trapdoors open and the dirty butts vanish into its ashy bowels.

My parents would often take my grandmother out in our black Ford Popular on summer day trips. Southend-on-Sea was a favourite, and Martin and I would sit trapped in the back of the car, windows closed, while Nan puffed solemnly away for four or so hours on her Player's Weights. These were pre-service-station days, and Nan's bladder had to be emptied in numerous lay-by bushes along the route, making it a journey of immense proportions, but at least allowing us some respite from the fug. We'd finally arrive, set her down on a deckchair, put a plate of whelks in her hand, and play in the mud for a few hours before the return journey home and another gassing.

I could leave her there, in the back of the Popular, heading home towards Shoreditch, or maybe jump-cut to 1978 and the last time I saw her, waving me goodbye from her hospital bed, ancient against the smooth, fresh pillowcase; either way I would be doing this woman a disservice, the woman I never knew, the one that existed before the broken version that I met. So I want to wave goodbye to you again Nan, and try to see the young, cockney girl who once fell excitedly in love; the woman sadly resigned to the constant disaffection of her husband; the mother who was forced to say goodbye to her babies at a wartime railway station; the fighter who worked all the hours she could to feed her five children; and the brave widow, who once crawled from a shelter to see her home and all her lovely things crushed by a German bomb.

The Duke of Clarence was a busy Victorian pub, full of etched glass and polished wood, with a well-worn upright piano pushed against a nicotined wall. Part of the terrace, it adjoined our house and was the venue for my parents' wedding celebrations. Of a winter's evening, returning from shopping or a family visit with my mother, I would hear the liquored ribaldry coming from the smoky warmth inside, and through the swinging door witness flashes and hints of this secret, prohibited place of adults, brilliantly lit in all its bottly glitter. My parents weren't drinkers – I don't think they'd been inside a pub since the night of the broken gas mantle – and so the people within held some kind of illicit attraction for me. My father would occasionally have a bottle of brown ale on a Saturday night – his glass perched on the mantelpiece as a symbol of the weekend – and manage to make it last the entire evening, whereas it would take at least a wedding for my mother to drink. My bed was next to the pub's adjoining wall, and at night I would lie and listen to the muted devilish sounds of the piano accompanying hearty, raucous singing. Those old, boozy music-hall songs that swam through the wall – still part of the prevailing culture in the mid-sixties, albeit waning – became my lullaby, and to this day I'm home when I hear them.

Once a month, local mods would converge on the pub and I'd stare out of my bedroom window, thrilled by the scooters gliding down the street, a dream in white sparkle and mirrors, reflecting the sharp, neat lines of their riders. This was certified mod country – a greased rocker wouldn't dare walk the Essex Road. Young men here took a feminine level of time in their grooming, and my cousins' boyfriends would be all slim suits, burned-in partings and geezer sovereigns.* The mods would reincarnate themselves here one day as soul boys and I would join them, but that's for the future. Right now, my Aunt Dolly is drinking inside, blonde and beehived, her voice warm with rum and black.

Dolly lived two doors away from us with her mother and her brother, David, and she'd occasionally pop in on her way to the pub. I'd never smelt perfume before, and she was all sweets and smoke on our sofa, with a great big laugh that denied the cancer swelling within her. When she died, David's 'mum' revealed to him that she was really his grandmother, and that Dolly was not his sister at all, but in fact his real mother. I was beginning to realise that it was what people thought you were that was important, even if it wasn't the truth.

In front of me is a grainy black-and-white photograph of my family, taken in the Clarence's upstairs function room during the wedding reception for my pretty cousin Janice. It's about 1967, and she has just married one of the Nashes, an appropriate moniker for the family who ferociously dominated the Islington underworld. Here's Ted, my

---

* *Local legend has it that you could purchase these huge masculine rings, sotto voce, at the sarsaparilla and apple-fritter stall in the local market. The trader, apparently, kept them secreted at the bottom of his fat fryer.*

great-uncle who fought in the First World War, standing proud in a three-piece suit, face as white as his hair, homburg settled on a cabinet behind him. Here's Aunt Flo, looking mischievous and twinkley in winged spectacles, and here's my cousin's husband, wearing a pin stabbed through his collar and, like the other men in the picture, hair trimmed neatly and Brylcreemed. The men wear dark suits, white shirts and sombre ties with small, hard knots pushed up to strangling point. The younger women have their hair high in beehives, while the seated, older ones look comfortably ample and matronly as they contribute to the ashtrays that spill over on the table. My parents are both sporting tans, telling me that we must have just returned from our annual summer visit to my Uncle Tom and Aunt Joyce's family home in Swansea, and that there had been good weather that year on the Mumbles. I'm stood behind my brother, but you can only make out the top of my head, hair newly trimmed – probably by Dad's do-it-yourself shearing tool.

Staring at the photograph now, I'm reminded that I may have been a little tipsy here. The reception had deteriorated into post-speech raggedness, the children starting to be ignored in favour of flowing booze and knees-up music. Women were kicking off shoes and dancing in stockinged feet on the now sticky carpet that had, over the years, cushioned many a cockney do. Lured by fascination with what my parents had claimed was a reception full of bookmakers and villains from the Angel, an area of Islington where Essex Road met Upper Street, I wandered around the edge of the room. I was attracted to a mucky, lipstick-stained glass of thick, yellowy fluid, and, lifting it from the deserted table, drank its sweet contents. The elixir was – magically, I thought – called a Snowball; is it any wonder that I wanted to drink one of those? Head curiously light, I loitered around the male conversations at the bar, now heavy with cigar smoke and braggadocio. It was here, in hushed tones, that I overheard a cousin mention the Krays to another man. Was it a gang? A new musical group even? There was such reverence and awe in his voice that it struck me, even at that age, that whoever or whatever they were, they were to be feared and, disturbingly, this wedding was somehow bringing them closer to my door.

And then the bragging men were rushing past me. A fight, outside somewhere, between some of the wedding party and a gang of interloping rivals. The excitement that suddenly swept through a number of the male guests as they ran into the street was palpable. Someone told me to stay where I was but I was thrilled by these heavy, bristling blokes, hot in their bri-nylon shirts, as they strode back into the hall, pumped with adrenalin and beer, cigars still smoking in hands, breathlessly recounting what had either just or, more realistically, almost occurred. Many years later, these would be the kind of men that I would draw on when asked to play one half of that feared East End fraternity.

With friends from show business and politics, and pictures of them by Bailey and other society photographers, the Kray twins, Ronnie and Reggie, were supreme rulers of London's underworld, and their name had fast become a byword for proletarian power. They dressed in the stark, dark uniform of the working-class male, which owed more to the sartorial sobriety of the forties and fifties than anything that could be considered 'swinging' in this new age. The Krays put the Nashes in the shade.

We poured out of the Clarence and into the warm night air. It felt grown-up to be part of the noise in the street, the noise that usually woke me, and I was thrilled by our loud, carefree voices echoing off the redbrick housing estate opposite. Bentham Court had been built in the hole that the doodlebug had made and it would be there, within the next year or so, that I would meet a dynamic young Irish woman who'd set my life on a course that would one day take me to Broadmoor prison, and a meeting with Mr Ronnie Kray himself.

CHAPTER THREE

WE ARE THE BOYS AND GIRLS

The year 1968 was one of revolution: Tariq Ali, striking a symbolic hue in his red mac, raging against Britain's embattled blue line; Vanessa Redgrave, Joan Bakewell and a horde of angry young people storming the steps of the American embassy; students sitting-in and, at various points of confrontation around Britain, taking up arms and flowers. Change was in the air. My parents, however, were busy looking after us at the time, and anyway, we were all watching telly.

The revolution never came to our street, although we heard the Beatles singing about it on the new Radio 1 station. My parents preferred the group's earlier numbers and style, but anything was better than the band they considered to be dark and filthy miscreants – the Rolling Stones. I attempted a moment of pre-prepubescent rebellion around then and told my parents that the Stones were my favourite group, even though I had no idea what their music was like, my only record being a Pinky and Perky one that Aunt Lil had bought me.

The hippy extravagances and their worship of all things floral and herbal were not to be seen on our impoverished side of the Essex Road, but as through that swinging door at the Clarence pub, the glimpses I managed were intimidating yet tantalising. Camden Passage, a narrow lane of antique shops, Italian restaurants and men walking poodles, was also home to a mini-commune. We sometimes passed through this Islington lane when going to the market, and one Saturday morning, on our way to buy cut-price cleaning goods, underwear or maybe a pie-and-mash lunch, I peered in through a window, into an orange-painted room hung with posters where a group of long-haired men and women lounged in strange, pantomime-like clothes. It's hard to imagine now how shocking and exotic long hair looked on a man back then, but a divide was occurring between my parents' generation and these new adults and, even at my age, I was aware of the tension. For people of my parents' age, who'd lived through the war, it was a snub to their struggle; but the new generation was looking for their own identity, and their own battles to fight.

The mods no longer frequented the pub, having split in two directions: the aspirational, better-off ones began making their own version of San Francisco somewhere in property-owning North London, growing their hair and collars, morphing with the middle classes, trading pasties for pâté, and finding an accent somewhere between the Harrow Road and Harrow School; the other half shaved their heads, shortened their britches and donned the braces and boots of an earlier generation of proletarian males, forming a tribe of symbolically deloused Roundheads.

My father was a Labour man and my fifth birthday brought an extra reason for him to celebrate: Harold Wilson had brought Labour to power, albeit with a small majority. The anachronistic, Edwardian-styled gentlemen of politics, with their euphemistic cricketing metaphors, were making way for the ordinary man. Maybe even a bottle of brown ale was opened at 138 Rotherfield Street. Even so, Dad was part of an age that unquestionably toed the Establishment line and respected the institutions that ran the country; after all, they had witnessed and suffered the war in order to keep them. But the counterculture of Baby Boomers was here and beginning to affect everything. Anna Scher was part of that revolution, and in 1968 she began something that would change my life.

Stephen Brassett led me to her. An angelic-looking ten-year-old with hair as white as a Midwich Cuckoo, he had recently lost his father, and his mother was now looking for her deceased husband at local seances.

Stephen dipped his chip into a blob of brown sauce and blew on it. 'You should come to my drama club. It's on tomorrow.' He folded the chip into his mouth.

I was around at his for tea. On the settee his mother was skimming the latest edition of her *Psychic News*, in front of her, on the coffee table, a Ouija board held an upturned glass like a telephone on the hook.

'Go on, Gary, why don't you go with him?' Like my mother, Mrs Brassett tactically disguised commands as questions. 'Stephen likes it, don't you, Stephen?'

As with music, theatre was not a part of the Kemps' culture and I have no memory of putting on any front-room performances for my parents. The only time we went to a show was to see the Black & White Minstrels one Christmas. Children's drama schools tended to be the place of wealthier working-class kids whose parents could pay the fees. This often meant the progeny of the more successful villains – the Little Princess pushed up on to the kitchen table with guests forced to watch her singing songs from the shows, as Dad swallows back tears of pride, convincing himself, and Princess, that one day she will be a star, and thus creating a permanently dissatisfied social monster.

The Anna Scher Children's Theatre in Islington, to give it its full title, was different. First, it was a club, not a school, and second, there wasn't any singing or dancing, although some of the parents were probably villains. Stephen had gone to her drama classes when she'd first started teaching in his annoyingly long-trouser-wearing school, Ecclesbourne,

Rotherfield's rival primary and the home of our tormentors. Now, at the end of '69, owing to high demand, she'd moved to the community centre in Bentham Court and, given its proximity to me, it seemed churlish not to have a look. In any case, I was a little frightened by the kind of people Mrs Brassett could talk to through her board.

The following afternoon, without telling my parents where I was going, I left the house and crossed the street. The community centre in the middle of the estate's central open space was an unloved, soulless, two-storey brick building. On entering I made my way up its wide stairs and past its communal washroom and notices for judo meetings and women's groups. A girl's voice reverberated from the hall above. She seemed to be in an argument with another girl. Maybe this was a bad time to go in but, reaching the hall, I peered through its glazed double doors.

At the near end of the room, on either side, chairs were stacked into small uneven towers and stood like sentinels, while in the far half of the room about twenty kids, mostly a year or so older than me, sat in a loose semicircle facing the other way. In the two seats directly in front of me I could see the backs of a woman and a man, blonde and dark respectively. Everyone was watching two girls argue at the end of the hall, one sitting on a sofa, the other standing with arms folded. Behind them were boxes and hats spread on a large table; a small mobile bus stop stood to one side, and a red-and-cream Dansette record player was perched on a small stage. The attractive standing girl furiously shouted something at the fat seated one and with a spin stormed off to the edge of the room. The fat girl stared after her, then turned her head sharply and looked at the woman, who immediately started to clap. The kids quickly followed her lead and relaxed in their seats. I took the opportunity to push open the heavy door and walked in.

I had the self-conscious awareness of the outsider as I stood in the open space, committed to the moment between piles of watching chairs.

No one had seen me enter but, thankfully, I spotted Stephen sitting among the group and willed him to notice me. He did, and, smiling, crossed and spoke to the woman. I felt the room grow silent and slowly turn its focus upon me. Outside I heard boys playing football. Maybe I should have been with them.

The woman stood. She was young.

'Hello, Gary,' she said, 'it's lovely to meet you. I'm Anna Scher.'

Her beaming face and the lightly tongued Ts of her Irish accent rapidly melted me into the semicircle of people and, with a fragrant hand upon my shoulder, she introduced me as though I were the answer to all their problems, the missing piece to their puzzle, the most important person to ever enter the room. This was her skill and it made me stay for the next eight years.

Anna Scher was a diminutive, twenty-three-year-old Irish Jew from Cork. Coming to England at fifteen, she found her desire to be an actress squashed by her authoritarian father and, as a compromise, she went into drama teaching. Her long, blonde hair, plump mouth and honeyed complexion were made all the more striking by her fierce control of some of the wildest kids from the borough. She managed to exert this power while dressed in miniskirt and suede boots. I fell in love with her.

The man sitting next to Anna, with long, dark hair and skinny-rib tank top, was Charles Verrall, Anna's assistant. He gently played second fiddle to her strident lead, yet they seemed to quietly harmonise. Although their relationship was never apparent to the students, he was in fact Anna's lover. Tall and thin, with a patient temperament, he'd studied to be a scientist at Oxford but found himself enjoying the rewards from teaching working-class kids how to act. Charles was everything we weren't: upper-middle-class, well spoken and gentle, but contrary to the fashion of the time, neither he nor Anna attempted to be one of us or change themselves to suit. Yet the respect that they received was palpable.

Anna's technique was praise mixed with discipline and she delivered it for just two shillings a lesson. Even if your kernel of talent was extremely small, she would highlight it and sing its praises. Many of the children had never experienced approval or encouragement and this was hard for them to trust, but very quickly their spirits grew.

Her method was improvisation. We never looked at scripts or texts, and Shakespeare or Pinter were never mentioned, although Martin Luther King and Gandhi may well have been. We were, on the whole, not literary creatures, and generally frightened of books or anything that resembled schoolwork, so, without any level of condescension, Anna cleverly built her classes around what we could create ourselves. She would get us to play out mini-dramas based on problems that we all knew uncomfortably well: communicating with teachers or parents; issues of unfinished homework or coming home late; and, more importantly, bullying.

It might begin with one of us playing the role of the Parent and the other the Child returning from school or play, trying to hide the fact that he or she is suffering; a simple exercise that was set in the world we knew. As a by-product we'd gradually learn how to deal with those situations and, by acting them out at Anna's, exorcise any frustrations that we felt in real life. It was a kind of gestalt therapy by default, spooling out our inner anxieties, giving them a voice and, to a certain extent, freeing us of them. Acting is about tapping into one's emotions and, with Anna's kids, the emotion that poured out initially was anger.

At that time, we were mostly young people from the poor side of Essex Road, but Anna's would gradually become a meeting place for the different classes and cultures of the Islington kid. The borough was divided into two distinct sides by its main road, which ran from Newington Green to the Angel. On our side, the treeless streets of council accommodations, rough and rented; on the other, the leafy lanes of mortgaged Georgian homes, proud and well-proportioned. Here, three families to a house; there, one (plus, of course, an au pair or two). The child of the printer will also meet the child of the professional at Dame Alice Owen's grammar school, but that is for the future, a future that will have Anna take her theatre across the Islington divide and lose it to a group of trustees, and the attractive standing girl and the fat one from the sofa become household names. But for now we are at the beginning, and it is gloriously innocent.

'I'm going to be in a film.' Stephen was behaving quite normally considering his news.

'What is it?' I asked.

'It's called *Junket 89.*'

He was about to take on the lead role in a Children's Film Foundation production. His mother seemed unimpressed and carried on with her tidying, but then, to our parents, born before the age of desperate celebrity-craving, it was all childish frivolity, and to be too excited would only encourage us to let it get in the way of normality. A picture of Stephen's father looked on stoically. I glanced at the upturned glass on the Ouija board. It remained unmoved.

As for me, I was amazed and envious. Every Saturday morning from the age of six, I'd walk up the Essex Road to the Ancient Egyptian-styled ABC cinema. In my jeans pocket (not Tesco Bombers, but some equally cheap market-stall pair) I've two bob, round my waist maybe a snake-belt, on my feet possibly Trackers (the ones with the animal footprints on the sole and the tiny compass in the heel – on the other hand, it could have been the later design, Grand Prix, with the racing-car tyre tread), and in my mouth an anatomically pink Bazooka Joe. I was on my way to Saturday Morning Pictures.

I was an ABC Minor and would faithfully belt out the song that began the morning's programme: '*We are the boys and girls well known as the Minors of the ABC ...*' as about two hundred of us, wired to the tits on Jublees, Munchies and Kia-Ora, infested the cinema with such virulence that even the toughest usherettes would scurry off to cleaning cupboards for a couple of hours and smoke themselves sick. But the manager, in our case a balding Uriah Heep, hard bitten and seasoned from years of abusive children, would have no truck with us urchins, and if the noise became too much – which was inevitable, given the combination of parental absence and unnatural food colouring – would halt the film in a second, march down the aisle in his tired maroon blazer, and threaten us with early expulsion into the light.

The first half of the programme had not changed since my father was a boy and invariably started with a cartoon. This was followed by a non-sequitous episode of either the 1930s Flash Gordon or the original 1940s 'fat' Batman serial, and then a Western. In accordance with some long-forgotten lore of cinema, the cavalry coming meant you had to lift your seat and drum your feet rapidly on its underside until the manager turned the lights on or the cavalry arrived.

The programme would always end with a Children's Film Foundation movie. This might be a fifties, black-and-white, gritty, Osborne-for-kids, kitchen-sink morality tale, with a gang of malnourished children with dirty knees finding a stolen FA Cup or whatever else would have them and a dog scurrying over a bombsite; or it could be a full-colour, contemporary story, set in a world where children looked like us and were always right.

The CFF had been making movies for Saturday mornings since 1951, all shot on 35mm and aiming for a high quality of directing and acting. *Junket 89* was to be their next production and it would co-star a thirty-six-year-old Richard Wilson – who would later become popular as the grumpy old man from *One Foot in the Grave* – as an absent-minded science master, and my mate Stephen as his eponymous pupil. The other child roles and minor parts were all to be filled by Anna Scher kids and, as I would soon find out, that would also include me.

The story has Junket stealing a 'matter-transporter' from the science master and keeping it in his locker, number 89. It allows its user to 'jump' to different locations. A 'returning device' is in the shape of a cricket ball, a ruse to end up at Lord's Cricket Ground and have the real Gary Sobers appear as himself. On the way there are many high jinks involving two stupid bullies who get their comeuppance, a tap-dancing mummy's boy whose mother (played wonderfully by Fanny Carby, one of the original members of Joan Littlewood's company) becomes embroiled in some clothes swapping with the headmaster, and the Benny Hill-style appearance of a sexy French maid.

I have a tainted recollection of filming *Junket 89* that summer of 1970. The producers and the director, Peter Plummer, had been coming to watch us at Anna's and picked their leads without auditions. I was to play one of Junket's classmates, a non-speaking role but one that required quite a few filming days. Around then I became the brunt of some hurtful teasing, or, more correctly, bullying. I was a skinny new boy, not good at football, shy with girls and getting lots of attention from Anna. I was very close to Stephen and always sat next to him, all of which prompted two or three of the lads, including a spiteful one named Norman, to decide I was a 'poof' and 'definitely queer'. I didn't even know what it meant. For them, Anna's 'therapy' wasn't quite working yet. One day's filming became horrendous for me, with some brutal teasing. I wasn't physically scared of them, just humiliated, a painful experience that still makes me wince to remember. The pain had everything to do with separation and not belonging. The next day I didn't want to return.

The meeting place for everyone was on the corner by the post office opposite my house, where a bus would take us to the set. I peered through the net curtains and saw them gathering there like a storm; all friends; a clucking gang. My mother was having none of it, and to my horror, marched across the street to talk to Anna. I cringed as the main antagonists watched the conversation. Oh my God, she's made it worse. I will be killed if I go there now. I sank lower behind the sill. She returned, and with a tone oddly sharp, considering she was on my side, told me that it'd be all right and to get over there now. With stomach-churning apprehension, but abiding faith in Anna and my mother, I crossed the road and went immediately to Stephen. Thankfully, she was right, and Norman et al. never made another snide remark about me again.

Recently a series of the best of Saturday Morning Pictures was issued on DVD and *Junket 89* was one of them. With some curiosity, I slip the disc into the machine, hit play, and the movie fades up. The CFF opening titles have a familiarity that comes from being burned into a fresh young brain. The shot is of the fountains at Trafalgar Square with St Martin-in-the-Fields dominating. The bells are ringing out across the square and then the feeding pigeons suddenly take wing into a perfect sunlit sky. It's a symbol of Britain at its Ladybird Book best. Fade out and up on to hands filling the screen and a football-terrace clap begins. And here's Stephen, blond and squinting in the early seventies sunshine, just how I remember him. And there's Linda Robson, the attractive 'standing girl' from my first visit to Anna's, in miniskirt and long white socks. Twenty years later, Linda will become nationally famous in the hit sitcom *Birds of a Feather*, along with her best friend, the 'fat girl' from the sofa, Pauline Quirke. Pauline will appear any second now, in her sulky ten-year-old incarnation, but before then the camera pans down a school building and follows a young Christopher Benjamin as the pompous headmaster. A school bell rings for playtime and here's an interior shot of kids coming down the stairs, screaming and fighting. The faces are all familiar. Here's my good friend, Tony Bayliss, the coolest dresser I knew at the time. He's the only one wearing Levi's, narrow, of course, and also a Brutus check shirt with button-down collar and a half-pleated back (both bought from a small boutique at the Angel run by ex-mods), a real suedehead look, and one that I would soon aspire to. He's already ahead of the game and starting to grow his hair. Here's Ray Burdis, who would enter my life again twenty years later as one of the producers of *The Krays*. And here is Mario, playing the 'mummy's boy', who, in a few years' time, will try to seduce me to the sound of a Diana Ross record. Hopping down the steps comes a sweet-looking black girl, hair pinned up. I can't see her clearly, but now she appears again, face smiling, and I see that it's Hyacinth, gaily unaware that she would, sadly, only have a short life.

Cockney voices sing the title song: '*Who takes the cake then lands in 'ot wa'er? I know because he's a mate o' mine. It's Junket eigh'y nine!*' This was what the producers wanted when they picked Anna's children, genuine street kids, not drama-school fakes or hams. It's a different cockney to the London voice of a ten-year-old today, but this is the London of my memory, and here I am, coming down the stairs.

During this process of thinking and writing about my past I suppose I've envisaged myself as a slightly smaller version of who I am today, albeit younger, obviously. But as I rewind and play again, the boy I see here is not the one I've had in my mind; he's fresher, with no great experience or aspirations; he's not seeing this moment through any nostalgic haze or wry cynicism, and hasn't even thought about playing in a band yet. He comes from a different world to the man watching him now.

I suddenly feel a sadness, a pathetic desire to speak to him, and, with a deep sense of loss, realise that I miss him; because he no longer exists.

CHAPTER FOUR

WATERLOO SUNRISE

The guitar was awkward to carry. I held it by the neck, my skinny arms aching as I fought to keep it from hitting the pavement. I had its body tied in a plastic shopping bag, probably from some peculiar idea of decency – it felt wrong to parade the thing exposed through the street, especially its two mournful 'F' holes. A late spring sun was starting to warm the air as I walked the few hundred yards to school. Apart from where Bentham Court now stood, our street had survived the Blitz – and the developers – and the little front gardens of the more privileged tenants blossomed with roses and hydrangeas, their morning scent reassuring. Being so close, school felt part of my home, my little universe of four blocks that included the swings, shops, family and friends.

Every lunch break I would come home with Martin for 'dinner'. Dinner was always at one o'clock – the evening meal at six being 'tea' and usually something like Spam or fish fingers (sometimes Mum would boil a pig's trotter as a 'treat' – a pink and often hairy amputation in a bowl of broth that you'd tug at with your teeth until it was mutilated). But dinner meant chops, sausages or mincemeat, and Dad would come back from work for that hour and we'd sit together as a family. It was wonderful but, with some sadness, I was already anticipating its loss. In September I would begin at the local grammar school, Dame Alice

Owen's, and today Rotherfield leavers were to receive their end-of-school prizes. The headmistress, Miss Bannatyne, would make a little speech, hand out the books and then, at some unrehearsed point, I was to provide the entertainment by performing two songs that I'd written.

I'd had a choice that Christmas: to ignore the guitar and sulk until it was returned to the music shop in Holloway Road for the five pounds it cost, or make an attempt at learning it. I soon found myself becoming obsessed with the thing. I loved it most of all for the privacy it gave me. This was different to the solitary wonder of books and comics; here *I* could create the atmosphere I wanted and the sound of it soon became a close friend.

Bert Weedon was a London guitarist who'd had some success in the fifties. A smiling, unassuming celebrity, he based his style on Les Paul and enjoyed a hit with 'Guitar Boogie Shuffle'. *Play in a Day* was his successful tutorial book for the guitar. Its red cover with black-and-white photo of the smiling, freckled Bert looked dated even in 1970, but inside was a method based around chords and rhythm that was simple for the novice. Hours were spent with Bert attempting to get my fingers into the correct positions, which wasn't easy as my guitar's steel strings were like cheesewire on my young fingertips. The usual guitar for beginners was the nylon-stringed Spanish version; however, the sound and style of my guitar, picked by my father by chance and from budget, were much more rock'n'roll. And it also looked damn good in a mirror.

And then something odd happened. I'm not sure what inspired it or why I did it as I had no concept of writing a song, but once comfortable with some prosaic chord changes on the cheese-cutter, I began to sing my own melody over them. It was thrilling and I couldn't stop la-la-ring it. Mr Allison, my class teacher at Rotherfield, was a guitar player too. Young and geeky, in Buddy Holly glasses and tweed jacket, he offered to help me with my playing during break times and I showed him what I'd come up with. A friend, Gary Jefferies, was present, and Mr Allison suggested that we both try writing some words to go with the tune. As it was the end of March, he thought that it might have an Easter theme.

My mother had deep beliefs, but like alcohol, church was only for weddings, and though within a year or so I was, precociously, to dump all spiritual belief, Religious Knowledge was at that time one of my better subjects. Equipped with the story the lyrics for the song came easily and the first verse still remains firmly in my head. With soft rhymes and bad grammar, I was obviously made for pop music.

> *Jesus rode through Jericho on his way to the cross*
> *He met blind Bartimaeus, who his sight had lost*
> *Jesus touched his eyes and Bartimaeus could see again*
> *So Jesus rode on safely to Jeru-oo-oo-salem.*

Probably under the influence of a recent Roger Whittaker single, I decided to intersperse the verses with an annoyingly whistled phrase, but Mr Allison was impressed, and within the week we had a group of children from my class singing it. We performed my first song in front of the school just before Easter – whistling included. My parents were thrilled; their gift was worth more than they'd thought.

That weekend Dad drove me and my guitar to Waterloo. In the novel *Brighton Rock* the anti-hero, Pinkie, records a nasty message for the innocent Rose in an acetate-booth at a railway station. The booths were the size of telephone boxes and once inside you'd pop a coin in a slot and through a window you'd watch a smooth acetate disc being lowered on to a turntable. A needle landed and as you spoke your voice would be etched into the disc's soft blankness. When finished the disc would slide out, equipped with an envelope for you to post it to a loved one or, as in Pinkie's case, not so loved. In 1971 on the concourse at Waterloo Station stood what must have been the last booth in London, the telephone now being ubiquitous, except of course in our house, where we'd have to wait another four years for that modern pleasure.

I slipped the plastic bag off my guitar and, holding it ready to play, stepped into the booth.

'Dad, my guitar won't fit in.'

'Go on, I've got to shut the door, you'll be all right.'

He lifted the guitar gently and I bent sideways about ninety degrees. The guitar's arm was now facing downwards. Dad carefully closed the door and I shuffled farther in.

'Hang on,' he said, opening it again, 'I've got to put the money in.' His arm reached through and the door banged against the front of my guitar as I pressed tighter against the opposite wall. 'OK, it's ready. Wait for the light. It lasts a minute.'

A minute? How long was my song? He closed the airlock and it went silent. I saw the fresh, black disc drop and the needle approach its edge. The red light went on and I looked outside at Dad, who was mouthing 'Go on' through the glass. I began strumming.

'*Jesus rode through Jericho on his way to the cross ...*'

The station was busy with Easter trippers and I was aware of people glancing at us while I sang and Dad proudly guarded his young artist's recording studio. I reached the final verse and saw that the needle was only a few revolutions away from the end of the disc. I sped up, trying to fit it all in. The final bars were now frantic as I began racing towards the end; and then the light went off. The needle lifted and the disc whirred and started its sedate little journey towards the exit hole. I hadn't quite finished.

Nevertheless, I'd made my first record. It felt warm and smelt of summer pavements. I clutched it all the way home in the car, staring at its grooves and wondering at the fine impression my song had made. I played it over and over on my parents' gramophone until its tiny trenches, ploughed that Easter weekend on Waterloo Station, wore into each other and my voice became a soft shadow, receding into the distance, until eventually I was gone.

The school hall was abuzz with excited pupils. No classes made it too thrilling to behave in any way other than berserk, and the staff were struggling to get everyone quiet and seated in class rows. I settled at the side, my guitar on my lap, plastic bag removed.

At the end of the little hall, thin Miss Bannatyne stood next to a tall, grey, stately-looking man in a long maroon robe. His huge chin supported a wide friendly grin. Around his neck hung a heavy plain cross. 'Good morning, everyone. I'd like to welcome the Bishop of Stepney, Trevor Huddleston, who has kindly agreed to hand out the prizes today.'

There would have been some singing and some recorder playing, and a long-drawn-out giving of prizes to the leavers. At some point during the proceedings, I was called up and sat on a chair in front of the school. My now minuscule shorts rode up tight into my crotch and the guitar felt cold on my bulging, naked legs that were being drained of blood by the second. Uncomfortably, and unseasonably, it being midsummer, I played and sang 'Jesus Rode Through Jericho' – an encore from Easter that my headmistress had insisted upon – followed by a new song. The record-buying and private listening having influenced my playing, I'd written a more contemporary follow-up to the now dissolved first acetate.

My mother was upset about the title. '"Alone"? You can't call it that! They'll start to worry about you.' She already had.

Writing songs was a lonely process, it seemed. Although a dark, maudlin number in a minor key, it still somehow managed to contain a whistling refrain. But a pattern, thank God, was not forming, and it was to be my last in the whistling genre.

Strangely, and with some measure of foresight, my headmistress recorded the performance on reel-to-reel and I still have it. Listening to it now, what fascinates me most of all is not my child's voice, surprising lack of nerves or dreadful whistling, but the noises of the children in the background, children I knew, shuffling, coughing, talking as though it were yesterday, and yet now into the final half of their lives. It's a distant moment of sublime naivety that I want to reach into and pull out. And somewhere, just off to the side of the singing boy, silent, but to me very present upon the tape, the bishop, making a decision that would help create the man now listening.

In the January of 1971, my brother and I decided to buy our first records. We both had money saved from our paper rounds and together we walked the Essex Road towards a little record shop in Cross Street, painfully called Pop Inn. For such an important event we needed to be attired correctly, and Martin and I were both dressed de rigueur in Brutus shirts with buttoned-down collars.

I had begged my mother for this essential fashion item the summer before, knowing exactly where to purchase it. At the Angel a shop run by some tasty ex-mods was a windowless little grotto of working-class style. Oh, that giddy sensation when I first saw the Brutuses and Ben Shermans, as one of the shop's oh-so-fashionable owners slipped them off the shelves and laid them out for my delectation. Folded oblong in shape and protected inside their crisp polythene wrappings, they were like perfect portraits of what shirts should be like, all stiff and pleading to be bought. Some were gingham, others a confectionery of ice-cream colours, and all impossible to choose from. I wanted to own every one of them, collect them with the same eagerness that I'd collected World

Cup coins the year before, but I had to make a choice and my eyes kept returning to a pale yellow one. I pictured myself in it; I pictured Tony Bayliss and Stephen Brassett looking at me in it; I pictured myself walking into Anna's in it. The power of making that choice left me light headed, almost a little nauseous with excitement, and then the owner was slipping it into a brown paper bag and I was desperate to get back home.

The smell of the fresh cotton as its lemon folds fell open and caught the light had me falling further in love. Little vents and buttons flawlessly set off its short sleeves, and, as I slipped it on, my skin had never felt such bliss. Leaving its straight-bottomed tails hanging out over my trousers, I would be à la mode that winter, but what terrible trousers they now looked next to my new shirt. These were awful. They had to go. More begging ensued.

Dad took me to a little Jewish tailor he knew of in the East End, and I picked out the electric blue-and-green mohair myself. By the following weekend, the bespectacled cutter had made me the sharpest parallels I could imagine, and although they were unlined, the roughness against my legs was worth suffering. As well as getting a few cast-offs, my brother was quick at catching me up with his own begging, and so there we were, a couple of real tasty geezers in two-tone tonic strides, marching up Cross Street in search of our musical identity.

Two pairs of mini-brogues with Blakies hammered on to the heels clipped their way into Pop Inn. Presented with a large tray of 45s, the baby suedeheads were bewildered as to what they should pick as their first buy. The bearded shop assistant indulged them by languidly playing a few. Martin heard the double-tracked vocals of the Tremeloes' 'Me And My Life' and made his choice. For Gary, the minute the car horn sounded and the singer's lazy London drawl spoke to him, he knew what he wanted.

'I think I'm so-phisticated ...'

The Kinks' 'Apeman' was my first record on a consumerist journey that would not only shape my life, but would eventually pay me back in spades.

Thursday night was *Top of the Pops*, it had been since 'Hot Love' reached number one in March. Marc Bolan's T.Rex was now being scrawled over my exercise books, and my second single was soon bought. As Marc flicked his corkscrew locks from his glitter tears, I knew the button-down collars had to go. I grew my hair, had it 'feather-cut' in a new 'unisex' salon called Stanley Kays, and graduated to a turquoise-patterned tulip collar – probably worn under a knitted black tank top with rainbow hoops – and the ultimate playground desirable, a suede Budgie jacket. Adam Faith's eponymous TV character, Budgie, became a clothes peg for the West End store Mr Freedom, and we all wanted what Budgie wore. My Budgie jacket was cream with a green yoke. I can still smell its urban opulence, although mine was almost certainly tainted with the pungent smell of burgers from Brick Lane, where my cheaper version was bought. I never extended to the white clogs Budgie also made fashionable, although the star of our playground, a boy called Chris Lambert, certainly did. Captain of the football team, and a magnet for girls, he had everything, and so long before you did that by the time you'd realised you wanted them, his were already worn out. Toppers, Selatios, Wedges, whatever shoe it was, he'd kicked them to bits while you were still begging your mum for them. He laid down the playground's sumptuary rules of clothing and we followed them as best our parents' pockets could afford.

T.Rex's follow-up to 'Hot Love' was all pouty plosives and hissy breathing, with a dark, feline groove that crawled all over me the minute I first heard Tony Blackburn play it on Radio 1 while I was getting ready for school one morning. After watching them do it on *Top of the Pops*, I pestered my mother into buying 'Get It On' while we were out shopping the following Saturday. The bearded hippy from Pop Inn looked unimpressed as he dropped it into a paper bag and handed it over. I was dying to get back and bang-a-gong with the Puck-like Marc, but on the way home we had, frustratingly, to stop and buy saveloys and chips. As soon as we were in the house I dived into the shopping bag and lifted the record out from underneath the hot chip bag; but it didn't feel like a record any more. 'Get It On' had warped into something resembling a piecrust or a small fruit bowl with crimped edges, the kind Nan would own. The hot chips had destroyed it. There was no way I was going to get another one so I put it on the turntable anyway. As the needle bobbed like a boat on the high sea the sound left everyone in earshot feeling nauseous. I suffered the indignity on behalf of Marc, and in between gobfuls of the now cold, shameful saveloy, I sang along anyway. Oddly enough, as with that familiar vinyl scratch we all know and love, I now miss the wow and flutter of an unwarped 'Get It On'.

It was on a Thursday that the bishop came round. I can say that with some certainty because *Top of the Pops* was on telly. My mother and father were packing as we were going off to a holiday camp in Westward Ho! at the weekend. The doorbell went and I ran to the window. Below on the doorstep stood the tall man in the maroon robe from prize day. Local kids on bikes wheeled around, staring at him. Someone must have died.

'It's the bishop.'

'What? For us?' Mum sounded a little frantic.

'The one from prize day.'

I'd already told her that he'd spoken to me after I played that day, and that Miss Bannatyne was very excited by it, but I wasn't sure she'd listened.

'Well, go down, then, and see what he wants.'

I went downstairs and opened the door. The kids tried to look into our passage, probably for signs of grief. On top of all the maroon material the bishop's grin sat high on his jutting chin.

'Hello, Gary.' He was holding a large plastic bag. I stared at him. 'Are your mother and father in?'

'Er … Yeah.'

He seemed huge in our little place as he went up the stairs in front of me. His shoes looked worn and dusty underneath the richness of the cloth, as well as a bit odd, as if he were a man in a dress. It seemed a bizarre outfit to be wearing in the street, especially around here, but I assumed he must have come straight from work. I could hear my mother plumping the sofa as we climbed the stairs. I pushed open the front-room door and went in.

'Hello. Mrs Kemp? I'm Trevor Huddleston. I saw your son perform his songs at Rotherfield. The headmistress gave me your address. I hope that's all right.'

'Oh, right. Come in. Sit down. Would you like a cup of tea?' She had a different voice on. Oh God, not that voice.

'Yes please.' She vanished. 'No sugar. Thank you.' He took Dad's chair, putting his bag next to his feet, and I returned to my place on the sofa. 'I thought you were *wonderful* at the prize-giving, Gary,' he said, giving his fist a little shove into the air in front of him. 'I loved your songs, especially the one about being alone.'

I could feel my mother flinch. 'We like the Easter one, don't we, Frank?' she shouted from the kitchen.

My father came in from the bedroom. He brushed his palms together and shook the bishop's hand. 'Nice to meet you. Yeah, we have a record of it we made at Waterloo Station.'

'It doesn't work any more, Dad. You can't hear me.'

The bishop seized his moment. 'Well, that's exactly why I'm here,' he said. I wondered if I'd done something illegal. Maybe even immoral. 'A few years ago I worked in Africa.' It occurred to me that that was why his shoes looked so dusty. 'While I was there I met a young black African boy. A wonderful trumpet player. Still *is* a wonderful trumpet player.' His two large hands came out like paddles. For a moment I thought he was going to pray. 'I gave him a trumpet, to help encourage him. And it has.' He stopped. Was that it?

Mum came back in with the tea. 'Turn the telly down, Frank.' She put the steaming mug on the mantelpiece above the flickering fake coals. 'Would you like a biscuit?'

Top of the Pops was being ruined.

'No, thank you, this is lovely.'

They're clapping on the telly and Jimmy Savile is back on introducing the next band. Except for the blond hair, he looks like a younger version of the bishop.

Dad leant across to lower the volume a little and I shuffled to the end of the sofa, closer to the telly. The singer seemed to be impersonating Mick Jagger, but I loved his feathery haircut.

'Don't look at the telly!' my mother snapped. 'Look at the bishop!'

'Eh?'

'He's come to see you.'

The bishop smiled. 'I bought this for you, Gary. If that's all right with your parents?'

Out of the plastic bag he pulled a box with a photograph of what I thought was a radio, but my peripheral vision was still half-concentrating on the telly and the guitarist and bass player, who were running around like a couple of cheeky schoolmates.

'It's called a cassette recorder. Easier than reel-to-reel. I'd like you to have it.'

I wasn't sure what this meant and stared at the box as he handed it to me. *Philips*, it said.

'Every time you write a song I'd like you to record it on to a cassette, write down the lyrics and send them to my house in Stepney.' I didn't know what to say and carried on staring at the gift in my hand. 'Would that be all right?'

I looked up to see he was asking my father the question and took the opportunity to glance once more at what was too fascinating to ignore. They had a football out on stage now, and their skinny legs and high platforms lazily kicked it around while the mandolin player, or whatever he was, did a solo.

'That's brilliant,' said Dad. 'Thank you. Thank you very much. What d'ya say, Gary?'

'Thank you very much.'

The singer was singing something about finding a rock'n'roll band. The bishop could see that I was distracted and a little taken aback by the gift. 'Do you like pop music, Gary?'

'Er, yeah.'

'I've just been helping to put on a charity pop concert with a famous guitarist called Pete Townshend. It's going to be at the Oval cricket ground. We're helping to raise money for Bangladesh.' To my pleasure and relief he turned to the telly. 'He'll be playing,' he said, nodding at the screen, 'Rod Stewart. With the Faces. And the Who.'

He knew them!

'That's nice,' said Mum.

Clapping announced the end of the song and the band looked relaxed and pleased with themselves, tousling their funny hair and shuffling around onstage as if they were too full of energy to stop. It looked like the kind of gang you'd want to be in. And suddenly it came to me: that's what I'm doing. I play guitar; I write songs; I could do that. I *will* do that. It was a moment of clarity, an epiphany, delivered by a bishop.

I turned back to him, sitting there in Dad's chair, swathed in cloth, a heavy cross resting like a sleeping bird on his belly. 'Thank you,' I said, glancing down at the box. 'I'll do that. I've got another song already.'

I will meet Trevor Huddleston, Bishop of Stepney, for a third and final time, but not for another fifteen years. By then he will be an archbishop and the president of the Anti-Apartheid Movement. It will also be an extraordinary coming together of his two protégés: the boy with a guitar from Islington, and the boy with a trumpet from Africa.

CHAPTER FIVE

TWENTY-FOUR FRAMES A SECOND

The screaming engine of the silver Lotus Elan pinned me back into the leather seat and shot me down the empty backstreet. It was exhilarating enough to be nearly horizontal in a speeding car but to have a voluptuous, miniskirted blonde driving me, her slim leg pumping the heavy clutch, was beyond my pubescent dreams. What made it sublime was that the woman with a kid glove on the vibrating gearstick was the pulchritudinous star of the *Carry On* movies, Liz Fraser.

I was making another 'Saturday Morning' picture, but this time I was starring in it, and Liz, who was playing the lead villain's moll, was taking me for a spin in her new toy. Catapulted from my black-and-white telly to full glorious colour in the driving seat next to me, I'm sure she knew to what wonderful places she was also driving this twelve-year-old's imagination. *Hide and Seek* followed the rules of most Children's Film Foundation movies: kids rise above the bumbling inadequacies of authority to help capture a bunch of no-gooders; on the way, they have a bit of slapstick at the adults' expense and learn some lessons about themselves. I played Chris, a policeman's son, who finds an absconded borstal boy, Keith, hiding in a basement under the house of Roy Dotrice's grubby Mr Grimes. We soon stumble upon a heist that, with the licence of cinematic coincidence, involves Keith's father, who's also the gang's leader (played by the swarthy Terence Morgan), and his henchmen, Johnny Shannon, Alan Lake and Robin Askwith. The denouement is played out over classic CFF territory – the bomb-site. With cameos from Alfred Marks, Bernard Spear and Graham Stark, as well as the delicious Liz, it had a cast list equal to any of the major British comedy productions of the time.

What thrilled me even more was that I had to take six weeks off school to make it. Of course, I had a tutor, but what kid wouldn't rather be here, although in saying that, Deptford was not in my comfort zone. The local lads gave us as much trouble as they could without gaining the attention of the police. It was common for me to have to dodge the odd flying milk bottle during filming, and a bunch of fey film types are never great at standing up to that sort of thing. It was usually left to one of the female chaperones to defuse the wrath that our presence instilled in the local gangs. A few cakes off the buffet would also help. Noticeably, it was always quiet when Johnny Shannon was around. Johnny, bald and heavyset, was a fighter turned actor and had notably played the arch villain, Harry Flowers, in Nic Roeg's *Performance*. Johnny was a friend of the Krays and someone that would come back into my life during my preparation for *The Krays*. But at this moment I'm a skinny kid with a bad haircut courtesy of the assistant director, who was given the job of chopping it after the producer felt my 'feathercut' too trendy for Deptford. I cried bitter tears when I later saw it in the mirror above our fireplace at home. Dad could have done a better job with his K-Tel special.

Alan Lake and the young Robin Askwith soon became the set's bad boys, and though they teased me in a good-natured way throughout the filming, they took me under their mutual wing. A stalwart of British television, Alan was famously married to Britain's answer to Marilyn Monroe – Diana Dors. Sadly, five months after Diana died of cancer in

1984, Alan, laden with grief, would unburden himself by unloading a gun into his head.

To a boy of my background one of the added bonuses of making films was money. In those days the authorities felt they needed some promises before trusting what might be devious working-class parents with cash that belonged to a child. And so my mother and I, dressed in our best, went along to County Hall to see a haughty representative from the Inner London Education Authority for an interview and a large dose of condescension. Over a pair of reading glasses my mother was scanned for honesty, and made to understand that a third of the money had to be put away until I was sixteen. Flinching under the wagging finger of authority, my deeply moral mother must have been appalled by the suspicion laid upon her. I'd already been earning my own money working Saturdays at a local greengrocer's, my father insisting that I put a third of it towards the housekeeping, as he felt that it would give me a sense of financial responsibility. But with this additional sum, I knew what I wanted to do – go electric. As soon as I got the money from the film, I took my old cheese-cutter back to Holloway Road and exchanged guitar and earnings for an amplifier and an Epiphone electric guitar in cherry red. The acting was starting to feed the music, but the music I wanted to play was from outer space.

One Thursday night, while watching *Top of the Pops* on a friend's colour TV, we both agreed that we'd seen the future and it had white nail varnish and orange hair. T.Rex had made way for Slade, but here was someone to make them all look like piffling nonentities, a troubadour to welcome in my sexual awakenings. A Mephisthophelean messenger for the Space Age, expounding a manifesto that was almost spiritual in its meaninglessness, he spoke his words through a grinning confidence that had me signing up to whatever he was selling for the rest of my life. Pointing his long finger down the barrel of the lens he sang: '*I had to phone someone so I picked on you,'* and I felt that he had. And oh, but oh, when that guitar solo clawed and choked its way out of the Gold Top Les Paul, brandished like a musical laser gun, the Starman Bowie threw his arm around his golden-suited buddy and I wanted to go to that planet. For a generation, a benchmark was being drawn as to how pop music should look – not the boy next door, nor the corkscrew-haired changeling, not even the hyper-lad of the Faces, but a theatre of glittering aspiration that one could only ever dream of entering. I walked home through the decrepit streets of Islington and planned my future. *If we can sparkle he may land tonight* ... But it would be a few more years before touchdown.

Phil Daniels was a wiry King's Cross kid whose twisted smile revealed a cynicism that belied his young years. Small, dark and feral, he seemed more cultured than others, and having just added himself to Anna's swelling number, I was drawn to him. He also had an electric guitar.

Phil and I started to meet up and make music with Peter Hugo Daly, another one of Anna's new recruits, but a patchouli-scented one from the other side of the Essex Road. When Peter's keyboard was in charge we'd play strung-out jams based on Pink Floyd tracks; if it were Phil's guitar it would be the Faces; and if it were my Epiphone taking the lead, anything from *Ziggy*. We rehearsed in Duncan Terrace at the house of a middle-class kid called Miles Landesman, brother of the future writer Cosmo, and his place was a revelation to me. Although his parents Jay and Fran Landesman owned their own home, I was shocked at how strangely out of joint everything was: old rugs thrown about on rough planks; photographs, old paintings and revolutionary posters hanging on scuffed walls; an odd frying pan that they called a 'wok', unwashed among half-empty bottles of wine – the first I'd ever seen – in a spacious pine kitchen that smelt sweetly foreign and tantalisingly decadent. Even the rice, left cold in a large pot, looked dirty and brown, not the starched, white stuff I'd seen before in a Chinese takeaway. Obscure, dog-eared books were scattered on shelves and tables, while a tennis racket lay discarded on the stairs, waiting for another summer. But what shocked me the most was that the sofa and chairs in the living room didn't match! And yet his family were so at ease within this shabby chaos, it was as if nothing mattered or belonged to them enough to care about. The truth was *everything* belonged to them, unlike in my own house, where Wilson the cat was the only thing not on hire purchase.

I sat in their living room and tasted my first 'real' coffee and thought how horrified my mother would have been by the lack of curtains or nets on the windows. Without nets, she'd once told me, people will think we are poverty stricken. In her mind their absence inferred some kind of moral collapse. I started to become upset with my own home – why didn't we read newspapers that had more words than photographs? Why didn't we have books everywhere? Why were we not discussing theatre, politics and macrobiotic diets? Regardless of the spoonfuls of love I was being fed at home, my newly formed taste for garlic pâté and roasted coffee beans was turning me into a bitter young snob.

My father had been struggling at work, both physically and mentally, and the result was turning into depression and a potential breakdown. He would come home and sit slumped in his chair, complaining of pains and dizziness, and we had lost the do-it-yourself man we loved. My worried mother felt he should go to our local GP, a trip full of fear at the best of times for my father. He'd grown up with no National Health system and when, after the war, he finally saw a doctor, it was a man with an upper-class accent and a university education – an absolute alien, as far as my father was concerned. Dad would sit like a child, not asking any questions, convinced that the professional was 'looking down his nose' at him. Nevertheless, he took my mother's advice and made the visit. The doctor, who was not quite as disdainful as Dad had imagined, sympathetically recommended a change of job, and so for a while he considered leaving the print and working for the Post Office. He even toyed with the idea of leaving London and we spent one day visiting the sixties-imagined future that is Hemel Hempstead. We stood in the middle of the toytown and imagined our future there and, luckily for this story, promptly returned home.

And then they made him redundant; a real blow for a breadwinner with little savings. It was a dreadful time for him, but after searching he managed to find work as a guillotine operator for a print firm in Old Street. My father recovered his spirit, we stayed as Londoners, and almost as a symbol of regaining his old self, he built me something. A dulcimer is a beautiful four-stringed folk instrument played on the lap. He painted it orange and black and I hung it on my wall, proud of my growing collection and my skilled father.

Although my aspirations flourished, the band with Phil didn't. We didn't even bother to give it a name, let alone play a gig, and we soon drifted apart. Three years later we reunited for an Anna Scher television programme. Written by Charles Verrall, *You Must Be Joking!* was a children's sketch show for Thames TV that featured many of the Anna Scher kids. A teeny-band called Flintlock supplied the music, but on the first show Charles asked Phil and me if we would play a song. Somewhere in the basement of a television studio lies a tape of the boy who would eventually star in the movie *Quadrophenia* and his mate, sitting on stools, strumming acoustic guitars and singing America's 'A Horse With No Name'. Why we didn't do something cooler I have no idea! Probably too much time spent in Miles's mother's pine kitchen soaking up Joni Mitchell et al. Hopefully the tape will never be found.

To everyone's surprise *Hide and Seek* was released with the flourish of a royal premiere. The film was shown at the ABC cinema on Shaftesbury

Avenue one Saturday morning in October 1972 in the presence of Her Royal Highness the Duchess of Kent and an invited audience. It was the twenty-first anniversary of the Children's Film Foundation and *Hide and Seek* had been chosen for this prestigious birthday celebration.

Since making the film I had worked with my brother Martin in a small cameo role for the BBC's children's storytelling programme *Jackanory*. Playing two Arsenal supporters returning from a match and bumping into a friend (played by Stephen Brassett), it was hardly a stretch for us, but it was Martin's first role. Martin was a shy boy – he'd blush if he met a friend in the street – but after a few weeks under Anna's encouraging tutelage, his confidence grew, and it was now obvious that this relaxed ten-year-old's cheeky on-screen grin and ice-blue eyes were designed for attraction. I would have to work a little harder from now on.

My parents brought him along to the *Hide and Seek* premiere and they watched proudly as I stood in the line-up and shook the slight royal hand, the duchess a pale vision of creams and peroxide. Anna and Charles were there and so was a BBC camera crew for *Film '72*, the Barry Norman review programme. It was an enjoyable thrill, but the best screening of the film was a few weeks later in Deptford at a genuine Saturday Morning Pictures. The CFF invited its young cast down to present the film to an audience of local kids – thankfully not the ones who'd tried to bottle us. High on Jublees, they screamed, shouted and laughed in all the right places. Surprisingly, this time the manager didn't walk down the aisle and threaten to throw us all out.

Watching the film now, there's something wonderfully honest about the boy on screen: the accent is dated, yet true to his class, and the reactions are unselfconscious. It's a glimpse at myself before the advent of aspiration and self-design.

A week after the premiere I stayed up late and watched *Film '72* and an interviewer asking me if I planned to be an actor when I grew up. I was inspired by the story my father had told about having to leave school at fourteen and not being able to study for the job he really desired, and so my answer was for him: 'No. Not really. I want to be a journalist.'

It was a lie. I'd already set my sights on music.

Thirty years later, the wide-eyed Bowie boy from Islington would make an unexpected return. Working in Dublin, I spend an evening with Joe Elliott of Def Leppard. We end up in one of those drink-fuelled discussions where the aural highlights of your life end up scattered across the living-room floor while you claim that your growing pains had the greatest musical accompaniment of any generation. Being the same age, we concur on most things, and it's Bolan, Bowie and Bryan that litter the place, along with some crumbs of Humble Pie. Joe claims triumphantly to have experienced various rock epiphanies in the early seventies and shows me some of the evidence: a framed layout of ticket stubs from Sheffield City Hall, circa '71–75. Thinking fast, I manage to trump his yellowing memorabilia and brandish a dreamlike experience I had one October evening in 1973 at the Marquee Club in Soho.

Since that cathartic 'Starman' I'd devoured everything Bowie: weeping tears through the heartbreaking passion of 'Time'; crushing my feet into orange platform heels and even trying to reason out the ridiculous whimsy of 'Laughing Gnome'. I'd worn a white scoop-neck T-shirt that had tiny blue stars and long flared sleeves, and in a pair of loons from Oxford Street I'd felt David holding my hand as I sashayed uptown and went glam.

So it was with great patience that I'd queued for hours in a wet Wardour Street to see what was billed as *The 1980 Floor Show*. Bowie was to present songs from *Pin-Ups* and announce the writing of a musical soon to be released called *1984*, and all this was to be filmed by NBC for American television. With guest artists such as Marianne Faithfull –

dueting dressed as a nun – and mime artists from Lindsay Kemp's school, it would become legendary among Bowie aficionados. In bangles and baggies I rushed to the front of the stage and pressed into a mass of boys with painted faces and girls wearing baby-blue eyeshadow and antique fox stoles. The previous July, at the Hammersmith Odeon, we'd all shed tears as Bowie retired Ziggy and said farewell to the Spiders from Mars, but now, just for this show, the Spiders were back, Ziggy had risen from the grave, and I would watch the Pallas Athena of rock stalk the stage in heels. At some magical moment during the night he reached down, looked into my eyes and accepted one of my bangles as a gift. In return, he handed me the map of my future.

Sadly for Joe, he hadn't been there, but he's got it on a bootleg VHS and within moments of me mentioning it, we're watching the entire event on telly. Through the fractured twists and rolls of his distorted, multi-copied tape, I witness a moment from my past at twenty-four frames a second and it is glorious; a cabaret of decadence that had taught me how to dream. I remember it all as it reels before me. But then, as I watch Bowie lean into the crowd below, I feel weak, for there I am, right where I remember, just in front of the boots of Mick Ronson – a fair-haired boy, just turned fourteen, thrusting his bright face up into the temptation of glitter, lights and flesh; gorging on the glamour of it all.

I sit forward in my chair, open mouthed. Suddenly I can draw a line between then and everything I had done since.

'That's me, Joe! That's me!' I shout.

But then some white noise fills the screen, and I'm gone.

CHAPTER SIX

FAGS AND BEER

Like a fickle lover, the young fan of music thinks nothing of switching his allegiances and changes heart at the drop of a 45. As I browse through what is left of my record collection from the first half of the seventies, it flits capriciously from the glam pop of Bolan, Sweet and Gary Glitter, through the art-school histrionics of Bowie, Roxy Music and Mott, to the lad-rock of the Who, Humble Pie and the Faces, with a few Trojan Chartbusters and Motown compilations thrown in. What no longer exists in my dusty record cases are the ones that I covertly sold at Cheapo Cheapo's record store in Soho that summer of '76 when the Sex Pistols happened, the ones that if discovered would steam up the Ray-Bans of any discerning punk. These included the public-school bands Pink Floyd, Jethro Tull, Genesis, ELP and, of course, Yes; or basically anything with a Roger Dean cover.

Roger Dean painted the fantasy landscapes of floating grassy islands that so visually suited the dreams of young, sex-shy, middle-class boys soaked in Tolkien and real ale. It also suited progressive bands – photographs of the pale hairy musos themselves could potentially threaten sales. Roger's topographic panoramas were all the appetiser I needed before the needle hit the record and the sound of either Bachian or wistful prog filled my bedroom.

Dad had upgraded the front room's entertainment to a 'music centre', making Mum's ornaments suddenly homeless. I asked if I could have the old radiogram, and he pulled it apart and rebuilt the turntable, amp and a movable mono speaker into the gap in the wall behind the headboard of my bed. In 1971, when Arsenal won the double and the outside of our house became decorated like a battleship, in red and white bunting, my brother and I placed the speaker on the window ledge to blare out the raucous 'Good Old Arsenal' to the entire street. But now, lying on my bed, immersed in folk-styled fantasy lyrics of namby-pamby desire, I'm leaving my humdrum Islington reality on a floating hillock of Roger Dean's design, and probably passing some 'Watchers Of The Sky', or even a 'Siberian Khatru'. From here I can see the remnants of my discarded bands spread out below me like fallen idols, while I gloat from above, aloft on my own smug superiority.

What had caused this levitation in musical taste was grammar school. Dame Alice Owen's had brought together the working-class and the middle-class kids of Islington and the battle played itself out in the quad of cultural choice. Bowie boys lined up against prog rockers; lager drinkers foamed at the mouth against the anti-fizz brigade of the Campaign for Real Ale; while tartan-scarfed geezers, with their war cry of 'Rod is Guv'nor', fought tooth and nail with the yeomen manqués of the English folk revival. Intellectually – and technically – prog felt superior to pop and embraced my desire for something more challenging. But my journey on that floating tuffet said more about my aspirations within the playground than any real musical taste. Somehow, with skilled diplomacy and a lot of hot air, I managed to hover disgracefully between all camps.

When I arrived at Owen's, the school still had one foot in its public-school past of classics, fagging and gowned teachers, some of whom were permanently lost in their own brown studies. The other foot, platform-shod, stomped its way forward into the comprehensive future that was planned to happen in 1976. This schizophrenia seemed to embody itself in the architecture: two buildings, one Victorian and musty with cloisters and ghosts for the boys; the other – keeping the girls tantalisingly separate from us – was a sixties vision of the future, all glass and sexy steel geometry. We were to be the final intake on this site, whose foundations in Islington went back to 1613 and the charitable dream of the eponymous Tudor lady. The school was to relinquish its grammar status and move to Potters Bar.

Over the years, Owen's had spawned some famous names, the ancient actress Jessica Tandy being the earliest that people knew of, followed by the actor Joss Ackland and, the one we were most proud of, the legend of Owen's reviews, the film director Alan Parker. There must have been great politicians, judges and curers of fatal illnesses, but frankly the media names impressed us the most. Three years above me, Steve Woolley would play a part in the making of Spandau Ballet before going on to run Palace Pictures and produce the hit movies *Mona Lisa*, *Scandal*, *The Company of Wolves* and *Absolute Beginners*. In his year a chirpy cockney kid called Chris Foreman would leave at sixteen and, with his mates from Camden, form a ska band called Madness. It was this frisson of clashing cultures and class that led to its rampant creativity. The working-class boys would be there on creative merit and charm, and the arts, not the bar, were where we saw ourselves as potential champions.

Those first moments in a new playground are a feverish jostling for status that can brand a boy for life, and I was terrified on my first day there. My mother had bought me a pair of trousers big enough to give me as much wear as possible, and so the turn-up inside went up to my knee. They looked ridiculously wide and my fear was I would be confused for a 'wally' and they would condemn me to the infamous and terrifying 'Fag Cage'. The Fag Cage was a tall gate in the quad that when pushed back against the wall would create a tight little medieval prison for the poor first-year boy chosen as torture victim. Thankful that it wasn't me, I stood, hands in pockets, desperately pulling my flapping trousers in as tightly as I could, while the chosen quarry was dragged screaming from a group of new boys and placed between the wrought-iron gate and the wall. His back scraped the red brick as he slumped inside the cage, while large, acned lads prodded and abused him until a bored member of staff strolled over and set the blubbing, permanently scarred creature free. Unfortunately, being the last year's intake at the school, we never got the chance to pass that particular baton of cruelty on.

There were six of us working-class lads who'd made the grade at Rotherfield and every one of us was named Gary. My name gives a lot away: middle-class kids are just not called Gary; neither, it seems, is anyone born later than about 1965. However aspirational I would try to be, no matter how much I would smarten my accent, 'Gary' is always the giveaway and has me bang to rights when among the Simons and Julians.

I was probably very lucky not to make the Fag Cage, given that I took time off to make films and occasionally carried a guitar to school. For a moment there was a rumble of discontent about it in the year above, but being in films was something that seemed to give me an aura of protection, a veneer of something otherworldly – they weren't sure how to despise it as it was way off their map of things to hate – and playing guitar was generally considered a lot cooler than swotting at schoolwork, being too fat to do sport or playing the violin. A friend of mine, Neil Barnes, who fearlessly brought his violin to school, took some terrible lashings for what was considered to be a symbol of great queerness. Neil would have the last laugh, though. Small, glasses-wearing Neil would eventually grow to stand tall in contact lenses, and become extremely successful in an electronic band called Leftfield.

Blessed were we that the school's trustees happened to be the guild of brewers. From the first year we were given what was called 'Beer Money', a subsidy and stamp of approval for our drinking. We boys were taken to Brewers Hall in the City and, with Masonic-like ritual, silently lined up to approach the Master of the Worshipful Company of Brewers and receive an old crown coin in return for a silent and respectful nod.

'Boys, you must promise to save this money,' the Master said piously, surrounded by grand heraldic ornamentation, 'until you are old enough to spend it on beer.'

At Owen's this was about thirteen and a half. At that point we were allowed to spend our annually increasing payment in the Crown and Woolpack, a pub that adjoined the school building like a classroom for extracurricular studies. Here, certain members of staff openly encouraged our loyalty towards the ancient livery of brewers that owned our school. This dedication was visually borne out by the crest emblazoned proudly upon our blazers: a shield containing six sheaves of barley and three barrels of beer.

If I were to blame anyone for my journey into prog rock then it would be Ian Bailey. Ian was three years above me but we both took guitar lessons in the music room of the girls' building and I befriended him immediately, looking up to his musical talent and superior knowledge. Slight, with thick, curly black hair, glasses and a soft-spoken voice, he played rock keyboards like a professional and we soon started playing together around the piano in the music room.

Once a week we had open assembly and pupils could contribute to that morning's events in the musty, oak-panelled hall. Ian and I, along with a drummer from my class called Chris 'Ossie' Ostrowski, decided to perform two songs in front of this yawning, captive audience, one of which was 'Light My Fire'. I sung while Ian took the opportunity to go for the full Keith Emerson, his hero at the time, and placed his Bontempi organ at right angles to the piano for full prog-rock simultaneous double-keyboard playing. To excite the audience even more – and probably himself – he wore a denim jacket slashed to the waist with nothing else but a gold medallion underneath. Being but measly third-formers, Ossie and I had to put up with wearing our school uniforms, and were bitterly envious of Ian's real rock chic. The assembled boys, used to sermons from our begowned headmaster, Puddyfat, lapped it up.

After our triumph in the school hall, I'd visit Ian's house in Stoke Newington, where we would jam around the sitting room's upright piano while his tiny Jewish mother served us tea and encouragement. Here, we would write songs together for what would soon become my first proper band. Ian had started working Saturdays at Howarth's Music in Camden Passage, a middle-class area dominated by antique shops where I'd witnessed the hippy commune in 1968. By the early seventies the London hippies had moved their spiritual home from San Francisco to LA and accordingly had swapped sandals for cowboy boots, Afghans for jean jackets and Love for Crosby, Stills, Nash and Young. The Western front had arrived in London and chilled-out desperados with tight denims and pasty faces roamed the knick-knack stores of the Passage. A few of these lonestars, when they weren't drinking over roll-ups in the Camden Head, centred themselves around Paul Howarth's shop. Two of them, Ian Fox and Mickey Ball, were looking to form a band and both fell upon Ian Bailey. Of course, Ian wanted to include his schoolmates, and within a few days, Ian, Ossie and I were rehearsing with these guys in the cramped basement of the shop.

Mickey, with Zapata moustache, played bass. He was an old mod turned urban cowboy who loved soul, while Ian Fox, on second guitar and whole-earth beard, was strictly a country cockney, and being the most organised, became leader. He introduced me to Little Feat and the Doobie Brothers, Southern-fried funk that I loved to play on my guitar.

Actually, the confusion between the two Ians I'm experiencing as I write was the same for us in rehearsals and led to Ian Bailey's renaming. At that time Jess Yates (whose daughter Paula I would meet in just a few years) was a household name for his Sunday evening religious programme, where he sat smiling behind his organ. Ian Fox took to calling Ian Bailey 'Jess' as a tease, and, sounding more cowboy, it stuck.

Our first public performance was on the pavement in front of the music shop during the Camden Passage festival in October 1974. Our set included a Beatles song, a Herbie Hancock instrumental and an Average White Band number; it lasted half an hour and when we finished we started again. But what made that cold night particularly auspicious was the appearance of two guys from school who'd come down to watch, hang out and help us with the gear. Both were called Steve.

Steve Norman was a good-looking blond boy that I vaguely knew from my class at school. He was learning to play guitar and I'd spotted him in the music room watching me once as I sang 'The Highwayman', an Alfred Noyes poem that I'd set to music. The other Steve, Steve Dagger, was in Jess's year. He was obsessed with music and its history, especially Motown and the Small Faces, and was the first mod-revivalist I knew. Along with his Chelsea boots, Sta-Press and matelot top, he sported a blond, mod haircut that made him stand out from the crowd. An only child and a fellow son of a printer, he lived in a high-rise in Holborn. Fervently left wing, Steve had views upon everything musical and political, and although he was subdued and thoughtful, his company would become inspirational.

The gig was a local success and after some additions of Kemp/ Bailey numbers to the set, Ian was out looking for gigs. The Same Band was typical of Ian's dry sense of humour and given that we were anything but unique, the name he chose suited us. Pub rock was happening, and the pubs were full of bands wanting to be the Band – Ducks Deluxe,

Brinsley Schwarz, Bees Make Honey – all playing American-style boogie. So we added ourselves to the list and the Pied Bull near Chapel Street market and the King's Head in Upper Street became our usual stages. But most of all, we rehearsed. And made our way through drummers.

Ossie could never turn up on time and after grander and grander excuses culminating in a lie about a burst blood vessel in his arse, we relieved him permanently of his drum stool. The next drummer seemed to be Camden Passage's main drug dealer, which kept him busy between sets but left him a little vague about arrangements. And then Mickey retired at thirty – at twice my age he must have been feeling the strain. Ian took over on bass and I became the only guitarist. Still hovering on Roger Dean's floating mountain, I wrote a Tolkien-inspired ballad called 'Lothlorien'. It was born out of my latest inspiration – folk.

With Steve Norman I'd started visiting a folk club at the Florence pub near Upper Street, a real finger-in-the-ear, knit-your-own-beer sort of place. The English folk scene was going strong, and although it was a home for nervous, intellectual introverts, I had a deep feeling for the music, even getting up one night to sing my 'Highwayman'. The early-seventies folk revival seemed to come from a general desire to return to the loyalties of a simple past, a reaction to the sixties op-art future and Wilson's 'white heat' utopia that never came. And by early 1975 it definitely hadn't arrived in our street.

The Kemps were still in their rooms in Rotherfield, with no bathroom and one outside loo shared between three families. My parents, far from interested in middle-class folk nostalgia, were desperate to get the luxury that their friends in high-rise places had, and they quite rightly craved an avocado bathroom suite, a warm, dry loo seat, and maybe even a small area outside for greenfly to gather. When my memory is lit by the candlelight of Ted Heath's Three-Day Week, the place takes on a certain Dickensian nostalgia, but in reality the enforced

Victorian living conditions only added to the coldness and grimness of our situation. In any case, my brother and I were getting a little too old to share a bedroom, and had to satisfy our daily desire for teenage privacy in the damp shed of that smelly yard toilet.

The opposing walls above our beds reflected our separate interests in a kind of face-off of passion. While mine was hung with a growing collection of stringed instruments, Martin's was a riposte of kung fu posters. Martin, who played football for Islington and had had a trial for Arsenal, was much sportier than I was, and he invariably beat me in our occasional fisticuffs. And so his burgeoning showmanship found its stage on the football pitch, with his deft attacking touches enhanced by a customised pair of football boots that he'd painted sky blue and lined with fake fur from Mum's sewing bag. He balanced this with some wonderfully intelligent acting – being given the chance to co-star in *Glittering Prizes*, a drama for television starring Tom Conti – and being offered a place at the other Islington grammar school, Central Foundation.

Although 138 Rotherfield Street meant a sparse and cramped existence, it was a rock of love for my brother and me to venture from and return to, a place of safety where we found confidence and therefore a growing success in our lives. My parents, on the other hand, deserved better.

My acting career with Anna had fallen away, owing mostly to my growing lack of attendance because of my obsession with the band and music, although I did keep my thespian leanings going at school. A teacher called Roger Digby, a large bearded bear of a man who played a squeezebox and Morris-danced in his spare time, had the inclination to pull together some ambitious school productions. The first was *The Boy Friend*, where I charlestoned as Bobby Van Husen, and the second was an even camper musical, *Salad Days*, in which I was given the lead.

Things weren't going so well with the Same Band, though. Flicking through the music papers one day, we saw a gig listed for none other than the Same Band. But it wasn't us. A trip to meet them was made. The confrontation went something like this:

'How *long* have you been the Same Band?'

'We've been the same band since school.'

'No, how long have you been *the* Same Band?

'I'm sorry, but we've been the Same Band longer than you have. I've never heard of the other Same Band.'

'But *we are* the Same Band. We've done lots of gigs. You can't have the same name as us – people will think we're the same band!'

'What?'

'We can't have the same name. One of us has to be another band.'

'*Another Band*? That sounds awful.'

Pause.

'Oh, whatever … Shall we toss a coin for it?'

We lost.

In 1975 Islington Council were in the process of renovating the houses in our area, and with great excitement we were suddenly relocated two blocks east to Elmore Street and a 'modernised' Victorian terrace with our own front door and all the amenities we'd craved. My room was small, but at least after a hot bath I had my privacy. Mum got her avocado suite, and Dad finally had a garden to play in. To us, it was a mansion. In the summer evenings I would sit alone with my guitar on the little six-by-six square of grass, and watch the sun dancing upon our washing line. But my meditative little tuffet was about to crash against an accelerating new wave.

CHAPTER SEVEN

FOLLOWING THE DRUM

'We have to go to this, it's gonna be amazing.' Dagger was standing under the glittery lights in full Chelsea-mod regalia. He'd just arrived, and his declamatory statement, given while brandishing a black-and-white A4 flyer, had all the pub's smoky heads turning towards him. He held the page up for us to see. On it was a Xeroxed picture of a short-haired singer and a young, similarly barbered guitarist. Above them, in an aggressive scrawl, was written THE SCREEN ON THE GREEN PRESENTS A MIDNIGHT SPECIAL SUNDAY AUGUST 29TH MIDNIGHT–DAWN. Below that it said SEX PISTOLS. *What a name*, I thought.

It was bank holiday weekend and Steve Norman and I were sitting in the Camden Head. Since the Same Band (or whatever we were now going to call ourselves) had started rehearsing upstairs, this cut-glass pub had become our centre of operations. Fundamentally a soul boy, Steve had inspired me with his Stevie Wonder and Motown records that he played at his home on the Bourne Estate in Islington. His father, Tony, a cabby whose passions were London, the voices of Mel Blanc, and commentating upon the soap opera that was going on inside his tropical-fish tank, had passed his typically North London sense of humour on to his son. But what drew me to Steve was his instinct for music. He had a sharp ear for what was going on in the arrangements of records we'd play, comfortably transcribing them to our guitars, and we soon performed a morning school assembly together, playing 'Light My Fire' and 'A Horse With No Name', albeit to a hall of half-awake kids, still lost under their bed-hair.

We usually talked music on our Saturday nights out, but this time we were both contemplating our imminent move up to the new school in Potters Bar. We'd just received our 'O' Level grades and I'd pulled in six; good enough to begin 'A' Levels in Economics, English and British Constitution. I'd also received the F. E. Cleary prize for music, which was odd and slightly embarrassing, as music wasn't one of my given subjects. They did manage to spell my name wrong on the certificate, though. The final day at the old school had been celebrated in infamous Crown and Woolpack style, ending up a wild, lustful affair, with all 'beer money' correctly spent. But now, with holidays coming to an end, we were kicking our heels.

'I got it from Woolley,' continued Dagger, reverting to his usual calm manner. Steve Woolley was a mate of his from the same year at school. A movie fanatic, he had left Owen's at sixteen to assist a guy called Roger Austin in managing the Screen on the Green, an arthouse cinema in Upper Street and just across the road from the Camden Head. Woolley was destined for greater things in the movie business, but right now he is a spotty kid with glasses and lank hair, and an insider tipping the wink on what was about to be one of the most influential moments in our young lives.

Dagger paid for his pint of lager and, smoothing his mod sideburns, joined us in one of the pub's booths. Three years above us, he'd just finished school and was about to begin his degree course in politics at the University of London.

He settled into his seat. 'The Clash are a new band.' Dagger was reading the names of the support acts mentioned on the flyer. 'They've only done one invited show in London so far, in a rehearsal room, but they're gonna be huge.' He curled his lip over his beer glass, content in his own authority, and then studied the page once more. 'Buzzcocks. They're from up north.'

Dagger was an oracle for our musical knowledge. He'd tried everything contemporary but still hadn't found anything that he could connect with apart from the music of the sixties. Growing up in the West End, he'd become gripped with the notion of 'Swinging London', but by the time he was old enough to join in, it had stopped swinging.

Folding the flyer, he delivered a final morsel of intelligence to his faithful two: 'It's called punk.'

In the July of that hottest summer on record, two bands had started duelling residences at the Marquee Club. One was a blokes' band from Essex called Eddie and the Hot Rods, the other was an ear-piercing Australian mob known as AC/DC. They were both breaking attendance records every week, cramming over a thousand into a space meant for less than seven hundred. Something was developing out of the pub-rock scene that demanded more sweat and muscle, more showbiz and glamour; a rejection of the laid-back denim and beards; something just a little ruder. Along with the two Steves, Martin and I had been part of the sweaty masses that had attended both of these bands' gigs on a regular basis that summer. We were thrilled as AC/DC's boy guitarist stripped to his underpants, entered the audience on the lead singer's shoulders, and stood vulnerably next to us while playing a cocky solo. A few days later we'd be shouting the refrain of 'G-L-O-R-I-A' towards the shirtless singer of Eddie and the Hot Rods as his band ripped out their frantic R&B. Both shows seemed to be about a crowd interaction – we were as one, the band and the audience, creating an event together. It was a growing philosophy that would excite us for many years and it was one that punk was to utilise like none before.

And so it was with some anticipation that we three gathered that night after Dagger's dramatic annunciation. He was still carrying the now dog-eared flyer, and we gathered around it as though it were some kind of religious relic. Outside the old cinema, Roger, the tall, arty manager, was striding nervously up and down, thrilled by the 'happening' that he was helping to create. Recognising Dagger, he lurched over and told us that they'd hired a print of Kenneth Anger's *Scorpio Rising* to run between the bands. We'd never heard of it, but it sounded suitable. As we entered the small cinema, the congregation that greeted us was a shock: here was a girl, brazen in a cup-less bra, fishnets and a swastika armband, camping it up with a boy in a bright pink mohair jumper, shades and bleached hair; a young girl with a severe, pink buzz-cut and exaggerated eye make-up; a man dressed like a charlady but wearing white sunglasses; a large posse of extraordinary yet knowingly arch young people, all hugging and grooving to themselves. I suddenly felt very self-conscious about the plain, flared jeans and sweatshirt thingy that I was so blandly wearing, while Steve fidgeted in his new, but suddenly not-so-cool, Foster Grant Easy Rider glasses.

When the bands came on, the clique feigned exaggerated boredom and shouted catty remarks up at the stage, which the bands batted back with equal wit. I loved this – watching rounds of one-upmanship, where everyone, regardless of whether they were onstage or not, vied to be the night's main attraction. The event was enthralling, but Steve and I expected someone to come up at any minute and say, 'Sorry, there's been a mistake. We've spotted your nerdy look and you'll have to leave.'

It was when five men calling themselves the Clash stepped on to the stage that we knew we were witnessing something seminal. It's difficult now to relate the shock of seeing clean-shaven boys with short, spiky hair in such hirsute times. With tight, paint-splattered suits, and legs as wide apart as humanly possible, they played low-slung guitars at a frenetic, angry pace, and spat out little sound-bites of song. They were modern; we were abuzz.

And then, at around 3 a.m., without any announcement, and just as Dagger and Steve had gone to the loo, four slack-jawed lads swaggered onstage as though they were about to steal it. Their mischievous followers, to show they'd seen it all before, continued their wry, artful game and sat in affected silence. But dressed in the flags and schmutter of their tribe, the Sex Pistols were a gang like no other and I immediately wanted to take their shilling. They had something of Old London about them, a comic familiarity and yet shockingly new; it was a kind of vitriolic vaudeville. The singer, dressed in ragged pomp, looked like a crooked kid from a council estate, a boy with a capacity for hatred, not like any of the fake West Coasters that pub rock had thrown up. Squaring up to the audience, he pulled the microphone sharply towards himself and, with a loud thump from the PA, smacked it into his snarly grin.

Dagger and Steve were taking a piss when Johnny Rotten slammed through the toilet door and up to the sink.

'Fuck! I've knocked me fucking tooth out!'

Dagger looked over his shoulder. 'Oh. Fuck … are you … are you all right, mate?'

'No. I've knocked me fucking tooth out on the mike!'

Disturbed by the singer's intimate proximity and fear that they might be discovered as impostors, Dagger and Steve zipped up and made a swift exit. They got back just in time to see the bloodied Rotten retake the stage and, with his cohorts, launch into the most thrilling performance of Young Turk rock'n'roll we'd ever witnessed. I was enthralled – behind the arrogant, swashbuckling guitar and the Bash Street Kids vocal was pure pop, an amalgam of hooks lifted from the great London writers that had come before: Marriott, Davies, Townshend, Wood. In the end, even the hard-to-impress charlady bloke was dancing.

Just after 4 a.m. we fell into the daylight, reeling like the victims of a hit and run but convinced we'd just taken part in the kind of event we'd read about happening in the sixties in places like the UFO club. We felt changed, and Dagger, high on adrenalin, had at last found his contemporary musical connection. I thought about the kind of music I was making with my band of older guys and how there was no cultural connection there for me at all. Saying goodbye, I realised that the answer was in front of me: my best friend, Steve Norman.

I turned back down the Essex Road and walked towards home, my ears still ringing with the future.

'I'm sorry, I wanna leave.' We were standing in the empty pub, about to start rehearsals. Over the last week, since seeing the Sex Pistols' *Midnight Special*, I'd made up my mind that I needed my own band of young punks.

Ian and Jess didn't seem to react to the news, or my newly chopped haircut. 'Well, actually,' said Jess, 'I'm off to uni in October and I'm not gonna be able to do this much more anyway.'

Ian was his usual calm self and carried on making his roll-up. *Was that it?* There was probably some hugging and a collecting of equipment, but with mutual acceptance, it was over.

At the same time, I left Anna's. I was on a mission.

The new school was a mass of ill-designed, low-rise blocks surrounded by leafy lanes, and felt sterile compared with its London original. They'd brought the gates up from Islington and a few oil paintings of ex-heads and even a stained glass of the Dame herself, but they sat miserably in the bland seventies architecture, as did we.

For a few of us though, the centre of gravity became the music room – a self-contained block where Steve and I would spend our lunchtimes playing guitars and making music with a dark-haired drummer-boy called John. A year above us, John Keeble lived with his parents, Stan and Doris, and younger sister Jackie, in an old tenement block in Kentish Town. He was a little shy and would often defend himself with a bluff manner, but he had a sharp eye and a strong sense of ambition, and his drumming was as tight and as solid as his wiry frame. On the bass was Michael Ellison. He wasn't really considered one of the lads but he owned his own PA, so he was in.

The first songs we did were the Kinks' 'All Day And All Of The Night' and an amphetamised 'I Wanna Be Your Man'. Dagger's sixties influence was working upon Steve and me and a punk version of Gary Puckett's 'Young Girl' was also knocked out. At that point, Steve and I were sharing the singing, but neither of us wanted to be the frontman. We needed to find one. As word got around, one of the boys started to announce himself as a contender.

Tony Hadley was well over six feet tall. Topped by a brush of black hair, he was not easily ignored, yet I'd never spoken to him in the five years of going to Owen's. He seemed to aggravate all of John's year and was forever in scrapes with them, as well as members of staff. I was fortunate and never got bullied at school – sometimes you just have to keep your head below the parapet, but with Tony that was physically impossible. It could have been his manner – a little too perky and Tiggerish – but whether in his overly long school scarf, or with his fluffy Bowie cut, he became some people's favourite moving target.

'What about Hadley?'

John was fixing his bass drum to the floor but the question made him jump up. 'No way! If he's the singer I'm not playing drums.'

'But John, he could be good. He says he can sing.'

'He says he can do everything.'

'That's true. He's always asking Salisbury to play him as centre-forward in the first team. It annoys everyone.'

'But John … *annoying people* might be good. And anyway … he's got a leather jacket.' The leather jacket was the symbol of punk cool at the time.

There was a pause. Steve and I looked at each other. John went back to his bass drum.

'What do you want me to sing?' Tony was excited and as Tiggerish as ever. It was lunchtime in the music room and Steve and I were playing it cool while John was openly belligerent. A few people loitered, but the room seemed equally split between those wanting him to succeed and those wanting him to fail miserably. Michael, as usual, didn't seem to care either way.

'"Oh Carol"?'

'Sure.'

Hadley took the mike and John raised his sticks.

'WHUTOFRIFOR!'

Like all our other songs, it was a version that started as fast as possible and ended faster. But he could sing; he was brilliant; even John agreed.

The next lunchtime we took Tony through the songs, including a version of the Animals' 'We Gotta Get Out Of This Place'. We'd found our man. And he wore the jacket well.

I'd always worked Saturdays. My father had insisted on it ever since I turned ten. After the paper round I started at a greengrocer's on Essex Road. I'd arrive at 6 a.m. to put the 'show' up, boil the beetroots and make the price cards (including the requisite intrusive apostrophes). I'd sell cabbages to one side of the Essex Road and avocados to the other; one I'd learn to call 'mum', the other 'madam'. Occasionally the young owner's father, who often worked there, would get me to hold the shop while he had sex with a customer on top of the sacks of potatoes out the back. After a couple of years Martin began working there, and we would run the place on our own, shouting out our wares in that traditional singsongy way. Eventually an older couple took it over. He only had one ball, she only one eye, and their elderly assistant, one leg. I got out of there before I too developed some sort of mono-affliction. A few years later I was to be diagnosed with having only one working kidney from birth. Unknowingly, I'd been perfect for the job!

I took on Saturday work at Greenfield Millets in Holloway Road. Here the manager would tell me to stand near the front of the shop and warn him if any 'coloureds' were coming in. I never did and he would berate me for it: 'The trouble with you is you're a socialist!' The advantage of working there though was that I got cheap walking and camping equipment, which supplied my new growing obsession.

Going to the mountains was a very grammar-school/*Lord-of-the-Rings*/real-ale thing to do in the early seventies, and an inspirational teacher, Jon Townsend, introduced me to it. It became a passion that I carry to this day and have passed on to my eldest son. In 1977, along with two other students, I received a travel bursary from the school, and with Jon and two more teachers, we all flew off to Morocco and the Atlas mountains; our ambition: to climb Mount Toubkal, the highest peak in North Africa.

The Kemps had never flown; in fact we'd only been out of Britain once. A few years previously my father, impressed that I'd started to learn French, decided we should take an overnight boat and train to Paris for a day. Deposited at the Gare du Nord, we stumbled into a culture shock of smells and visions. We seemed to have little idea of what to do or where to go and wandered its avenues in a daze, unable to communicate with anyone. In a café, we sat in hungry astonishment at the bloodied meat we were presented with. My mother, being a great believer that nothing can be cooked too much, ordered us to just eat the chips. That afternoon, heads in hands, we all fell asleep upon a random park bench before taking the train back to the welcome familiarity of Rotherfield Street and Dad's concluding statement: 'Well, I wouldn't bother with that again.'

Triumphantly standing on that cold, snowy, African giant, 13,671 feet above sea level, I looked out over the shimmering endlessness of the Sahara and felt that I'd come a long way from home. For ten days, camped at 3,000 feet below the summit, we lived on rehydrated food, and so hungry were we that every evening, whatever the subject discussed, we always managed to work it back to food. And so, on our exhausted return to Marrakesh, we offered up our emaciated stomachs to its steaming food stalls, and ravaged unnameable bowls of vegetables, meats and fish. The next night, while sleeping under the stars outside Agadir airport, I deposited all of it into my Greenfield Millets sleeping bag.

A few hours later, weak and shaky, I stumbled into the flyblown airport. As we entered customs, looking like burned-out hippy-trailers, we were hauled over by a gleeful officer in search of a bonus. The surly, armed and moustachioed guard confronted me first and, enjoying his moment, stared into my face while slowly opening my rucksack. Suddenly his whole body jarred. It must have been the impact of the stench that came from the hideous, squelching sleeping bag that I'd placed on top. With a weak wave of his hand, we were free.

The band was ready to play its first gig. Of course, we needed a name, and the Roots must have been pulled from an extremely unimaginative shortlist indeed. It was a fourth-form Christmas party in the big hall that gave us the chance. Our set lasted twenty minutes and when we were finished we did it again. Tony was brilliant and the fourth-form girls loved him. He'd been too much for the school playground – too tall, too loud, too unique – but on stage he was just right. He'd found his place – high up, above the rest – and the bullies were left awestruck. We weren't as musically proficient or as sophisticated as the Same Band, but in my gut it felt real, fresh, and something of the age. It was a band I could be proud of and one that I could imagine going all the way with. There was one problem: Michael didn't really fit in.

Short, tubby, and a little straight, Michael was also partially deaf, which gave him a speech problem and some cruel nicknames, but the real issue was we didn't consider him punk enough. He seemed good at organising, though, and helped to arrange our first public performance at the Queen's Head, a large, old-fashioned pub in Turnpike Lane. We were using his PA as well as his brother's guitar, a Les Paul copy, so his musician father was there to help keep an eye on things. We were a little overexcited and a few too many Bacardi and Cokes were sunk with the travelling fourth-form females before we went on; as a result I couldn't get my guitar in tune, and Michael's father was getting increasingly angry with me. Punk was in its infancy and there was much animosity to this new, high-energy music; but we were determined to throw its shapes on and off the stage, and this seemed to upset the landlord and Michael's fastidious father. When we got onstage, we were loud, too loud for the pub's DJ, who pulled the plug on us after only a few numbers. In my anger, while leaving the stage, the Les Paul copy fell off its stand and broke in two. Somewhere in the jeering crowd, Dagger was smiling – *this is just how it should be*, he thought.

Michael managed to arrange a couple of pub gigs supporting the up-and-coming Tom Robinson – one of which had Robert Plant and John

Bonham in the crowd – but our relationship had soured, and we finally asked Michael to leave. We changed our name to something more aggressive, the Cut, and Steve temporarily switched from guitar to bass.

Dagger, Steve and I started seeing the growing plethora of punk bands playing in various pubs in town. The Roxy was deemed the first punk club, and one night, with Martin in tow, we saw Generation X there. They were absolute pop, with the lead singer quite unarguably calling himself Billy Idol. All peroxide sex and baby-sneers, Billy was the first pop star of punk, and with his sidekicks he had the tunes to match. Full of hip sixties references, Generation X delivered a sound far more accessible to the charts than any other punk outfit before or after. We immediately fell in love with them and the next day, in the art room, Steve and I desperately tried to emulate their abstract screen-print T-shirts. We were no longer punk but 'power pop', and we needed some pop songs to match and, in order to put Steve back on guitar, a permanent bass player.

Richard Miller was a short, chirpy character with a Cheshire grin that split his face. Being the only other guitarist we knew at school, he was an obvious choice to take up the bass position, and he filled it with relish. Another name change, the Makers, was picked by Steve to suit our sixties pop sensibility, and songs started flowing, fizzy titles like 'Fantasy Girl' and 'Pin-Ups' to match our bright shirts, white jeans and growing mop-tops. With our ready-made school audience of mostly girls we landed a regular Sunday residency at the Pinder of Wakefield in Gray's Inn Road. But it wasn't enough, we wanted more, and the man who might deliver it was standing right in front of us.

'Would you like to manage us?' Steve and I were back in the Camden Head and offering ourselves to Dagger over a pint. He was a regular at our gigs and, along with Martin, helped with the gear-shifting. But

Dagger knew more about the history of pop than any of us, and his obsession with rock's great managers – Loog Oldham, Epstein, Meaden – revealed his interest in a particular niche not usually glorified by teenage boys. While Steve and I wanted to write the best song in the world, Dagger dreamed of designing the best band. This, he thought, could be his opportunity.

For a moment he stared at the white swirl on his lager. Thunderclap Newman was singing *because there's something in the air*. 'Yeah ... all right. I can do that,' he said, raising his head. 'I'd love it.'

Dagger's first booking had us supporting the punk band Chelsea at the now infamous Roxy. John's dad brought the gear down the narrow Covent Garden street in the back of his lorry and we humped it into the graffitied basement of the club. We were beautiful and clean compared to what its ravaged crowd were used to; a fresh-faced bunch of shiny popsters looking out on to an addled crowd of second-wave punks. Afterwards, as we collapsed inside the tiny dressing room, Chelsea's lead singer, the speed-driven Gene October, unsuccessfully attempted to poach our drummer. We were getting closer to the centre, and now with a hip, young manager, this school band was seriously thinking about a record contract.

But the punk scene was losing the pizzazz that I'd first recognised in Islington, and the original glamorous support had melted away, either forming their own bands or going back to the disco. Hijacked by the jetsam of suburbia, the movement had lost its direction, and McLaren, on the brink of creating the new Who, had turned the Pistols into his own self-destructive art project; either that or he'd lost his bottle for world dominance. Steve and I were drifting back to our love of soul and visiting clubs such as Crackers, Global Village and the Lyceum, dancing with the soul boys to American imports. Dagger, now at the London School of Economics, was a political animal. Angered by the

Orwellian image of the working class as portrayed by punk and its designers, Vivienne and Malcolm, he felt strongly that we should visually represent the real, contemporary extension of mod, the genuine article: the soul boy. Here was the true working-class youth movement, dressed to the nines in all its aspirational glory, every hard-earned penny spent on clothes, haircuts and American soul imports; a detail-obsessed, dancing Narcissus.

Inevitably, we fell between two stools, neither musically appreciated by the soul fraternity nor understood by the power-poppers. And even though we were happily playing venues such as the Rock Garden and the Hope and Anchor, with a regular crowd of supporters in tow, Dagger had spotted another problem that he felt stood in the way of his perfect band.

Visiting a photographer to pick up some photos that we'd done at his studio, he had an awakening. This had been our first 'professional' shoot and we were all excited about how it would look.

The photographer slipped them out of the envelope.

'How are they?' said Dagger.

'Good. They look all right, but, well ...'

'What?'

The photographer pointed at our bass player, standing on one side of the line-up. 'It's just this one here. He shouldn't be in it. He doesn't ... fit in.'

It had been on Dagger's mind for a while but this was confirmation. He knew he had to let blood. And he also knew who could make it better.

The Tibberton Arms was an Islington soul boy hangout opposite the public baths where I'd once lain horrified, calling for more hot water. Small, dark and empty of seating, the pub was chock-a-block with the bleached and unnaturally tanned aristocracy of North London, and Dagger and I were pressed against its sticky bar. Through the clamour of flattened vowels and geezered glottal stops, I wasn't sure that I'd heard what he'd said correctly.

'*What*? Instead of Richard?'

Dagger smiled back at me with a tight grin, visibly excited by his contentious new concept.

'Are you joking, Steve? Martin can't even *play* the bass!'

My brother was now sixteen. He'd left school and, following in Dad's footsteps, found a job as a typesetter in a print shop. Apart from roadie-ing for us, he also had a little punk group called the Defects that rehearsed in the basement of a friend's family's dry-cleaner's. As a punk, he'd chopped his own hair, worn his pyjamas to go out in and hung a metal coat hanger around his neck for jewellery, presumably as a symbol of his band's dry-cleaning roots. He adequately played the three guitar chords that they needed but this was a different matter – Richard was a very good bass player and Martin had never touched one before.

Dagger was adamant and shifted his weight to the other foot for a fresh attempt. 'The thing is, he's the best-looking bloke we know. Look at him – he looks like a fucking movie star!'

I looked down the bar to where Martin stood with his huge smile and a floppy wedge of black hair, holding back a swell of frothing girls, all attempting to fall into his pool-blue eyes.

'Yeah … OK. I'll think about it.'

Four or five days later I was teaching him the bass lines. With a guilty nod of inevitability we deferred to Dagger's better judgement and accepted the cull of poor Richard. Tony had left school and was working at IPC magazines and hating it, and we were all desperate for that elusive record contract. *Whatever it takes*, someone said. Hunched and lily-livered, we gathered in the Camden Head minus Richard and

Dagger. Richard had been told that a band meeting was to be held in another pub, but arrived to find only his erstwhile manager waiting for him like a debt-collector. Getting Martin into the band was to be one of the most important ideas Dagger would have. Richard accepted his fate and we accepted our new, younger bass player.

The Gentry was meant to be ironic, an anti-punk statement. The name suited our look of browns and beiges, wedges and waistcoats, and reflected the aspirations of soul boy culture. Martin was note perfect and we were happy that he'd transported his sexual magnetism on to our stage rather than being the most female-attended roadie in rock. It felt visually more harmonious and I was lifted by having another Kemp onstage. But soul boys playing guitar pop was a cultural contradiction that seemed to be alienating all sides. One night, drowning my awful 'A' Level results, brought on by lack of school attendance, Dagger confessed that he thought the band was going nowhere. We were stuck in a rut, he said, and needed to find our audience, a crowd that we could connect with. Not for the first time, he recounted the story of how Peter Meaden, in order to find success, had redesigned the Who to suit a mod audience. But not being American, or black, and playing essentially rock, left us wondering who we were to relate to. Where and what was *our* scene?

On a wet autumn night, at a little club in Soho, a strange, exotic crowd was beginning to gather, and our moment was about to arrive.

CHAPTER EIGHT

REVOLT INTO STYLE

Many years previously, the young Kemp family had taken a Sunday afternoon bus ride into the weekend hubbub of the West End to see a film that my father had waited expectantly for. Sitting in the velveteen comfort of the London Coliseum – recently converted to accommodate the wide-screen experience that was Cinerama – we watched *2001: A Space Odyssey* and felt intellectually weightless. That afternoon, Dad became acutely aware that a subject he thought he grasped had been snatched from him. Dan Dare was dead; art was now in space. Baffled, we stepped into the early-evening shadows and across into the flickering neon of Soho.

Sex on the telly would always reduce our chattering family to a gnawing silence. Time would slow down intolerably and we would wait motionless with discomfort for the intimate scene – and thus our embarrassment – to end. Walking through Soho that evening, we hunkered down into our familiar, burning speechlessness as all around us loomed photographs of naked women in various arrangements. The narrow streets were an entanglement of fleshpots: every other doorbell carried cards announcing 'models' waiting on first or second floors; shop windows revealed little but intimated much, while behind their luridly tasselled doorways, cold lights lit a mostly pink world that circled around the grubby groins of whispering men. Soho was a cockpit of sex, and our bus stop seemed a long way away.

By 1978 nothing had changed. No brasseries or boutique bars yet, and the only people eating al fresco were sitting hunched on the kerb. Amid this sordid square mile lay a basement club called Billy's, and the owner was on his uppers. A sad disco ball pointed its fingers of dissatisfaction at a lonely dance floor and its surrounding empty booths. That is until a fey Welsh boy and his cockney sidekick stepped in.

The usual oracle informed us. Dagger and a friend from Owen's called Simon Withers, a willowy, well-spoken boy, now practising fashion at Saint Martins College on the Charing Cross Road, had already been there.

'Bowie Night. Look.' Dagger shoved something across the bar. It was another flyer. 'Every Tuesday at Billy's in Soho. Bloke called Steve Strange runs it. And Rusty Egan – you know, the old drummer from the Rich Kids. He plays the records; not just Bowie, plays Roxy, Iggy. People in amazing gear. All very glam.'

Simon lit a cigarette and gave it a few sharp, feminine puffs. 'Yeah, a lot of fashion people from my college go there, and some of the old soul and punk crowd – you know, who went to Louisa's. It's wonderful, really. Quite arty.' His lips pursed and grabbed at the filter. He was wearing a plain, geometrically cut top that looked a bit sci-fi am-dram; on it was pinned what looked like a diamond brooch that spangled as he talked.

'That's nice,' I said, pointing at the thing.

'It's diamanté. Steve Strange is totally camp on the door but Rusty's like a barrow-boy, a sort of spiv throwback. It reminds me a bit of how punk felt at the beginning but with no bands. Doesn't it, Steve?'

I looked at Dagger. He was sporting a sharp red bandanna, cowboy-style around his neck, his blond wedge adroitly ironed over one eye; he was suddenly all angles, a look I hadn't seen before. Whatever this place was, it had clearly made an impression on him. 'You have to go,' he said. And he meant it.

On the flyer was printed an enticement: 'FAME, FAME, FAME – JUMP ABOARD THE NIGHT TRAIN.'

The boy in the doorway was a svelte Cossack with a quiff. He waved his cigarette over our heads as if he were delivering a magic spell into the air, and Dagger, Simon and I stepped up. The blue-black, shiny roll of hair was folded expertly into his forage cap.

'Hello, Simon.' The Cossack strung out his vowels, in that lazy, punk manner Johnny had invented, but a Welsh accent lingered. He wore a single long earring. Diamanté.

As he stared through kohled lashes at me, I burned and suddenly had Roxy Music jumping into my head – *There's a new sensation, a fabulous—*

'Who are *you*?' His fearless queeniness was intimidating. Earlier that evening, unsure what to wear, I'd chosen black pegs and a plum Woodhouse shirt that I'd buttoned to the top; cool and neutral, I thought, but now I felt decidedly underdressed.

Simon introduced me. 'This is my friend Gary.'

'It's two quid,' said the Cossack, and he went back to waving his wand.

As we walked down the stairs, Dagger pulled me to him. 'That was Steve Strange.'

'He's *our* age.' I was surprised to see someone so young running a club. Inside I could hear the erogenous pulse of a slow, chiming synthesiser. It grew clearer as we approached.

'*She's a model and she's looking good* …' A stark, Germanic voice set the tone of *zum cabaret* as we walked into the smoky cavern. On the dance floor two boys, one in a shoulder cape and cummerbund, the other a military shirt with Sam Browne belt, danced what looked like a slow jive – holding hands, moving close then apart, turning their heads away from each other as they came together again. Mirroring these, two girls in black taffeta, glam with gothic trim, twirled hypnotically.

'*It only takes a camera to change her mind ...*'

Along the bar an androgynous thing with a shaved head, false eyelashes and a ruff laughed with a tall, thin boy wearing a pencil moustache, softly visible beneath pan make-up, and a black shirt, pinned at the collar with another diamanté broach. A red sash crossed his body like a proud fashion wound. The neckerchief was in evidence everywhere, mostly paired with high-waisted, bright-coloured pegs; winklepickers and quiffs finished a bizarre, fifties-meets-the-future look, whereas Chinese slippers and winged collars were a combination as yet untested on a British dance floor. Billy's was a costume-box of a club that I immediately knew would dance its way into my heart and wardrobe. Here were Bowie's spiritual children, formed many years earlier by the sparkle of Ziggy; here was a post-punk generation finally allowed to flaunt its roots; here, in this tiny room, was my generation, come of age.

'*She's going out tonight, loves drinking just champagne ...*'

Even the music toyed with irony – the lyrical version of wearing winged collars; nobody in this room could afford champagne. This was fashion student meets street-flash; sewing machine meets Oxfam; style on a student grant. Here, the sulky pout of young punk was painted with cheap rouge and puckering to be kissed.

'Hello, chaps.' It was a stocky boy, sweating in tweed, spats and a monocle. His Welsh accent was as strong and as masculine as his pomade. He sucked on a can.

'Chris, this is Steve and Gary.' Chris was easily the most spectacularly dressed young man I'd ever met. Immaculate in every detail, he could have stepped from an Agatha Christie novel. With him stood a skinny boy with Irish skin and a red, floppy wedge. He held his beer high in front of a silver sash that wrapped a blue T-shirt with large shoulder pads. It made his torso appear cartoonishly triangular. Dagger knew him from the LSE. His name was Bob Elms and he was a cockney with the vocabulary of Nietzsche. He was bursting with words, even when silent.

'But Steve, it's a classic dialectic …' They were in deep conversation now, excited by their own presence, but my eyes were still enjoying the room. The young, copper-headed geezer in the DJ booth, with LOVE and HATE on his knuckles and a rejuvenated fifties suit, followed Giorgio Moroder's 'The Chase' with Iggy's 'Nightclubbing' and the floor filled as the glitterball spun happily above painted heads. A matelot from a Jean Genet dream; a girl in an asymmetric suit; a kabuki punk in a kimono; a powdered Bo-Peep; a rockabilly; all moved in slow motion. This was new, something to do with punk, disco, rock, glam; disparate styles, all of which I loved but until now couldn't bring together.

A tartaned Jacobite smelling of L'Air du Temps appeared by my side. 'You know this was once the Gargoyle Club?' He was in my ear, and I could feel his lacquered hair on my cheek. 'Full of the Bright Young People. You know – Noel Coward, Evelyn Waugh, Tallulah Bankhead. And now … *ME*!' He spun away in mock triumph and I turned to look at Dagger. He was smiling straight back at me and I knew just what he was thinking: *this is exactly what we've been waiting for.*

I may have left school with low results but I had some high self-belief: *our band would succeed.* Until then, I had to get a job. For a while I worked at Islington Health, in the same office as Tony's mother, and apart from some lazy admin work I occasionally went out to schools to tick off names of kids having BCG injections. It was terribly dull, and I soon left to join the *Financial Times* as a prices clerk. The office was full of young, tailored men rushing around with market prices and exchange rates, but most of my time was spent dreaming up song titles and performance fantasies. One dismal afternoon, it was my turn to calculate the dollar exchange rate, and after phoning the BBC News desk with my answer, I sent it down for the next day's paper. As I arrived the following morning there were tuts and whispers from the other clerks, and one, a fat boy with thick glasses, looked at me and slowly drew his finger across his throat. I was called in to see a furious editor and informed, in no uncertain terms, that I'd calculated the wrong dollar rate and, disastrously, it had been printed in that morning's paper. I survived, but like to think that I did more damage to the capitalist system than all the copies of *Socialist Worker* ever sold.

The whole band were now Billy's regulars and sparkling with diamanté. Coming from Islington, we became known as the Angel boys. The Gentry seemed like yesterday's men, and the fact that we were a band was never mentioned to the discerning yet impecunious Young Turks of Soho.

Oxford Street's Woodhouse had been usurped by a little shop in Neal Street called PX, the brainchild of Acme Attraction's Steph Rayner and Helen Robinson. Steve Strange was their gossiping shop assistant. Here were the geometric, shoulder-padded space-shirts like the one I'd seen Elms wearing. As usual, Mum insisted on running up a couple of copies for her boys, as well as some super-baggie electric-blue pegs that she cut from our own design. She made them out of two pieces of material and, annoyingly, they had no fly. The next home-made shirt I wore I bought from one of the Saint Martins students at the club. It was a white, blousy, swashbuckling number, and he'd scrawled his name in blue felt-tip pen inside the collar: GALLIANO.

The key instrument in the new sound we'd so recently been dancing to was the synthesiser, and the five of us, plus Dagger, chipped in to buy one – a Yamaha CS10. I took it home and it buzzed in my hands, a dirty great garagey buzz that rocked Elmore Street. You could only play one note at a time and so I started riffing on it, fiddling with the filters while tapping my feet four-on-the-floor. All fancy rock patterns had to go. Buzzed on blues, our drug of choice, we'd discussed it at the club: these new songs would be to a disco beat; there would be a cull of all the old power pop stuff; our future sound had to be like the one we heard every Tuesday night. If we were to attempt to be the band that represented this new cult, then we had to be absolutely ready.

In February 1979, while London subsided under a weight of rubbish, bursting from black bin-liners piled like steaming turds on every street corner, we ignored the Winter of Discontent and followed Strange and Egan through this septic Hamelin to Blitz. (The pimps – who'd used Billy's for their regular business – were annoyed that we weren't hiring their girls, and chased us off their patch. In any case, we peacocks needed more room for our expanding feathers.)

Blitz was a wine bar in Great Queen Street decorated with thirties memorabilia. It suited our theme of dancing while Rome burned. Strange wore his hair and heels high, and tottered at the door with a silver-topped cane, while hundreds, desperate to burn brightly in these dark times, blocked the street outside.

In the club, the young meteors were already aflame. The Saint Martins crowd were dominant at Blitz: the great British milliner-to-be, Stephen Jones, along with his muse, Kim Bowen, who'd dress in one of his high hats and a regal DIY frock; Stephen Linard, the tartaned Jacobite I'd met on my first night, with his Kenneth Williams voice and white make-up, who'd go on to design couture; Melissa Caplan with her single spike of hair, and glamorous Fiona Dealey, who'd brought them all down in her white van. Other Saint Martins students included Sade, who at that time never thought she could sing, and, of course, John Galliano.

George O'Dowd, not yet the Boy he would become, was dressed in tartan bondage with feathers and boas, and worked in the cloakroom with a pouty girl called Princess Julia. His coterie included Jeremy Healy, dressed like a George Cruikshank drawing in crushed stovepipe hat and Artful Dodger trousers, and a beautiful blond boy known as Marilyn, who if you asked what his real name was would breathily tell you, 'Norma Jean.' Their mentor in high bitchiness was a slightly older queen called Philip Sallon, whom I'd first seen dressed as the charlady dancing onstage at the Screen on the Green. Graham Smith, a graphic design student, photographed events; John Maybury filmed them; Bob Elms put them to words; Chris Sullivan, with his armoury of historic clothing, set the standard of dress for the straight boys, and Christos Tolera, Martin's best friend, simply lived it.

Other Blitz regulars that would find fame in their chosen fields were Michael Clark, Mark Moore, David Holah and Stevie Stewart, Sara Dallin, Keren Woodward, Baillie Walsh, Carole Caplin, Caryn Franklin, Perri Lister, Dylan Jones, Stephen Webster, Perry Haines, Richard James Burgess, and Cerith Wyn Evans. The only person with any level of celebrity at that moment was Midge Ure, who was still yet to replace John Foxx in Ultravox. Something was happening here, a critical mass maybe, but certainly a competitive desire to claim the territory that was opening up in front of us. Unfortunately, at that moment, we were all skint.

We'd arrive in our much-deliberated-upon splendour, cobbled together from Oxfam or under hot sewing machines, brazenly kiss Strange at the door – a public gesture that signalled power to the waiting hoards outside – and sashay in. Kraftwerk's 'Schaufensterpuppen' might be pulsing through the system, or Gina X's 'No GDM', maybe even Telex's 'Twist à St Tropez', but once the grand entrance was over, we couldn't afford to buy a drink and spent much of the night attempting to steal bottles of wine from the bar and other people's tables.

Downstairs in the toilets (where proper boys were expected to visit the ladies) you bought your fun from Barry the Rat. His white pet rodent would twitch upon his shoulder while he fiddled in his bag for a nice speckled blues, and then he'd slip your bill, folded, between his gum and lip. Now we were speeding on into the night and Bob and I, chemically improved and highly impressed with ourselves, shouted at each other about Italian futurism, Russian constructivism or English hooliganism, until either our ideas or our mouths dried up. Bowie arrived one night and was fawned over; Jagger arrived and was refused entry; while Dougie Fields, Zandra Rhodes, Andrew Logan, Molly Parkin and Nicky Haslam were the few allowed in to represent London's older glitterati, the omnipresent baby-boomers that Peter York would go on to call the Thems. As most of us were under twenty-one and planning a social *coup d'état*, this was frowned upon, but Strange, a class-jumper of fabulous grace, was always aware that he might need an invite to a dinner, or simply a nice bed to sleep in.

Every seminal moment in British youth culture had had a band or artist that represented it: skiffle – Lonnie Donegan; rock'n'roll – Cliff Richard; mod – the Who; psychedelia – Pink Floyd; glam rock – Bowie; punk – the Sex Pistols. We knew, even then, that Blitz and all it entailed and encouraged was going to be an important chapter in the story of London youth and their street-found fashions; and so, in a basement studio on Islington's Holloway Road, the Angel boys were busily trying to create a band who'd embody this latest twist in the tale.

Halligan's was in the same building that had once accommodated Michael X's commune for black consciousness – the Black House. Here, in the early seventies, John and Yoko would pop down for a cup of tea and the exchange of some political chutzpah. Now it was a music shop and rehearsal rooms run by a shabby Irishman, and we were there developing a sound for our new identity, one that, for the first time, felt like our own. But how we would spring the result upon our potential audience, we had no idea.

We finished playing the four or five songs we had and faced Dagger. He was pleased, I could see, but his words were frantic with concern.

'We have to get it out there quickly. This is gonna explode sooner than we think. I met someone the other night that told me he was the Steve Strange of Salisbury! And that fucking Gary Numan song, have you heard it?'

'He can't even get into Blitz! Anyway,' I said, 'that's futurist bollocks, Steve, not what we're doing.'

'All I'm saying is we need to be ready soon.'

We added Iggy Pop's 'Funtime' and a version of John Barry's 'On Her Majesty's Secret Service', but the minute we started playing the riff for a new song that I had, we knew we were ready. 'To Cut A Long Story Short' was garage-band stuff – short, to the point, and very English. With its portentous refrain of '*We are beautiful and clean and so very, very young*' it seemed the perfect manifesto – or at least lyrical sound-bite – for the Blitz generation. It was time to reveal ourselves, and Dagger had an idea how.

But there was a little matter of a fight to be dealt with before then. As Steve Strange refused entry to so many, a rival club had sprung up. We pooh-poohed it with knowing disdain and mocked the poor futurists who frequented it, still trapped in last year's sci-fi clothing. Studio 21 was run by a tough Scot and ex-manager of the Roxy club called Jock McDonald, and one night, Chris Sullivan, while out with Dagger, had a run-in with him. It ended up in a fist fight over the bonnet of Phil Lynott's car, with the Thin Lizzy frontman trapped nervously inside with his girlfriend. Jock escaped from the clutches of the historically dressed Welshman (apparently that night it was the French Resistance), but not before issuing a threat that he and the futurists of Studio 21 would come to Blitz and take it.

The following Tuesday night the club was full to bursting and jumping with expectation. True to his word, Jock arrived with a bunch of bruisers and, ignoring the door policy, muscled passed the terrified Strange, while leaving his futurist followers sensibly outside. There was silence as they pushed their way through to Sullivan, who stood waiting in the middle of the bar area. Now Chris, not one to underdress for an occasion, had that night decided to go for his Harris tweeds, spats and monocle and created quite a picture as he nosed McDonald. Within seconds it went off, and fists, bottles and hair were flying. Bizarrely dressed people fought tooth and painted nail with Jock and his heavies. A friend of ours slammed a chair into the back of one of them and it splintered like a prop; the more effete ones, screaming, found tables and chairs to stand on and from which to aim their bottles and barbs, while I, pushed against the bar, flailed my arms at anything that looked remotely dangerous. I saw one poor heavy try to make a retreat and get trapped in a corner. He was taking a vicious kicking from a boy dressed as a vicar, another in an Elizabethan ruff, a man in drag, and a person in full Highland battledress. Jock knew when he was beaten and managed to escape. As the club began to straighten itself, I found my brother – who'd been hiding in the Ladies – and we went to see how Chris had fared. He was left standing in his socks with his feet bleeding. His Oxfam shoes, being too large for him, had come off in the fight. He spat something out – it was a piece of someone's eyebrow.

I only wish I could remember what record Rusty was playing at the time … 'Ballroom Blitz'?

I'd never been good with girls, especially as a schoolboy. Not only was I threatened by the sexual banter that would go on in their presence, but

I also thought they looked odd and slightly ridiculous, with their make-up-stained faces and awkward shoes – although clomping along like Douglas Bader in my multicoloured platform boots, I was hardly one to talk. You also had to smoke if you wanted to hang out with girls, which made them part of the taboo geography that belonged to bogs and back alleys. I'd been forced into a 'lug' of a cigarette in the loos at Ally Pally ice rink by some predatory girls with red knees. I watched cross-eyed as the thick, grey smoke left my mouth like a serpent and they laughed with dry mouths at my inability to take it in. Real boys who had girlfriends smoked very seriously. They did it with the cigarette held between thumb and forefinger, the hot end hidden within the cupped palm of their hand. They also spat a lot. They'd flick the tip of their tongue up from the pool of saliva behind their lower teeth, and project a spray as far as they could manage, an art known to us as 'linking'. Girls did it too – lug, link, laugh, lug, link, snog. And so the world of kissing and sex – and therefore girls – I unfortunately associated with the smell of fags and toilets.

Then one day in 1978, I met the shy but floral sixteen-year-old Lee Andrews at a bus stop in the Holloway Road, and, after days of talking and awkward silences, she became my girlfriend for the next nine years. Small and blonde, she was a hairdresser at Molton Brown's, and at the flat she shared with her mum and sister – and at a relatively late age – I lost my virginity to her. Dressed in A-line skirts, she went from soul girl to Blitz girl and soon became the band's hairdresser. And for one Saturday morning in October, the band needed to look its best.

Dagger knew that we couldn't play any of the regular venues – this crowd would never come – and in any case, in such intolerant times, the way we all looked was extremely dangerous. If this was to work, then we needed the approval of the cognoscenti, so a private show was how Dagger saw our reveal. We needed to give the elite the privilege of seeing it first; a small crowd but *the* most important as far as we were concerned, and the direction of their thumbs would determine our future. We found an old black-and-white picture of a building collapsing, and printed up some passes that we handed out at the club to our chosen few. THE GENTRY, they said, with an address and time: HALLIGAN'S MUSIC – HOLLOWAY RD – 11 a.m.

The rudeness of the hour did not affect their dress that Saturday morning as most of them had been up all night anyway. Bob Elms, Chris Sullivan, Christos Tolera, Graham Smith, Kim Bowen, Melissa Caplan, Simon Withers, Rusty Egan and, of course, Steve Strange were almost the entire audience that shuffled into Halligan's, hung over, and full of cynical expectation. It would be a daunting forty minutes. These people had rejected watching bands to be the stars of their own show. Would they take us to their hearts? I'd chosen my Black Watch tartan trousers with buttoned ankles, white socks and green velvet slippers. A matching shoulder sash with the word *Reformation* written boldly on it completed the look. Simon had made it for me and I'd used this slogan as the title for one of the new songs.

We huddled for the ritual pre-gig tuning and worrying.

'You OK, Tone?'

The tall guy was drying in the mouth. 'Yeah, think so. Just wanna get it over with now.'

'You'll be great,' I said.

'This is mad, though. It's like we're on trial.'

The most opinionated young people in London had been gathered at our invitation, and I could see them beginning to turn their attention like a standing jury towards the stage area. *This is it*, I thought. We had no Plan B. 'We *are* on trial. Let's go.'

There were a few seconds of crackling leads and nervous testing of volumes as we assumed our positions. And then suddenly I had the synthesizer grinding out its gritty riff as Steve thrashed at his overdriven SG. John sat on the beat, disco style, while Martin borrowed octave slaps from Chic. The new songs allowed Tony to adopt a grandiose manner, which he delivered with belting confidence. I was looking for Dagger's face in the crowd, knowing that it would be a good barometer for the general impression we were making. For the first few numbers there seemed to be little reaction, just a slouching coolness. I could feel us trying to up the ante, then I spotted Dagger. He was standing between Bob and Sullivan and they were beginning to shout into his ear and I could see him nodding with approval. Bob was starting to twitch and roll his shoulders, a sort of standing sashay, and then John counted in 'To Cut A Long Story Short' and Steve Strange began to dance and we knew we'd been given their blessing.

Afterwards we all gathered in the rank Irish pub next door, the autumn sun warming its filthy windows. Chris was the first to book us. He and Bob had helped a young actress named Toyah Wilcox to put on a party at her Mayhem Studios – a large warehouse in Patcham Terrace, Battersea – and now wanted us to play there at a Christmas 'happening' they were arranging. Graham Smith suggested that he and Bob design the invite; Simon said he'd help with the lighting; Melissa would run up some clothes.

But never knowingly outdone, Steve Strange stood forward. 'I'm gonna be doing a Blitz Christmas party in a few weeks. I'd love you to play at it.'

That was it – we were to be their band. There was one problem though: they all hated the name.

'The Gentry sounds like a bunch of sixties hair models,' said Sullivan.

'Or a terrible TV series starring Roger Moore,' quipped someone else.

And then someone said, 'What about Spandau Ballet?'

'*What* ballet?'

'*Spandau* Ballet. It's a place in Berlin.' It was Bob. I should have asked how he'd thought of it, but I knew he'd just come back from a three-day pilgrimage there. It was preposterous but edgy; arty but aggressive; obscure but assured. It encapsulated all of the arch precious-ness we aspired to and we immediately loved it. We'd been blessed and christened by the elite. We were reborn. We were Spandau Ballet.

CHAPTER NINE

A CRASH COURSE FOR THE RAVERS

The Mayhem Party was living up to its name. Every young dandy – fabulous, fantastical, piratical – had arrived and was busy cramming him or herself into the now pumping warehouse space. The metal stairwell contained a continuous line of gloriously self-designed coxcombs and popinjays, all inching their way up to the entrance. On the ceiling inside, grainy porn flesh moved in colour Super 8, while psychedelic projectors panned across the revellers. Not having Steve Strange on the door meant that it wasn't quite as exclusive as Blitz, and ska boys, punks and a smattering of other urban tribes spiced the brew. It seemed only right that Bob, having conceived the name, should be the one to introduce us, and at midnight, dressed as a Parisian anarchist in black polo-neck and beret, he strode to the mike and announced Spandau Ballet publicly.

There was no stage so we'd set up on the floor, and it felt as though we were playing in the audience. I stabbed at my synth, nose-to-nose with a skinhead, while Tony sang confronted by a baroque pompadour belonging to a young androgyne in the front. People were hopping up and down or climbing on tables to get a better view. Owing to the unbearable heat and number of bodies, condensation started to drip on to us from the porn stars writhing ignominiously above our heads. It was hell but we loved it. We were of the moment and, armed with our electric weapons, the musical front line of a new tribe. And then, in the time-honoured tradition of the 'happenings' it aspired to, the police turned up.

In May 1979 Nanny Thatcher arrived to tidy the nursery and give us all a good what-for and a dose of her yucky medicine – or at least that's how the majority of the country wished to perceive it. Hunted by the media as good copy, we were detested by the left and right alike for elitism, 'gender-bending', dancing on the sinking *Titanic* and any other accusation that would appease their angry readers. Much to the annoyance of these stereotypers, we were mostly Labour voters – Dagger had physically stood in support of the miners during street protests – but regardless of what accusations we refuted, we absolutely loved the attention.

By now, packs of photographers and film crews hovered every Tuesday outside our spiritual home of the Blitz, while inside, one or two, wooed by Dagger or Strange, were allowed access. Peter York of *Harpers & Queen* duelled sound-bites and hyperbole with Bob Elms; David Johnson, the *Evening Standard*'s Jimmy Olsen of gossip, pointed his hungry camera and notebook at anything that pouted or sulked, and the *Mirror*'s Christina Appleyard flirted and named us all 'Blitz Kids'. We were learning on our dancing feet how to use the media, even if it just meant knowing when to antagonise them.

As far as we were concerned, the music press, dominated by the *NME* and *Melody Maker*, was run by embittered, middle-class, white college-rockers, who'd hated punk when it first arrived and then bandwagon-jumped a little too late. The only black music that they deigned to patronise was reggae; but soul, the real black music of America, and its cousin of the night, disco, were shunned for being too aspirational and not political enough. In any case, these writers couldn't dance and would never have understood our groove, so we turned it into a trench and prepared ourselves for an advance.

At the end of the decade there were no celebrity magazines, and only *Top of the Pops* and *The Old Grey Whistle Test* supplied televised music; this made it possible to build a myth. Instead of begging A&R men and journalists to come down, we did the opposite, and were perversely thrilled by them not being allowed in. No demo tapes were sent out, and although our name was spreading quickly around town and beyond, very few people knew what we sounded like. It made them want to hear us even more. It was bolshy and brave and we could easily have ended up with some facial egg, but all of it seemed carefully managed by Dagger. He also had an idea how to get our first review, and one where he'd have complete control of the copy.

Our Christmas Blitz appearance was rammed with London's sharpest youth. Being at the show was about belonging to something. Suddenly the band had taken on a credibility and a need-to-see factor that the last four years couldn't muster. Apart from the usual suspects – some dancing, some being flagrantly dismissive – lurked musicians from other groups: Japan, Ultravox, Magazine, Landscape, and Visage – a band Strange was fronting with the two ex-Rich Kids, Midge and Rusty. At the bar, Richard Jobson, Billy Idol and Siouxsie Sioux swapped stories; in fact, many of the crowd were from the contingent I'd first seen at the Pistols' Screen on the Green show. And somewhere, invited by a friend, lurked the cool head of Island Records, the white Jamaican who'd helped Roxy Music become a household name: Chris Blackwell.

Steve and I took the stage in wing collars, procured from a local Oxfam shop. I wore tartan trousers and green velvet slippers, while Tony and Steve went for small bow ties, and Martin, a trilby. It was Bright Young People on a shoestring, with wedge haircuts suddenly turning floppy fop. Steve had started wearing his guitar extraordinarily high up, almost in competition with his bow tie. It was an anti-guitar-hero position, but one that would catch on with every band to come in the next decade. Simon lit us like an Otto Dix painting as we gathered tightly around the single column that pierced the stage.

Apart from the two covers – 'On Her Majesty's Secret Service' and Iggy Pop's 'Fun Time' – they were my songs. All new, with faux-heroic titles like 'Reformation' and 'Age Of Blows'. We hammered out our white European dance music with all of the self-importance and earnestness that should be struck by youth defining their art. In the audience people did that stiff little clockwork dance – arms rotating in parallel circles at waist height, first clockwise then anticlockwise, while raising their knees alternately to the opposite side of the body, creating a hypnotic hip-swing. That was it – no other moves were needed; or allowed. It was an ordered dance that emphasised the incessant marching beat of the music. Often done in pairs, it was the futuristic cousin of that English rock'n'roll shoulder dance, made famous at holiday camps and seaside resorts in the fifties and sixties.

That night there were more people who wanted us to win than lose. We were raised on padded metaphorical shoulders before we'd even played the opening chord. As I pushed to the bar after the show, a buzzing Billy Idol grabbed me. 'Man! You guys are the future of rock-'n'roll!' Only two years before, I thought it was him.

We'd all grown up in a time still connected to a world of war; of bomb-sites and bunting, old soldiers and Old Holborn. But as we nodded a cursory goodbye to the seventies and all it had delivered to form us, we had no idea we were slipping across such a cultural watershed; a divide where the past would be so cruelly dismissed, disconnected, disfigured; where its people would be forgotten. We were convinced we were at the beginning of not only the most exciting decade of our lives, but also an era that would belong to all of us here. We accepted the baton and ran for the future.

First stop in the race was Island Records. Blackwell had found Dagger that evening and told him immediately he wanted to sign us. Meeting again the next day, he reaffirmed his desire. Three gigs with the synth and we already had an offer of a record contract. To the band, it was the miracle we'd been waiting for. As no one represented us legally, Blackwell recommended we get a solicitor. He gave Dagger three names to pick from, one of whom had just represented Johnny Rotten in his case against Malcolm McLaren and won; we liked the sound of him. Brian Carr was statesman-like, with no music-biz flash about him, and from the start showed great interest in my songwriting. On that, his guidance was clear: 'Don't sign a publishing deal if you don't need the upfront cash. Keep your copyrights as long as you can, they are the most valuable asset you'll ever have.' It was advice I would be eternally grateful for. The band immediately trusted him, and so Brian, with his wise-looking Abrahamic beard, became our counsel for all future business. His natural affinity for the artist, as opposed to the record company, made him a powerful ally, and one that Blackwell would regret recommending.

One morning in Hammersmith, the band, Dagger and Brian entered Island Records to meet the men who wanted to sign us, one of whom was, disturbingly, known as the Captain. On the walls gold and platinum records spangled next to huge, framed posters of legends. The faces and names were familiar: Roxy Music, Robert Palmer, Cat Stevens, Bob Marley, Free – names from our youth. It had us itching to contribute to the trophy cabinet. Some of us were even reaching for the pen. But the Captain, Blackwell's second-in-command, didn't seem to understand us at all, nor us him, and after going through the offer, our side retired to a Chinese restaurant for dim sum and a debrief.

Brian told us there was much that worried him in the deal. He went on while we ate: 'When we go back in I'll put our requests to them, but if at any point I get up to leave, I'd like you all to do the same.'

Martin leant over into my ear. 'Does he mean we leave without signing?'

'I think so.'

'Shit.'

The dim sum a little undigested, we returned nervously to the fray. I prayed that Brian would stay in his chair, but suddenly, cued by an unsuitable riposte from the Captain, he rose; and true to our word, as Brian thanked the Island management and walked through the avenue of awards to the door, we followed.

Later, exhausted by our experience, we gathered in the Kemps' kitchen. Mum moved around making tea, offering biscuits of solace and pretending to ignore the growing debate. After four years we had had an opportunity to go professional and we'd walked away, literally. I'd recently left my job at the *Financial Times* to incentivise my desire to go professional and it now looked like more of the dole for me. While John sullenly waved off the offer of a placatory biscuit, Tony looked the most visibly upset. Both were understandably frustrated that we weren't by now Island artists. Only Dagger, dunking his digestive, stayed calm. He'd already taken the long view: there'd be more, and they'd be bigger.

'Janet Street-Porter wants to make a documentary about us.' Dagger was calling me at home on our new phone that Dad had proudly placed on the landing table. We must have been the last in my extended family to get one.

'Really? Who is she?'

'You know her, she's on *Saturday Night People* with Russell Harty?'

'Gary!' My mother was shouting from the living room. 'Y'know how much money that thing costs!'

'Mum, he called me! Sorry, Steve, go ahead.'

'She produced that Pistols documentary on telly. She's doing a new series called *20th Century Box*. I think it's similar and they wanna do one on us, the whole thing. They wanna film a gig. I'm thinking that we should play the Scala again.'

A few months earlier we'd played the Scala Cinema in a conscious effort to echo the *Midnight Special* Pistols gig that had forged Steve Norman and me together nearly four years before. The association was more than a homage, as the Scala, an arthouse cinema in Fitzrovia, was managed by Dagger's old school friend, Steve Woolley. Having assisted in the organisation of that Screen on the Green Pistols show, he jumped at the idea of helping to manage a similar event for this new movement – for that was how we were now describing it. In the first month of the new decade we'd played Blitz a second time, and the buzz was palpable, although we knew we had to grow beyond Steve Strange's clutches. We wanted our shows to be clandestine events, embracing the vanity and performance of our unique scene. The Scala was our first attempt and it worked. It also gave Dagger the opportunity to follow through with his idea for getting a good review.

On the Monday after, he collared the bleary-eyed Elms. Given Bob's deft verbosity and knack of creating tight, manifesto-like statements, Dagger had decided Bob should put his pen where his mouth was and fashion a review of the event. Dagger stood over Bob's shoulder, prodding, adding, deleting, until both were happy with it. Not wanting to waste time – nor let Bob have second thoughts – he frogmarched the freshly-minted writer down to Carnaby Street and the offices of the *New Musical Express*. Shoved through the door, on reception the nervous Elms met a boy that he knew called Danny Baker.

Danny had helped to create the punk fanzine *Sniffing Glue*, but was now working for the enemy. He guided him up to the editor. Bob walked in, slapped the review on his desk, and told him we were all gonna change the world. That Thursday, it was in. It was like nothing that had ever appeared in a music paper before.

> Shadows dominate a white backdrop as five young figures dressed almost too well exude a soaring, gothic dance music that conjures up everything except rock'n'roll ... An air of dandy dilettantism fills the air as wing-collars and cloaks come to the fore; Wagner lies with Classic Disco before they appear, and everybody poses for pictures ...

And posing for pictures is what we all had a chance to do come Scala II and Janet's documentary. Filmed in May 1980, it was transmitted in black and white, which added a patina of mystery and timelessness, and gave the film a ready-made nostalgia. Paradoxically, it made it all look a bit more expensive, masking our tawdry reality – although the scene outside John's family's flat, where we're shifting our own gear into the back of his van, has an honest innocence that looks incredibly dated in this celebrity-smart age. In fact, watching the film now, there's a naivety to many of the scenes, but nevertheless, it captures a unique moment in British youth culture, and one that went on to affect the world.

Here's Bob, slim and angular in a jaunty beret and ballet pumps, promenading through the bleak streets of Hoxton on his way to meet the young, reticent clothes designer Willie Brown, and choose something to wear for the night. Willie, along with his beautiful, half-Japanese model girlfriend, Vivienne Lynn, had opened a shop called Modern Classics in the then utterly unfashionable Shoreditch, where he sold his distinctive, constructivist-style clothing based on 'architecture and industrial design', or so we're told in the film. He also made skirts for men; for it was gentle Willie that started the unplaided kilt look adopted so infamously by Spandau Ballet on and offstage. Then Bob's in the Chelsea hairdressers, Smile, having his hair cut by the young über-barber and scene stalwart, Ollie O'Donnell, who's clad in a tartan suit, head crowned by a huge quiff. And then it's Chris Sullivan's moment. He's in his Kentish Town flat and sporting a straw boater and waistcoat before changing into his French Resistance look, complete with eyepatch. His cockatoo perches in the background while he talks. 'We select the past to create a future,' he explains in his lilting Welsh brogue. 'Hopefully a good one.'

As always, Graham Smith created the poster for the Scala II show and it was placed strategically around this small world of ours: Blitz, Smile, PX and Modern Classics, where tickets were also sold. The evening began with two short surreal movies by Buñuel as support: *L'Age d'Or* and *Un Chien Andalou*; although our real support was the audience. The film lingers on them arriving and posing, before choosing Christos – a major face – to be interviewed. 'If a person's got enough style they can get away with anything. Anything at all,' he says, with the brashness of youth. It's a statement that will be echoed much later for the *Krays* movie tag-line. And then we're about to go onstage. But first it's Bob, in stark black suit with hanky and pin, attempting to echo Mayakovsky or Marinetti, by introducing us with a self-penned declamatory prose poem.

'*From half-spoken shadows emerges a canvas. A kiss of light breaks to reveal a moment when all mirrors are redundant. Listen to the portrait of the dance of perfection – the Spandau Ballet.*'

After the show we towelled down in Steve Woolley's office. Janet Street-Porter was thrilled with what she'd filmed that evening and so was Dagger. She was telling us how fantastic both us and the audience looked when in stepped the brusque, old-school music publisher Brian

Morrison, followed by his keen sidekick, Mark Dean. He was wreathed in a cloud of his boss's rich cigar smoke. Dagger and I had been courted by Brian for a while now, but this was the first time he'd seen the band. He held his arms out wide and his camel-hair coat flapped to reveal its Savile Row lining. 'Boys! I gotta tell ya …' And then he stopped. Brian loved a pregnant pause.

'What, Brian?' said Dagger.

'I'm like a virgin in love.'

We thought it outré at the time, and certainly un-rock'n'roll, to be interviewed for Janet's programme in one of the new drinking establishments appearing around central London. Known as a 'wine bar', Jacques', on Russell Square, was one of the first of its kind and also an early-evening meeting place for Blitz kids. This was where Dagger had insisted that I make one statement he'd carefully thought about. 'I don't care what else you say,' he told me, 'but make sure you say this.' He knew it would irritate the previous generation of music people, and with this one line, we helped kick-start a new cult of aspiration. Wearing a Willie Brown collarless number and a rather Germanic-looking puff of blond hair, I gave the interview and, at the appropriate moment, delivered Dagger's sound-bite: 'They all know,' I start earnestly, referring to the record labels, 'that we are gonna sell thousands of records.'

I presented it as bald fact. It was certainly one that us six lads hoped would come true. But to mix popular art and the immodest desire for money and success was quite a subversive cocktail in a post-punk era. The Sunday it was screened on London Weekend Television, it antagonised many. But, as Dagger foresaw, it also pricked the ears of every major record company in Britain; although that weekend, we were all on a beach in St Tropez.

*

'You've got to be joking, Steve.'

Dagger had come over to Halligan's to tell us some news. He was obviously excited. 'No. They want us to do a two-week residency there. It's right on the harbour. They'll pay us, put us up and feed us. I think we should go.'

'What's the club called?'

'The Papagayo. Parrot apparently.'

Out of the blue Dagger had been called by an agent for the club looking to fill an early-season slot with what he'd been told were the hottest new group in town. We jumped at the chance – we were on the dole and going to St Tropez. More than that, we thought it perfect as part of our campaign to irritate the rockist media. We were also children brought up on Bryan Ferry and suntans.

The thing is, Bryan would have flown down to the Côte d'Azur in a Learjet, with Jerry sprawled out among the Sunday papers; unfortunately we were attempting it in a minibus, and that included all of the musical equipment plus as many friends as we could fit into the space left. Simon Withers wanted to come, so did Graham Smith and Bob; after all, they were respectively our lighting designer, graphic artist and artful spin-doctor. Inserting everyone and their wardrobes into the hired bus was a physics equation that meant windows had to be climbed through and gear slotted in afterwards. Individuals were practically incarcerated within small, dark niches, all of which had to be unravelled and re-formed every time anyone wanted to stop for a piss, which was frequent given the amount of booze being drunk on the way. On top of all this lurched a roof-rack of luggage that looked like a giant game of Jenga.

Two miserable nights were spent in cheap board as we travelled down the spine of France, with some people – including my brother, much to his annoyance – kipping in the bus to guard the equipment. So it was with huge excitement that we finally drove over the mountains and down into the shimmering heat of Provence.

Simon freed a hand and passed over a cassette of the European national anthem 'Ode to Joy' and we all started singing and shouting. My eyes drifted to Tony at the wheel. He looked different. He'd stopped singing. Suddenly I saw him steer without the bus making any corresponding movements; and then we were veering sideways at great speed, careering across the carriageway, the wheel spinning through his hands.

'What's happening?'

Amps and speakers teetered around us as the bus turned and made its way back across the busy road.

'I don't know!'

So we were to die. I secretly knew we never deserved St Tropez but it seemed a little unfair. Cars were swerving around us as the van skated sideways and angled itself towards the mountainside. I instinctively pushed hard at the back of the seat in front and braced myself as the crag moved rapidly closer; and then … stillness.

In the silence the roof-rack groaned as its tall load leant to one side. Apart from the guys at the front, no one else could get out without help and suddenly panic set in. But Tony was immediately outside, calming us down and dealing with our extraction. The smell of rubber was in the air as I fell from the window on to the hot tarmac. We got the van unloaded, and surrounded by our equipment stared hopelessly at what was left of a flayed tyre. The bus, hired from a friend, carried no jack.

'Bollocks. We're gonna be late.'

'When's the first show, Steve?'

'In about three hours.'

I couldn't drive, and not being very mechanically minded either, decided it was not my responsibility. I sat at the side of the dusty road pompously waiting for someone else to take the initiative. Luckily someone did, and after they'd thumbed a lift to a garage, returned and got technical on the bus. Two hours later (and all carefully reinserted) we were driving along one of the world's richest harbours, salivating at the prospect of two weeks in Bardot's paradise.

Apart from my climbing experience and the family visit to Paris, the only other foreign experience I'd had was the Costa del Sol, for a lads' unsuccessful attempt at being deflowered. Nevertheless, the smarting of burnt skin and the smell of Bergasol were in our genetic make-up, and Spandau was drawn to the sun like the proverbial Icarus. I'd grown up being stripped for the beach by my mother and then spending sore nights caked in calamine lotion; it was what you did. But for some, getting a tan was considered a very vulgar thing to do. The middle classes shunned the sun when on holiday for the shade of a straw hat, a Penguin Classic or a church interior. Suntans revealed your class, your vanity, and vanity was vulgar. Paradoxically, the rockist view of a suntan was that it was *un*-working-class, preferring the Orwellian ideal of the pale, ricket-deformed shadow-lurker. Dagger didn't miss a trick – he knew that soul boys and soul girls the country over were at that moment turning pink, red or blistered on the beaches of Bournemouth and Benidorm. It was *their* hearts he wanted to win and he insisted on photographs of us soaked in factor-two, legs akimbo, brazenly bronzing in Speedos. As if to not let the class theory down, Simon, the only middle-class chap among us, refused to take off his shirt and spent his days on the beach wrapped in a Vivienne Westwood bondage suit and black balaclava.

A whiff of scandal accompanied our posse right from the off. First, the club had offered us free drinks all night at the bar – *how foolish* – and within a few hours everyone was trashed on champagne cocktails, and, given that a beer was £7, we'd run up a bill that had cut straight through the management's purse. We were immediately demoted to free beer only. Second – and more alarmingly – after swanning around town in berets, jodhpurs and Sam Browne belts, while putting up Graham's poster displaying a stilettoed S&M jackboot, that whiff had become a stink. Rumours were abounding and the local tattlers had us fingered as fascists. When Bob had suggested our name it never occurred to us that some might query its Germanic origin, and it was only later that we learned Spandau was the town where the Nazi war criminal, Rudolf Hess, was imprisoned. Naively, to us it had simply sounded exotic. Someone said Bob had got it from a toilet wall in a club in Berlin – *could it be that there was already a band with that name?* By now it was too late. That first week, a disparaging, accusatory article came out in the local press with a priceless headline, and the only part of the piece that was undeniably true: *They Drink Beer.*

The accommodation was unfurnished apart from some mattresses on the floor and a small kitchen. Mum had given her two sons packets of Savoury Rice and Vesta Curry, which we lived on for as long as possible (there was a time in the early seventies when it seemed that all our food was powdered: stew, mash, soup, trifle – we ate like landlocked astronauts). Other friends arrived from London and it soon turned into a foul den, although our clothes were kept with saintly reverence, sorted into outfits and hung like museum pieces from window frames and doors, awaiting their moment. One evening, while getting ready, I saw Bob dressed in a Milk Tray polo-neck and a Willie Brown kilt fly across the room. Someone had told him drugs were hidden behind the plug socket. He'd looked and put a finger in.

For us, St Tropez was like walking into a Roxy Music cover. We'd strut out every night like peacocks from our rancid nest and attempt to shock this cradle of chic. At first our music sounded strange to the club's clientele, but within days we were filling the place, our sartorial obsessivness and fanatical posturing somehow suiting the archness of St

Tropez. Although penniless, we made it our own and were taken to their hearts. Jackboots and all.

The day after *20th Century Box* hit the screens, I was in the bar down on Coco Beach when a barman called me over. There was a phone call for one of us so I took it. At the other end of the line a well-spoken English voice crackled. 'Hi. Are you with the Spandau Ballet?'

'Er ... yeah.'

'Great. I saw your documentary yesterday. Fascinating stuff. I'm looking for a Steve Dagger. My name's Stuart Slater. I'm from Chrysalis Records in London.'

We returned to our home town as darlings of a rapidly expanding youth movement, flocking in from the suburbs, all keen to take a ride on this new fashion wave. It made sense, therefore, that their first stop should be a ship.

HMS *Belfast* stands – if that is what a ship figuratively does – permanently moored in all its matt, battleship-greyness upon the Thames, its guns proudly erect in the presence of the Tower of London. After conceiving the idea, Dagger approached the ship's catering manager with a lie about a small party for some Oxford graduates.

'Mmm. Sounds wonderful. Now what about food?' said the gentle purser.

'We won't be wanting any food, thank you. Just drink.'

'Oh no, you'll be wanting something to eat, surely. What about a nice cheese dip? It's very popular.'

'Fine.' And then, as though an afterthought: 'Oh yeah ... We may be having a small quintet playing, is that all right?'

'Lovely.'

Once we were back from France, Dagger's mum had handed him a notepad containing the contact details of every major UK record company's A&R person. The Monday after the show's airing, the phone in the Dagger family's little Holborn flat had not stopped ringing, and his mother had nervously taken on secretarial duties. Over the next week or so, he and I started visiting all of them. Their enthusiasm for the band was tangible, although they wanted to see us for themselves.

There had been a lot of press interest as well, and so we'd shot a photo session with Graham Smith in the infamous Warren Street squat. Run with efficiency by the matriarchal and frightening Melissa Caplan, Warren Street – as the squat was known to all – was a buzzing hive for exotic suburban runaways. Three storeys high, it housed nearly all the Saint Martins lot – Stephen Linard, Stephen Jones, Kim Bowen, Lee Sheldrick, Lesley and Jane Chilkes; David Holah – who would go on to form Bodymap – also lived there with his boyfriend, the film student John Maybury; and in the basement, the nocturnal Barry the Rat lay counting his blues.

Kim, the star of them all, had the most beautiful room – a little white pearl of a box, adorned with pale ruched hangings; a large gilt mirror sat on the floor against a wall. Our photo-shoot in that room is still the best we ever did – it set us in the correct environment and the creative synergy of the place affected the photographs beautifully. It became a look that influenced the times.

George O'Dowd lived in another squat around the corner in Great Titchfield Street with the boy Marilyn, Princess Julia and Jeremy Healy (although much bed-swapping went on between the two buildings). The day we did the shoot, George was over at Warren Street, cadging some sugar or eyeliner. His large painted face leered over the banister as we arrived. He was wearing chopsticks in his jet-black hair and looked as if he were preparing for a Gilbert and Sullivan moment. 'Oi! Spandau Ballet! I can sing better than your fucking singer.'

'Well, get a band, then,' one of us shouted.

That July, HMS *Belfast* was the only thing people talked about. Every newly formed Blitz kid, futurist, psychobilly and postmodern soul boy was trying to get a ticket (a wonderful Russian constructivist drawing of a battleship that Graham had pillaged and recycled). Even if they couldn't get in, they had to be there. By late evening, the embankment was full of exquisitely dressed urban buccaneers, all jostling to get across the gangplank and into the most important party to hit town in years. If you hadn't been at Scala I or II then you were even more determined not to miss this. One band of hard-nosed street-pirates, led by the charismatic rebel-rebel and clubman Dave Mahoney, made an audacious yet successful attempt to gatecrash by stealing a small rowing boat and scaling the side of the battleship. Once on board they were lost among contortionists, fire-eaters and a throbbing crowd – a visual confection that hadn't dressed quite so industriously for any event in recent memory. Rusty, resplendent in sailor suit, played the records, while the ubiquitous Philip Sallon arrived in a white wedding gown adorned with fairy lights, and then politely asked someone where he could plug himself in. He stood all night in the same spot, flashing and bitching, bitching and flashing, while his disciples brought him drinks.

The event almost never happened. Earlier, the set-up had been a disaster when Simon – not what you'd call a technical lighting designer, more the deeply committed aesthete with a vision – blew the ship's main fuse box while rigging the lights. I went into a blind panic at the thought of it being cancelled, but luckily a butch electrician with a quiff was found from among the gathering and the power was back on just before the ship's doors opened.

The space had a low ceiling with brutalist-looking riveted pipes that almost touched Tony's head as we stepped on to the room's small stage. Hanging menacingly from one of these while lit like Bela Lugosi by Simon's white-hot underneath lighting, Tony was all demonic power that night, as the band, pressed against the steely bulkhead, delivered its most exciting show to date. The same could also be said of the audience, for the event was theirs as much as ours.

Dagger stood to one side, flanked by our inner circle – a proud cadre, revelling in their cocky gunboat marketing. Just below me, with his coterie, George O'Dowd looked fabulous as a geisha boy, but almost certainly hated the fact that for the next forty-five minutes no one was looking at him. And somewhere at the back, a pinched-faced purser, shocked by the cross-dressing, flagrant drug-taking and lack of rented tuxedos, was demanding a constant flow of placating fivers to be palmed into his soft hand, while his cheese dip quietly formed a skin.

But looking weirdest of all among the crowd that night was a self-conscious party of tour-jacketed A&R men, including Stuart Slater from Chrysalis, all hand picked for the privilege by Dagger and the band. It was their first view of what was happening in this new London, and the following day, their chequebooks would go into battle.

CHAPTER TEN

THE JOURNEY BEGINS

Dagger pointed his long stride through his familiar West End. He walked everywhere; it reflected his nature – everything worked for and achieved under his own steam, that's how he liked it, with as few people involved as possible. Yet another record company was in our sights and as he attempted to brief me, I tried to keep up with him, both physically and metaphorically.

'The thing is not to make them think that *we* want *them*.' His emphasis punched the air in front of us. 'I'm not saying we shouldn't be nice, just stay a little aloof – y'know? They're desperate for this.'

At least I had something in common with them.

I'd fallen into the role of band spokesman quite naturally, probably because I was the songwriter, and so far had been to all the meetings with Dagger. Since the boat show we'd been flooded with offers – EMI, Chrysalis, Phonogram, Magnet, Arista. Our demands were high – we were asking for over £200,000 – but we felt could justify them. At the meetings, I never discussed finance; I was there to represent the band; 'The dog and pony show', as Dagger would describe me.

'Come in, guys. Coffee? Tea?' He sounded as though he might be American. We gave our orders to a cute-looking secretary and the A&R guy settled behind his desk. On a shelf sat a framed photograph of him in a beery man-hug with a craggy, long-haired rocker. 'Hey, I *loved* the show. Some *wild* looking people there too. Felt a little conspicuous, I have to admit. Y'know, I was gonna wear my old mod suit but my wife talked me out of it.'

We were always nice to them, that was our nature, but we knew what we wanted – complete control. How could you trust these men to understand what was going on?

'Among those people,' Dagger began, cutting to the chase immediately, 'are graphic artists, film-makers, photographers, journalists, producers, clothes designers, and nobody is older than twenty-three. What we want is the promise that we can have control over all those mediums: artwork, video, choice over whatever tracks are singles. And how we promote them.'

A&R seemed to be listening, rocking back in his chair, but was he taking us seriously? The history of band management had probably not seen someone quite as young as Dagger, and some of the companies had wondered who they *really* should be talking to.

I took over with some well-rehearsed sound-bites. 'This new club scene is growing and we're at the forefront. It's not just a band with an audience, it's a multimedia phenomenon – we just happen to have stepped onstage with guitars and synths, it could easily have been a needle and thread we'd picked up, or a pen, or even just dancing shoes.' I loved those fey, un-rock'n'roll suggestions; they left them either enticed, bemused or repulsed. The hairy rocker looked down from his frame at me. 'We're a mirror to our audience,' I continued, 'an applause, if you like. This is a new movement – the next stage in the evolution of youth culture that goes back through soul boys and began with the Teddy boy – and it's the first one since punk.'

The secretary returned and with her a moment's silence. Dagger took his coffee, and the baton back from me. 'Gary and the band want

'Somewhere between the rock and roll they fell in love.' Mum and Dad, 1952.

Above: The wonderfully named Eliza Ettie Ruth Crisp, my father's mother, in service, 1912.

Right: My father Frank (left) and his brother Percy, just before their evacuation at the beginning of the Second World War.

Left: My great-grandad John Crisp – a Hansom cab driver and sweet seller. He believed braces always needed a belt for extra security.

Below: My father and his sister Elsie on the step of 138 Rotherfield Street – where I spent the first 15 years of my life.

My mum and dad in 1952. Just courting, they sit in the 'bottly glitter' of the Duke of Clarence pub either side of my grandfather Walter (in the hat). They are flanked by Dad's sister Grace and her husband Tom.

At home in Rotherfield Street, 1960. My parents' radiogram stands just to the right.

Me in a school photo, wearing one of my mother's lurid wool creations.

The embarrassed winner of a 'Hat and Apron' competition at Prestatyn holiday camp during the late sixties. My brother, a close second, stands in the background.

At Lord's with Gary Sobers for the final scene of *Junket 89*. I'm at the front, third from left. Stephen Brassett, 'with hair as white as a Midwich Cuckoo', holds the clapperboard.

Shaking the hand of the Duchess of Kent during the line up for the Royal Premiere of *Hide and Seek*, October 1972.

Taking Ian Fox through one of my songs, while rehearsing with the Same Band in the basement of Howarth's Music in 1975.

Soul boy power-poppers – the Gentry play Camden School for Girls in 1978.

'Bright Young People on a shoestring'. Spandau Ballet's first gig – Blitz, 5 December, 1979.

With Steve Strange at the bar of Blitz, 1980.

The Soho contingent gather at London's Waldorf hotel, 1980. *Centre, seated, left to right:* Lee Andrews, me, Tony, Martin, Steve, John. *Front row, left to right:* Rusty Egan, Steve Strange, Stephen Linard, Steve Lewis. *Back row, left to right:* Robert Elms, Moses Mount Bassie, Ollie O'Donnell, Jimmy O'Donnell, Graham Ball, Daryl Humphreys, Dagger; Simon Withers, John Stevens, Graham Smith, Chris Sullivan, Melissa Caplan.

to make twelve-inch mixes of their singles too, which we can send to the clubs that are springing up all over the country.'

I interjected and A&R swung his head back round. 'The difference between the club Crackers and the Marquee is not just the few hundred yards that separate them in Soho. In our clubs, the people on the dance floor are the stars.'

'Every town has its own Blitz now,' said Dagger, whipping the attention back. 'There's Maestro's in Glasgow; a club in Sheffield. In fact we've just been to one in Rayleigh called Crocs.'

He was right. We'd seen two young electro-bands calling themselves Depeche Mode and Soft Cell in that Essex club, and the clientele had stood in awe of the arrogant Londoners who'd deigned to visit them. The bullish young manager of Soft Cell had even fallen on his knees in front of Dagger in a display of theatrical worship. Rusty and Strange patronised their counterparts and then the Crocs' visit from London club royalty was over.

'This is how we'll promote ourselves, instead of endless gigging. If they *do* do shows, they'll be events, like the one you saw the other night, not in regular rock venues.'

The A&R guy brought his chair back on to four legs, which suddenly stopped our tirade. 'We do that with our black acts. Twelve-inches, I mean. But ... Really?'

'Of course, that's all included in our breakdown costs,' Dagger continued. 'As well as clothes.'

A moment's silence.

'Sorry, did you say clothes?'

'Yeah. How the band looks is really important and they'll be needing new looks all the time.'

Before he could say any more I took it one stage farther. 'We also want our own label.'

Chrysalis Records had already done it with Two-Tone for the Specials, and we liked the idea. I remember how thrilled I was as an eleven-year-old when T.Rex got their own imprint from EMI called Wax. With an image of Marc and its serial number of Marc 1, it looked so special on my turntable that I wanted to frame it. We wanted that unique look for our label too – which, of course, Graham would design – and I already had a name for it: Reformation. It seemed to suit our philosophy of breaking with the old guard.

'The label thing might be difficult, Steve,' said A&R, desperate to show some power. 'And as for the clothes …'

'Well, *others* have already offered us that,' said Dagger. 'They're also cool about the percentages we're asking for. But we like what you do here.'

'Let me get my business affairs people to look at it again. We'd love to work with you guys.' He turned to me. 'Your singer has a great voice. He doesn't sound like anyone else either. He's a crooner. Almost … operatic.'

'You're right. His hero's Frank Sinatra.'

'Really? How funny.'

I got back to the demands. 'We also know what the first single is and who we want to produce. He's part of our scene – Richard Burgess.'

Richard James Burgess was another Blitz frequenter, although at twenty-seven, not quite a *kid*. An American drummer who'd studied at Berkeley, he played in the electro-jazz band Landscape. He'd also played drums on the Buggles classic 'Video Killed The Radio Star' and a plethora of Euro-disco tracks; he was champion of the four-on-the-floor groove. An ardent enthusiast of electronic drums, he had helped Dave Simmons design the first Synn drum, and as a friend of Rusty's he hung out at Blitz, choosing a more futurist look – canary-yellow jumpsuit and red Cuban heels was always a head-turner. With his hair quiffed and a flash of grey at the front, he had the swarthy look of a Thunderbirds character. He was hugely complimentary about the band, and one night Rusty suggested that he'd be a great producer for us. We put it to him and he jumped at the chance. We needed him right away.

We'd been sniffed out by Radio 1 DJ and drive-time star Peter Powell, at that time the most popular DJ on radio and in many ways the one who would be at the forefront of the eighties British pop boom. Powell's flatmate was a friend of Dagger's from the LSE, and so Powell had turned up at Scala II to see the band. He loved what he saw and asked us to do a four-song studio session for him that he could play during his show. We agreed and recorded them at the BBC studios in Maida Vale. During the recording, two record company executives, Roger Ames and Tracy Bennett from Phonogram, found out we were there and tried to get into the session in an attempt to woo us face to face. Dagger found them prowling the corridor and, in the nicest possible way, refused them entry to the studio. They left all the more tantalised.

The resulting tracks were highly potent, and the ever-ebullient Peter Powell played them endlessly, although one more than any: 'To Cut A Long Story Short'. In fact, the song started to appear as though it were a single before we even had a record label. We knew we had to get it out soon, before the Christmas rush, and before another band stole our thunder.

Nationwide, the BBC's tea-time TV programme led by the permanently sweatered Frank Bough, had shown a whimsical film on us and the scene; while *Newsnight*, the station's weighty news flagship, had a piece where reporter Robin Denselow earnestly placed us within the history of London's ever-evolving youth cults. Cutting back to the studio, the anchor man, a bewigged Peter Snow, wryly commented, 'Whatever next?'

The newspapers were also heating up. Dagger harnessed Christina Appleyard's enthusiasm and got her to write a piece on us for the *Daily Mirror*, while insider David Johnson was effusive in the *Evening Standard*. But it was a double-page spread and front cover of the music paper *Sounds* that gave the whole thing a name.

Betty Page, with her doll-like presence, became the only inky music press writer we would trust. Her nom de plume gave her cheekily decadent leanings away, and Dagger vetted her before the interview. It would be an odd first piece as the interview was given by Dagger and me alone. We'd decided that we'd reinvent our past as though the Makers and our power-pop period had never happened. We'd say we'd been inspired to pick up instruments by Billy's and before then we had only danced. It made sense to streamline our history – we were creating a myth, and although some band members didn't quite understand that, I was convinced of this well-honed spin.

It is disputed, but her article was the first time I ever saw the phrase that would go on to name a youth movement. Perry Haines, the Blitz kid who started *i-D* magazine – in which my brother and I modelled for its first issue – claims it was he who first gave us the soubriquet, but, as far as I know, Perry only mentioned the word 'romanticism' in his piece on the band for *Camouflage* magazine. But in *Sounds* that September of 1980, Betty coined the name with the title: *The New Romantics*. It stuck. Before then, Bob had dipped his white-socked toe in the water with a kind of sheepish anti-name in his first article for *The Face* magazine, calling it the clandestine-sounding *Cult With No Name* – a little too shy and long for a label, I felt. Betty's, though, seemed to sum up the anachronism of the fashions and the whimsical approach to clothes; to the mood-noise of the lyrics and music, with its conceit that it all somehow meant something grander; and above all – because of the name's association with the original Romantics, Byron and Shelley – it highlighted the cult of self, a powerful philosophy that would exemplify the coming decade.

Nevertheless, we were suddenly the New Romantics, and the record companies felt they were bidding for more than just a band. But *when* the signing would come was causing great consternation within the group. As Dagger and I were doing the meetings we had a perception of the game, but the others were getting increasingly frustrated. John was still working in a bank and Tony in the print, but Martin, Steve and I had quit our jobs and were unemployed, and so was Dagger, as he'd left his degree course at LSE to concentrate fully on Spandau. The four of us would stand at Holborn tube station handing out *Ms London* magazines for a few extra quid, before Dagger and I would go off to meet a record company or two. My parents were getting increasingly frustrated as we were still living at home and yet bringing very little money in. The band would often squabble in rehearsals over how long the process was taking, but I had faith in Dagger to get us the best deal with the best company. Eventually we settled on what Chrysalis Records were offering and they won. On the day that we signed I received a letter from the Social Security. I sat on the hall stairs and read that I would no longer be able to withdraw the dole as it had been six months, and that I'd now have to go on to a lower payment. Luckily, I never had to apply.

On a sunny October morning the five old school friends from Islington, plus a brother, gathered in the boardroom at Chrysalis's offices in Stratford Place just off of Oxford Street, and under the watchful eye of Brian Carr and the joint owner of the company, Chris Wright (whose first name was the phonetic opening syllable of Chrysalis), put their names on a contract. It was Martin's nineteenth birthday and we had our own label, a promise of full artistic control, and the additional promise from them to pay for 12-inch mixes and videos. It was the highest advance any unsigned act had ever been given in the UK. And it also included an allowance for clothes.

Six days later, on my twenty-first birthday, Richard Burgess and I took the finished master tape of our first single to the Townhouse studios in West London to 'cut' the record. This is where an acetate of the song is made, from which a negative is later drawn to press the records. I sat and watched as the diamond needle dug its little spiralling trenches of compressed Spandau Ballet into the smooth virgin plate. The warm smell reminded me of my first innocent attempt ten years before in Waterloo Station, and how long I'd dreamt of this moment. 'To Cut A Long Story Short' was taut, succinct, rude and uncompromising, with an all-in-at-once intro that sounded as though the door of the Blitz had been kicked open.

And now the youth of Britain were about to rush in.

As well as its new suburban satellites, Blitz had spawned other clubs in and around Soho, some of which were run by members of the vanguard. Chris Sullivan, Graham Smith and Bob Elms set up shop on a Monday night in Wardour Street at a club called St Moritz. This took our fascination with the Berlin of the thirties to its extreme, playing songs by Weill and Brecht, Marlene Dietrich and Edith Piaf. A new lounge-lizard look slithered into the night in the shape of Sullivan, Elms and Christos, while George, Pinkietessa and Philip camped it up to Doris Day and Billie Holiday. Occasionally, you'd hear *Cabaret*'s politically disturbing, but nevertheless emotive, 'Tomorrow Belongs To Me'. And, of course, everybody there believed it did.

The success of St Moritz had Steve Strange combining forces with Sullivan at a bar in the newly refurbished Covent Garden. The name Hell had people playing with religious iconography and ecclesiastical costume for the first time. Black was de rigueur. Here, I believe, were the beginnings of Goth, which would later fully embrace its satanic spirit in the Batcave, a club based at the old Billy's venue. When Hell was full, Strange would open the back door, which extraordinarily led straight out into a graveyard. We'd spend the night lolling on tombstones, creating a tableau of truly Gothic proportions. It became darker in other ways too. One night some bad acid was passed around and, with the proliferation of crosses and vampire face-paints, it transformed the club into a place more akin to Bedlam. Drugs were becoming darker and stronger among the few who dared, and one night a girl 'died' in the club, until paramedics miraculously revived her – a magic trick that to the more chemically expanded souls was proof of the occult powers they now commanded.

Towards the end of the Blitz, Steve and Rusty threw a joint birthday party for Martin and me. Mum and Dad came along and mixed happily with all the extraordinary youths. My mother got on especially well with Steve Strange, who'd often pop round to our house for tea. He'd sit in our kitchen in full make-up, hair in some vertical confection, chatting to my mother about his home life in Wales. One night, Chris Sullivan, dressed as an Edwardian gentleman, crashed out on my bedroom floor, where he lay in a fetal position for most of the next day. My mother vacuumed around him but even that couldn't rouse the sleeping Welshman. And then suddenly, at around teatime, he rose, and after reviving himself with a pot of strong brew, said, 'Thank you so much, Mrs Kemp. I'm sorry I've been such trouble but I've been very tired, you see.' He then picked up his silver-topped cane and left. She loved him.

In October 1980, on the eve of the release of our first single, and after a year and a half of partying, Steve and Rusty closed their Tuesday Blitz night, victims of their own ballyhoo. The street outside had become a riot of desperate dilettantes, all made up with nowhere to go, and Strange knew that, to its originators, Blitz had lost its enigmatic quality.

The same was happening on Thursdays and Saturdays at Hell, and in the same week it too ended with an operatic finale of police becalming a large assortment of angry Pierrots, rakes, futurists and voyeurs, who were all unable to gain access to the tiny bar. The owner took fright and suddenly London's freaks were homeless.

Spandau Ballet, on the other hand, were ready to give it to the nation.

Top of the Pops was Marc, Bowie, Rod and an endless line of epoch-defining acts that had threaded their way into my wardrobe and life for the last ten years. It was the new church for Britain's youth and we'd visit it piously every Thursday night, picking our way through the wheat and the chaff, the saved and the damned. Sixteen million people tuned in, and with its vibrant colour schemes and camera-fixated audience, it hadn't altered its style for over a decade. What changed were the fashions on show, and it was about to change once more as we prepared our wardrobe for Spandau Ballet's maiden appearance. But our arrival was to be less than glamorous.

The morning had started in stately fashion. My mother was so flustered when a black Daimler appeared outside our house that she instinctively started straightening the cushions. It's a cast-iron bet that a limousine had never been up our street before, unless it was lost. The neighbours poured out to watch the titfered chauffeur open the heavy rear door, revealing its teak secrets, and Martin and me crawl in over the leather. It was as if the Tardis had landed, ready to carry the two local lads off to places unimagined. In the real world, though, we'd rented a transit van for our equipment, which was all newly purchased from the advance and still in boxes. The placid Simon had agreed to help drive us there and set up the gear, but on arrival at the BBC studios had refused to get out of the van, suddenly stultified – as any good aesthete would be – by the blatant commerciality of what we were doing and what kind of a job he was being asked to do. And so, the group of young men most talked about as Britain's hottest new trendsetters were first spotted that day, humping their heavy cardboard boxes into the studio like the good, sweaty, working-class lads they really were. Thank God headbands were in. Proper roadies would have to be our next purchase.

Radio 1 was playing 'To Cut A Long Story Short' endlessly, it seemed, and the 12-inch dance mix – the first of its kind for a white non-funk band – was on DJs' decks in clubs across the country. The Tuesday before the television show, and the day before the chart was officially announced, Dagger had taken the call that the record had gone to number 43 and we were on *TOTP*. If anything, it felt like a greater high than signing – the culmination of all the work; the proof of arrival.

We took to the stage in a mixture of sashes, kilts, tartan and Edwardian military. It was a look as yet unseen on this great British institution, but would soon be copied on a thousand dance floors around the world. I thought of 'Get It On', 'Starman', 'Maggie May', and hoped that our moment could be of equal seminal status to a younger version of myself watching; I thought of the promises made to my struggling parents who'd kept faith as I quit my job and danced through Soho streets in a blaze of bizarre fashions; and I thought of the words that Dagger had made me say that summer on a television documentary, and I hoped he would be proved right.

The day after our *TOTP* screening – and after rustling up a few of our more reliable friends as roadies – we headed up to Britain's second-largest city and the home of the Rum Runner, a club that loudly insisted on its own importance within the *zeitgeist*. We were to play the Botanical Gardens in Birmingham as our opening foray outside of London and our first attempt to take the Spandau-slash-Blitz event to the provinces.

We would follow this with a show in another like-minded place, the Casablanca club in Cardiff's Tiger Bay, before returning, hopefully triumphant, to London and Heaven – a club that Steve Norman and I had frequented as soul boys when it was the Global Village. It wasn't a tour, more of a skirmish; and there would be some casualties.

We'd arrived in Birmingham via local radio interviews and a brief stop at Kahn and Bell's hip shop in the centre of town (there was, by now, always a shop. In Cardiff it was Mark Taylor's Paradise Garage). The gear arrived ahead of us in a transit van that Neil Matthews – our photographer and van driver for the day – had managed to impale on the roof of the entrance to the botanical hall. He'd hit it and then put his foot down to free himself, which jammed it even further. It took twelve of us to pull the van free.

We were finishing the soundcheck with Richard Burgess when I noticed Dagger in a difficult conversation with the local club guy who was co-promoting the show. I jumped offstage as Dagger walked over.

'What's up, Steve?'

'Apparently there's a local *Spandau Ballet*.' He said the name with a mimicked Brummy accent. 'They wanna support us tonight. I told him no way. He's fine.'

I felt a surge of jealousy. 'Rusty's DJing's enough. Plus our lot would hate it.'

Our lot were on their way up. Chris and Bob had arranged an away-day for fifty, a busman's holiday to Birmingham for a gawp down the nose at the local copyists. They'd all met (mostly late) outside Chris's flat, and he, Bob, Strange, Sullivan, Melissa, Christos, Ollie, George, Philip, the two Grahams et al. climbed on board a coach and immediately started downing Pils and pills. And pills and Pils.

A host of anxious Brummy Brummells and belles were gathering expectantly outside the gardens, adorned in their most angular accoutrements – hard-core New Romantics, hoping to be blessed by the metropolitan instigators, with a few simply waiting for the face-off. The London coach swung into the parking area where they were gathered, and bounced heavily to a halt. The Birmingham lot fluffed feathers and stood as one. They'd spotted Steve Strange through the misted glass and all wanted a view of what Soho was doing. In dazed dribs and drabs the original Cult With No Name spilled from the bus, hair matted, suits dishevelled, wrecked eyes squinting through the light and the MDMA they'd all popped. For a moment the two opposing sides eyed each other up in silent confrontation, as London, realising that they were being pronounced upon, gradually organised their clothes and posture. It was a shambolic show from the originals but, nevertheless, did not disappoint all of the faithful.

The show was a success, with Birmingham's finest dancing to Rusty's playlist and enjoying their first view of the Blitz house band. After the show had finished, and Sullivan had been retrieved, post-coital, from a bush with his girlfriend, we were all ferried off to the Midlands' answer to Blitz – the Rum Runner. We descended upon its dark, mirrored rooms with all the thirst of travelling pilgrims and proceeded to make bitchy sideswipes about the place. An unspoken dance competition then ensued, where zoot suits flashed with pantaloons, and quiffs with backcombed explosions. Winklepickers parried espadrilles as a whirligig of styles blended rapidly under the spinning glitterball. Eventually a breathless truce was announced owing to over-consumption of stimulants and the warring parties laid down their bodies in leatherette booths. Two local brothers oversaw proceedings. Tall and elegant, they paid for everyone's drinks and then escorted the dreadfully smashed Londoners back on to the coach. And then Spandau and a small coterie of friends and locals were quietly invited back to the local promoter's flat.

We sat on his floor and listened to Bowie and Roxy and swapped nocturnal tales, mutually fascinated by the parallel worlds we'd all created.

'I thought your kilt look was amazing last night on telly,' said one guy about my age with lots of prepped hair. I relished his obvious awe and tugged smugly at my can. '*We've* got a band.' he said, waving his hand at the small blond boy preening himself while talking with Steve Norman and Martin. 'The brothers who own the club manage us.' He lowered his voice. 'I'm a bit embarrassed actually, 'cos they'd asked if we could support you tonight but your manager …'

'Oh yeah, sorry. We're not into supports. What's your band called?'

'We got it from a character in *Barbarella*.' He was talking about the kitsch sci-fi movie from the sixties. 'It's also a club here.'

I waited for the name.

The small blond boy leant in. 'We're called Duran Duran.'

I knocked back my beer and felt the hairs stand up on the back of my neck.

There was a schism appearing between the gays and the straights of Soho, an internecine tiff between the ones who wanted to dress wilder – opting for the piratical look adapted by Westwood and McClaren, who were both desperately trying to hijack the scene – and the ones who wanted to find some old-fashioned urban masculinity in their clobber. The aptly named Le Kilt in Greek Street was the aural parallel to the oversized zoot suits and fob chains suddenly being worn by some of the straight half. Run by Bob, Chris, Graham Smith and Graham Ball, Le Kilt was back to funk. We'd all been soul boys and what with Top Shop now selling New Romantic clothes on Oxford Street – they were even being worn by Lady Di – we wanted to move back to familiar ground. It was also political: funk was the music most detested by the middle-class rock press – who'd only just got to grips with electro and Blitz – so we had another motive to sidestep and dance.

It also inspired me. We finished recording our first album – written more than a year earlier – but I feared it was already out of date. We'd started to strip back some of the synthesisers on the tracks and develop the guitar parts but I wanted to start writing again. I sat with my guitar in my bedroom and with the sound of the Fatback Band and Dr Buzzard in my head, I ground out a groove and made an attempt to write a song that combined funk with the stark European music that we had created already. The result was 'Glow'.

Steve, the most natural musician in the band, took to the congas and bongos as though he'd played them in an earlier life, and within a few days we had the song's staccato groove hammering through our rehearsal room in London Bridge. We were desperate to record it and get it out, announcing our credentials and proving that we were at the epicentre of Soho nightlife; but we still had an electro album to sell and singles to release from it.

Journeys To Glory was the title of a book I had on religious obsessives – people who'd crucify or flagellate themselves in the name of their beliefs. It seemed a perfect title for our first album: as well as being wonderfully pompous and presumptuous, it was made to irritate the enemy and clearly stated our intentions. Graham Smith's sleeve highlighted the title's classical allusions with a torso of a naked Grecian male statue (embossed white on white for the limited edition) and, except on the inner sleeve, no picture of the band (that would be too risky, given the speed at which styles were changing). It also included another futurist-style poem from Bob. We'd lived up to our promise of using 'in-house' people, but the only position our friends couldn't fill at that time was video director.

As with recording, I loved the process of video production, and would sit in during the edit, unafraid to make suggestions. My obsession with the design of Spandau was 360-degree and there wasn't an element that I didn't find fascinating or important. *Control freak* is a modern, derogatory term that reveals its etymological roots in hippy laissez-faire philosophy; I simply became obsessed with keeping all the bases covered and never letting a single aspect of the band's production slip by without focus. That's not to say we weren't all contributing to the process, because we were, or that I was always right in my ideas, because I wasn't, as I would later discover.

The video for the first single – directed by Brian Grant – was an opportunity to capture some of the flavour of who we were as well as educating the audience in the art of 'Blitz dancing', that solemn slow jive I'd first seen in Billy's. Two Blitz girls we knew who were exceptional dancers agreed to appear with us in the London Dungeons, a horror waxwork museum in the underground cellars near London Bridge. This being November 1980, they are in 'Hell' black taffeta, while the band are a mixture of Culloden and Edwardian Scottish military, designed and stitched by Willie, Melissa and Simon, with a sprinkling of finds from our favourite army surplus store, Lawrence Corner. Tony's holding my uncle's old WWII tank binoculars, an affectation that was meant to accentuate the battledress look and imply, I suppose, that we had the future in our sights. Chris, Christos and Ollie are card-playing extras in a dank, conspiratorial corner. But for me, the star of the video is Martin, who lives up to Dagger's original description of 'the best-looking bloke we know'.

That November, 'To Cut A Long Story Short' was all over the radio, as it hit top five in the UK. The journey had begun.

We returned once more to our native West End, and the Sundown was to be Spandau Ballet's biggest show to date. Outside, touts served up tickets at inflated prices, while well-dressed youths, trying to get in or simply just enjoying being there, filled the pavements of Charing Cross Road. As 1981 got under way, everyone seemed to be flying: Steve and Rusty had a spanking new venue to compete with the Embassy and Legends. Open to London's nocturnal aristocracy, it had the posturing name of Club for Heroes; they also had a band, Visage, with which they'd now had a top ten hit; Bob Elms was regularly writing for *The Face*, the hip, highly lauded glossy and arbiter of this new *zeitgeist*; Stephen Jones had graduated to his own millinery salon in Covent Garden, attracting the attention of, among others, Lady Diana; David Holah and Stevie Stewart were starting their fashion label, Bodymap; Melissa Caplan and Stephen Linard were designing for other pop artists; Christos and Chris Sullivan had a band called Blue Rondo à la Turk and were creating funky waves; Animal Nightlife and Bananarama were two other bands formed by Blitz kids and already heating up the charts; Midge Ure had joined the electro-band Ultravox and was hovering at number two in the charts with a song called 'Vienna'; Perry Haines had started the magazine *i-D* and was styling other bands; Graham Smith was taking on successful new commissions as a photographer and graphic artist, and George O'Dowd, no longer the beleaguered cloakroom attendant, was considering 'Boy' George and preparing to take on the world. Even the band that we'd first met up in Birmingham had a record out, and 'Planet Earth' was at number twelve with Duran Duran suddenly – and shockingly – our main competition.

This was to name but a few. The powerful everywhere were hunting out these once impoverished peacocks and trying to utilise their spirit and creative potency. For us, *Journeys To Glory* had arrived at number five in the album charts and our second single, 'The Freeze', had given us another top twenty hit and a national dance-floor filler. Tense, but excited, we paced the Sundown dressing room. It was that anxious moment before hitting the stage when you take on a reflective disposition and silence falls; the quiet before, as they say.

Dagger broke it. 'I was just thinking about the day we all first went to Billy's. It changed everything, don't you think?' He paused but we sensed he was still musing. 'It's funny, but it wasn't just walking into a club. It was like … walking through some magic door or something … for everyone who went there, I mean.'

Outside in the hall we could hear the anticipation building, and then he landed on it: 'It was like stepping through the secret door at the back of the wardrobe.'

He was right; I only hoped that we'd never have to leave.

CHAPTER ELEVEN

SOUL BOYS OF THE WESTERN WORLD

The Pan Am 747 touched down into a sunny spring day. On board was what would become known as the Gang of Twenty-One – twenty-one in number; twenty-one in average age. Their mission – to take London's new swing into the heart of New York.

It had been in the planning for a while. The instigator was a Blitz kid who'd recently found some success in NY. John Baker was a loquacious wheeler-dealer known to us all as Mole. He owned a stall in London's Kensington market called Axiom from which he sold the one-off designs of the Saint Martins girls and boys and attracted the attention of spiritual Blitz kids and documentary film crews everywhere. They all wanted a piece of the hip action. As a twenty-year-old student Mole took up to £3,000 on a Saturday and he used his cash and chutzpah to take him and his frilly shirts to America. They loved his New Romantic cockney-flyboy style, and within weeks he was making connections for like-minded types across the Atlantic.

Dagger knew it was the next step for us, and in 1981 he made his first trip to America. Mole immediately introduced him to the hottest young club manager in Manhattan: Danceteria's Jim Fouratt. Small, blond and with a voice not far below the dog-whistle of Truman

Capote, he was a major player in the quadruple-floor world of New York City's über-discos. I only wish I were able to illustrate the skilled, verbal mugging that Dagger and Mole must have performed upon the fey little New Yorker, but not being there, I can only assume that he fell head over Cuban heels in love with them, and became determined to bring Spandau Ballet to New York. But Dagger and Mole wanted more – context. The whole scene should come over, they said, and deliver itself not just to the music press, but to the fashion and art industry as well; an invasion, if you like. Jim swallowed the hook.

As the plane delivered up its young Londoners – who would scatter themselves throughout the city like a sartorially obsessed sleeper cell – New York prepared itself for our blitz on its Underground – a large club below the offices of Andy Warhol and his *Interview* magazine on Union Square. It would be our crucial point of attack.

We were becoming au fait with this method. A few weeks previously, we'd taken our music-slash-fashion event into the capital of decadence itself – Paris. Le Palace was home to Grace Jones, Thierry Mugler and the drag queens of Pigalle. The inheritor of belle époque, it was the Studio 54 of Europe. Steve and Rusty flew out with their record collection and entourage, and after the show we all enjoyed some disco détente. Unfortunately, Martin was still recovering from a very sore shoulder and a bruised ego.

While onstage my brother loved to hold his hand out to the reaching crowd and tease them between bass licks. That night at Le Palace someone grabbed it, and as he tugged back, his arm came straight out of its socket. The first I knew was when the bass stopped playing and I looked over to see Martin with one orangutan-like appendage swinging aimlessly around. Now one job that roadies have to do is watch for leads coming out of guitars. If it ever happens they scuttle on in a crouched position like a demented crab, grab the loose lead and jam it back in. In our roadie Nicky's mind, Martin's arm was a similar problem, and assuming the scuttle position, he went on, grabbed the flailing limb, rammed it straight back into its socket and retreated. After a severe jolt of visible pain, Martin, like the trooper he is, was back on his instrument as though nothing had happened. But the evening wasn't over yet for the brave bass player and his Sancho Panza.

Martin and I had come up with the idea after watching James Brown on TV and seeing him do such a trick. Towards the end of our last song, we'd agreed that my brother, feigning utter exhaustion, would faint onstage; then, while the rest of us exited, Nicky would run on only to find himself unable to revive his fallen man and so drag him from the stage. Cue great applause and an audience thrilled by total commitment. Stuff of legend.

That evening, coming to the end of our final encore, I saw Martin wobble and fall to his knees. He called upon all his Anna Scher experience to make the ruse work, and looked convincing as his eyes rolled, tongue lolled and he collapsed on to the boards. Ignoring him, we finished the song and left the stage. Now Nurse Nicky may still have been in shock from the emergency treatment he'd recently administered, but instead of running on to help our fallen hero, he followed us back to the dressing room.

A few minutes later Martin wandered back in. 'Where the fuck were you? Didn't you see me?'

'What happened, Mart?'

'What happened was I was lying out there like a prat. I had to pretend to wake up on my own!' He threw his sweaty beret with its tall feather cockade across the room. It landed on some cheese. 'People were laughing.'

It wouldn't have happened to James.

It didn't take the Twenty-One long to find their dancing feet in

New York. Dr Buzzard's Original Savannah Band was in town, and after we had watched his show, a meeting was arranged between August Darnell and his London acolytes. It was a bizarre mixture of flash cockneys, a bulky Welshman and a bemused but flattered Haitian gentleman from Canada, all wearing oversized zoot suits and swinging fob chains. The next evening we all dropped MDMA and kept up appearances at Bonds for the Debbie Harry concert, a pointless visit given our temporary heightened fascination with anything but her singing.

One of the Twenty-One who came along with us that night was a petite platinum blonde with a pixie haircut and a rock star boyfriend. Paula Yates was a precocious nineteen-year-old and as pale as a pearl. I'd met her at Steve and Rusty's Club for Heroes a few months before, where we'd both stood in shock as the great Pete Townshend was stretchered unconscious from the toilets after an overdose that, luckily, he survived. Not only had Paula never taken a drug in her life, she was teetotal; she certainly needed nothing to boost her in-your-face confidence. Her wit was as sharp as her dress sense – usually a natty choice of fifties peachy-keen – and her flirting ability had you feeling you were the only man in the room. That night, I walked her back to her scooter; it was white, to match her pedal-pushers, jacket and helmet. I'd just seen the movie *À Bout de Souffle* but I struggled in my imagination to be the Jean-Paul Belmondo character, and in any case, she lived with the extremely tall and intimidating Bob Geldof. Paula was now writing a perky pop column for the *News of the World* and flew with us to New York to write a piece on the Blitz invasion.

And the invasion seemed to be causing quite a stir. New York in 1981 wasn't all that difficult to shock. Unlike London, the streets weren't full of youth cults – no Teds, mods, punks, soul boys and definitely no New Romantics. The real working-class youth culture in

New York was black, but the streets we walked were white and full of flares. It was astonishing how easy it was to turn a New York head, but that summer a cable channel calling itself MTV would start transmitting and things would change. On its opening day in August, half of the videos shown would be British; it would open up a direct trading route for the more visually exciting Brits, and we would take a trip on it.

The abundance of British videos on MTV would be testament to their quality, and the man pushing the medium's so-far limited format was an Australian expat called Russell Mulcahy. Russell had come to everyone's attention with his dramatic video for Ultravox's single 'Vienna'. Before Russell, videos never took themselves seriously. They were either of leaping skinny-tied popsters against white backdrops, or full of Beatles-like cavorting in innocent shrubbery. 'Vienna' was cinema, though – cropped screen, slow tracking shots, backlit smoke – all a revelation in 1981; and we wanted some of it.

'Musclebound', the third single from our album, was a unique blend of constructivist propaganda, Russian folk music and slow-jive disco (pompous was fashionable then), all inspired by a typically Blitz-dreamt European nostalgia. It was begging for some larger-than-life treatment. And so the Lake District was substituted for the Russian steppe and dwarfs were enrolled to heighten the exotic flavour. We'd planned an evocative piece of pomp with burning fires, flailing sickles and the band on horses. *The band on horses?!* The thought of any equine posing was already making me feel sick.

We gathered at my parents' house, dwarfs and all, for the trip up north. Arriving early, a tiny Indian man who called himself a 'little person' came up to our front room, where my parents were having a drink with neighbours. As usual my parents and their friends were in fancy dress; a Saturday night ritual.

'HAVE. YOU. BEEN. IN. ANYTHING. ELSE. BEFORE?' My neighbour spoke to him as though he were a deaf child.

'Er, yes. Actually, I've just played Superman.'

Cue laughing.

'Honestly. They had me flying. It's for when they need him to be smaller on screen.'

Cue more laughing and thigh-slapping.

'No, really. You'll see me if you look carefully. Why are you laughing?'

Pause.

Cue embarrassed silence.

'Musclebound' was to be a day's filming on the high pass of Kirkstone, but on our arrival snow began to fall. All that day we struggled to film, the dwarfs especially, as they were getting lost in three feet of snow. We set up shop at the single pub that stands at the top of the pass and spent the next four nights trapped there. By the time the horses were taken out of their boxes they were skittish to say the least; on the other hand, the band were taken out of the pub bloated on scampi-in-the-basket and cheap wine. My chosen beast, a twitching thoroughbred, sensed my nerves in a second and, just as the cameras rolled, it reared up and smacked the back of its head into my face, throwing me unconscious across the field. No time for hospital. I revived in the pub and insisted on a stunt double. Tony, on the other hand, loved it all and even did his own stunts, the most difficult of which was riding a horse while balancing a tiny little Stephen Jones hat on his head.

Because of the extra money now available to the film company through weather insurance – and the enforced extra time spent up there – Russell shot yards of film and a small video masterpiece was created. It started a video war and soon our Birmingham counterparts would be begging their record company (and Russell Mulcahy) to make even more ambitious videos for them. Music videos became a new part of the British film industry, and MTV and America lapped them up.

But right now, we were a small vanguard in New York, and a shock to America's naturally conservative tastes. On the night of our show the Underground was awash with black polo-necks, dancing queens and the cream of New York club life. They had never seen anything quite like it before. The media were out in force, and when not clicking at a Brit, focused their lenses upon a small table where Andy Warhol sat surrounded by his doting devotees. From the DJ booth Bob delivered his Le Kilt blend of old funk, with a splash of electro for context, while his statement about creating a 'nouveau aristocracy' for the streets seemed to be coming true as locals hovered obsequiously around anyone who looked or sounded remotely British. And then the man who'd brought us all here, the diminutive Jim Fouratt took the stage.

'In 1981,' he stuttered, his high voice cutting above the New York hubbub, 'we present not just music … but London – a city and a lifestyle!'

Bob started spinning John Handy's 'Hard Work' and out came the freaks, like ornate figures from a town clock. For the next half-hour, sixty-one different outfits from eight new London designers stalked the Underground catwalk; from Sullivan's cartoonishly large zoot suits to Melissa's geometric cut-outs, it was a line of beauty that would inspire America's *Woman's Wear Daily* to give the band its front cover and report: 'Show*Blitz*ness has launched its American invasion … It is a conquest. Not since the heady days of Studio 54 has a Manhattan club crackled with such intensity.'

Our performance started rather oddly. Steve Marshall, our psycho-punk roadie, had dropped acid and must have thought we'd been playing for hours because after just two songs he decided he'd better call a halt to proceedings, came on and started to unplug the gear. He was rapidly dragged from the stage, told of his mistake and advised by

Dagger to go join the party out front. Steve Norman's rampaging congas echoed off the walls and Martin slapped his bass in agreement. We played extended versions of all our songs, including the Brit funk 'Glow' and a new dance number that we'd yet to record: 'Chant No. 1'. The New Yorkers approved and the club and the night belonged to London.

The following day the *New York Times* ran a piece by the aptly named John Rockwell, entitled 'London's Spandau Ballet':

> British rock bands make New York debuts frequently these days, but most of them sort of skulk into town, victims of record-company austerity and the new wave's own antipretensions. Not so Spandau Ballet, which gave its New York first local performance Wednesday night at the Underground with a full, nostalgically old-fashioned blast of hype, complete with a London vanguard fashion show and a disco full of exotically costumed trendies.

There's a much-used photograph of the so-called Twenty-One standing smugly outside a fashionable restaurant the day after the show. Some casualties (the ones who'd done acid the night before) deplete our magic number, but it's a wonderful document, not only of who was there, but of what London was wearing at the time. Here's the band, dressed in Robin Hood-style boots and baggy shirts tied around the waist with belts; Richard Burgess in a sci-fi black all-in-one; the irrepressible Mole in Errol Flynn shirt; Ollie O'Donnell and Bob in their zoot suits, a quiff and a buzz-cut respectively; Melissa Caplan (hiding a bequiffed Graham Smith) in her samurai stylings; Simon Withers in tartan jodhpurs and shoulder cape chatting to a proud, piratical-looking Dagger; and just in front of Bob, who's smiling fondly in her direction, is another young designer – a beautiful, mixed-race girl that I'd noticed on the scene but until then had never spoken to. Her name was

Sade, and at that moment she had no idea she could sing, let alone that she – and with much greater success than any of us – would eventually be the one to take America by storm.

That summer we rolled the show and its entourage out to a series of hot spots that read like an itinerary for *The Saint*: Rome (the Much More Club); Milan (Odyssey 2001); Madrid (Rockola); Florence and Ibiza. Ibiza was a hippy island, with no club culture at all. We opened a new place called Ku (now Manumission) and played under the night sky on a stage overhanging an open-air swimming pool. The place was full of bearded hippies, shocked at the raunchy behaviour of the young folk from England with coloured hair. They traumatised us in return with their ritualistic chasing of a young bull through the club, eventually hounding the poor beast into the pool. He was later brought around sliced and diced on a platter for our delectation. Ibiza was an odd place to go to dance in 1981, but on that night London liked what they saw. They went back every summer for the next twenty-five years. Balearic was born.

I don't think there are many songs that can boast the inclusion of directions in them. 'Is This The Way To Amarillo?' never gets a satisfactory answer; 'Do You Know The Way To San Jose?' has the singer pleading for a reply but getting completely ignored; and the song 'Somewhere' says '*there's a place for us*', only refuses to report where exactly. But 'Chant No. 1' gave you such a specific route that you could be led to believe the writer had done 'The Knowledge'.

> *You go down, down past the Talk of the Town,*
> *You go down Greek Street then it's underground.*
> *Well it's Soho life for this mobile knife,*
> *It's the place to shoot*
> *Friday night Beat Route.*

The only trouble was you probably couldn't get in anyway. Hundreds would huddle outside this Soho club on a Friday night like the aliens in *Toy Story*, waiting for the finger of Ollie O'Donnell to choose them; and that's if you were able to get to Soho in the first place. But you could always buy the record, or watch the video set in the club itself, or sit at home in your bedroom planning your own Beat Route. Because in 1981 if there was one thing a young person believed, it was that they could take control of their nightlife.

What Blitz-culture had proved was that clubs run by twenty-year-olds for twenty-year-olds were possible. Punk always had its older Svengalis, but as much as I loved it, punk made an art of complaining. Out in Thatcher's big bad world were millions of unemployed and a lost generation who might never work. With nothing on offer but despair, this was something you *could* be in command of. 1981 had young people starting clubs, designing bands, clothes, magazines, all for people of their own age; and if none of the above, at the very least they had control of their look, their dance, the shadow they threw. And, at a time when we needed it, that felt powerful.

Ironically, Thatcher got her own way – a generation of imaginative entrepreneurs; although unfortunately for her, many of us would grow to be New Labour-supporting media types and help send her party into the wilderness. But back at the beginning of the eighties everyone suddenly wanted someone with coloured hair. The newly formed Channel 4 dropped its 'minority' brief and decided to become a 'youth' channel; Perry Haines and Terry Jones's *i-D* magazine spawned *The Face*, *New Sounds New Styles*, *Blitz* magazine, *No. 1*, and all quickly employed coloured-haired kids as their features editors, etc. Record companies needed them; ad agencies craved them. Wild youth was suddenly in demand and infiltrating the establishment. Things would never be the same. Blitz started that.

There's a claustrophobia that emanates from 'Chant No. 1' that had everything to do with the club that's eulogised in it. Le Beat Route was a small and unfrequented dive that had sad Coconut Grove decor, a long central bar and a small stage at the far end in front of a square dance floor. Ollie the hairdresser had a charm that he'd quietly considered to be undersold. Others had succeeded with clubs, and now it was his turn. He started a night in this tired Greek Street dive that automatically attracted the ex-Blitz crowd and more. Ollie was a face and veteran of the scene, and so his appearance upon the door meant there was soon only one place to be seen on a Friday night. The film crews rushed from Steve Strange's Club for Heroes to focus upon the small red awning that curved discreetly into Greek Street. Inside it was hot funk, served up by our former electrician and saviour of our HMS *Belfast* gig – Steve Lewis. Steve was a soul boy from Ealing who had a huge black record collection and therefore an imme-diate job as DJ on Le Beat Route's opening night. He centred it around the intelligent funk of Was (Not Was) and in particular their menacing 'Wheel Me Out'. It became the anthem of the hottest club in Britain and had me banging my guitar and looking for the song that would, once again, place Spandau Ballet at the heart of London club culture.

Starting with its tetchy guitar riff, 'Chant No. 1' takes paranoia, throws in some gang vocals and a taut trumpet, mixes it with a soupçon of Raymond Chandler, and places it in the pressure cooker that was Soho 1981. We'd played it to our spin-doctor, Bob, at a rehearsal. I wanted to impress him and asked him to come over. The song was as sinewy as an all-night dancer, and finished on an unresolved chord as though it were the title-song set-up for a movie's opening scene – and the movie was yours. Bob loved it so much that when we took it to be unveiled at our Bournemouth soul-boys-on-the-beach Easter bank holiday show, he called for it ceaselessly all night. I knew immediately that we would keep the crown.

The idea to incorporate real horns came during our *Top of the Pops* appearance for 'Musclebound'. The Brit funk act Beggar & Co. were on and we bonded with them. It occurred to me straight away that not only would it be a great musical connection but that it was a subversive statement to boot. The conjoining of soul and rock had very little precedent then, and we knew that it would irritate the hell out of the rock press, as well as give us some extended credibility.

We recorded it at Utopia Studios in Primrose Hill, where John debuted his Simmons electronic drum kit for the track. With its hexagon pads, the kit that Richard Burgess had helped to develop would soon become synonymous with the period. Recording the music was fast and easy but Richard wanted something different from Tony. He wanted to capture some of the *film noir* quality of the lyrics by having Tony sing it quietly, restrained, and with a sense of paranoia. Tony has such a huge voice that Richard wanted him to relax it as much as possible, and after a few unsuccessful attempts had him singing while lying on his back. It certainly succeeded in making the poor guy paranoid, but delivered the song. Later, during the making of the second album, Richard would force Tony into even more embarrassing positions to sing, and in the process alienate him entirely. Nevertheless, at that moment his trick worked and the quiet tension is palpable in his voice.

We rushed to Le Beat Route with our white-label acetate and it conjured everything we'd hoped for. Even Boy George, sat in his catty booth, admitted to liking it; although he drew the line at dancing.

Russell Mulcahy's video gives you the Soho–Beat Route experience complete; a time capsule of British youth culture circa 1981. Tony, playing a strung-out lounge lizard, arrives at Le Beat Route and the camera takes his point of view as it passes a welcoming Ollie and descends the stairs to a dancing throng. Then it's long lenses and sweaty faces as Tony pulls off an incredible, Johnnie Ray-like performance. I wanted Steve Lewis to mime to my rap – DJs were rappers and it seemed a good addition to the time capsule to include him in it. As with Blitz, we were aware of the legacy the place was already promising. I also suggested that Lewis have his picture of Lenin in the shot. A communist DJ couldn't pass without notice.

That summer, Frankie Crocker was sitting having a drink at the bar of the Ritz in New York when 'Chant No. 1' – and with it a view into the Beat Route – came up on their newly installed video screen. It had been picked up by Ed Steinburg's *Rock America*, a video compilation reel delivered to clubs across the States. Frankie loved it, tracked it down, and immediately started playing it on his top-rated black music radio station, BLS. Frankie, America's number-one black DJ, was a soul legend of the airwaves and not afraid of a little showmanship himself – one night riding into Studio 54 on a white stallion! Frankie led the charge, and within a week or so KTU and KISS, both black stations, started to play the record. Dagger and I flew to New York to meet with the record company and talk about releasing it. On our first trip they said they wouldn't release anything unless it was on the radio. Now we were on the radio and one of the stations was the biggest in New York.

'The thing is, guys, it's *black* radio. It won't cross over into pop.' What he wanted to say was it wasn't proper radio and wouldn't be heard by white kids with cash.

It was frustrating. Chrysalis America just weren't willing to press the button on us. 'Story', and its attendant 12-inch – a package we immodestly felt represented a cultural shift in the UK – had no relevance to a company steeped in Pat Benatar and Huey Lewis. More than that, they seemed piqued by our arrogance. Nevertheless, Dagger and I thought that we should at least go in and give some interviews to these keen stations. Frankie was magnificent, formidable, even without his nocturnal white stallion, but in the other two stations our presence created quite a stir. The look on the DJs' faces when two cockney white boys arrived was one of open-mouthed surprise. I was thrilled. This London soul boy, who'd danced to black American music for years, had made a record that was being played on American black stations. Eventually it would be those very radio stations that would change my life for ever.

Back in England our office was sent a message. It was from the Clash. They wanted us to know that they thought the record was amazing. And even our enemy embraced us, as Martin and I arrived on the front cover of the *NME* dressed in zoot suits and key chains, crowned with a title that we couldn't have written better ourselves: *Soul Boys of the Western World*.

For me there's something utterly complete about 'Chant No. 1' and its accompanying video – a marriage of music, band, place and time that, even more than 'Story', positioned Spandau Ballet at the apex of what was happening.

But how long could we stay there?

I'm sitting on my bed at home with my guitar on my lap. I've been in the same position for about half an hour. On the wall opposite hangs my Reformation tartan sash, a poster from our first Scala show and a framed silver disc of 'To Cut A Long Story Short'. A book, *Great Mountaineering Adventures*, is discarded upon the floor. I consider picking it up but I'm obsessed with my mother's vacuum that's headbanging the stairs like a neurotic beast. I put the guitar down and fall back on to the bed.

Unlike second marriages, second albums are notoriously difficult. *Journeys* had been developed over some time and played live before we went into the recording studio, with some songs being discarded at the last minute. It was a mission statement, cohesive and tight, with none of the indulgence that often plagues follow-ups. 'Chant' should have set my course firmly towards the heart of the dance, but as the record went to number three in the UK, and clubs everywhere emulated the Beat Route vision, I felt a fear and a darkness clouding my direction. Or maybe it was just that 'Chant No. 1' at Le Beat Route was such a perfect homecoming that we had nowhere left to go. Basically – *follow that, Gary.*

'Paint Me Down' was my first attempt. It emulated the successful formula of including the Beggar & Co. horns and gang vocals but it somehow lacked the intensity of 'Chant' and followed poorly in its wake. Apart from some half-naked pagan high jinks up on Primrose Hill, the video was a series of clips from our short history. For the first time, we were being self-regarding and nostalgic instead of contemporary. The flirtatious Paula turned up to interview us on a day of filming and keenly agreed to take her top off and be shot with a droplet of paint running enticingly down her back. There were some rumours, though, that the BBC had banned it for nudity. I bumped into George and Philip on the street that week.

'Oi, Spandau Ballet, I'm sorry about your song. Someone told me it was *bland*!'

'Fuck off, George!'

Some things never change.

Flying around Europe doing TV shows is what we did a lot of. Having to race back for forgotten passports or being hung over and running through airports late had become our usual commuting experience. The Euros seemed to have terminally dreadful TV taste: in Belgium we performed 'Story' and later, when sent a video of the show, we were appalled to see they'd superimposed a grinning clown's face over the top of Tony's. German TV was always obsessed with creating faux beer gardens, and it wouldn't have surprised us if a group of dancers dressed as sausages came on to join us.

One morning in winter we took a flight on a single-engined plane to Brussels to do a TV show. The weather was poor and as we approached Brussels airport we got the news that it was too foggy to land. There was no way we were getting into Belgium that day and so the pilot turned the plane around and headed back to Blighty. We had all been drinking from the minibar and now, without any TV to do, we set about finishing it. The good news was there was plenty of alcohol, the bad news – there was no toilet on board. People were bursting so much that they'd started to sweat; and then someone thought of the obvious solution – the empty cans and bottles. With great relief some of us started to fill them up and then place them carefully at the back of the plane to be emptied on landing. Now some of our clothes at the time were a leather, fur and chain combination designed by Melissa; a kind of Good King Wenceslas meets village person; and so Steve's leather trousers were held up with a chain and small padlock. Unfortunately his trousers had no fly and the key to his chastity belt was in his bag somewhere at the back of the plane. After failing to slip out of them it was with some urgency that he pulled the bags down to finally retrieve his key, undo the lock and relieve himself into an empty can or two. For some people, the can method was too much and they begged the pilot to land at Southend, the first airport across the water. But as he approached the runway the fog just wasn't clearing, and then suddenly it was right below us and too late. The pilot pulled out of the landing, wrenching the plane steeply upwards. At that moment all of the bottles and cans at the back fell over and started rolling around the plane, emptying their contents out everywhere. We spent the next thirty minutes awash as bodily fluid sloshed backwards and forwards beneath our seats.

*

The recording of the new album was becoming far too erratic for its own good. Owing partly to Richard's now busy schedule (I played guitar for him on a Pamela Stephenson single he was producing) we couldn't get down to a solid run in one place and drifted through six different studios across London. But there was another problem. The group of songs lacked identity. I was torn between wanting to write commercially for the new funk scene, and at the same time wanting to attempt things in the vein of Bowie's second side of *Low*, or the mood pieces by Japan. I wanted credibility for us as a musical group and was probably channelling into my old days on that floating tuffet. But I could feel the album stumbling as we trekked between studios, and the focus upon developing material – or, in some cases, what we should have been cutting – was not happening. During the recording of the album, 'Paint Me Down' failed to get us on *TOTP* and stalled at number thirty in the charts. We ignored the crises and crawled on.

The men who should have been taking the rap were me and Richard, but unfortunately the scapegoat for everyone's frustration became Tony. Richard was expressing difficulty in recording the big man's voice, a difficulty that never arose on *Journeys*, and inevitably Tony was becoming emotional. Dagger felt the pressure too and arrived at the studio one day to see how things were going.

'Hi, Richard. Everything all right?'

'Hey, Steve. Yeah, I think so. We're doing some vocals at the moment.'

The band were at the back of the control room, perched and slumped all over a beaten chesterfield. The bored tape-op hit the red button and the machine clunked into action. The music jumped through the speakers and then Tony could be heard singing. I could see Dagger peering out into the dark studio, looking for his tall front-man, but he could make out only an old Turkish carpet that was thrown over something on the floor.

A little bewildered, he stepped back towards us. 'Where's Tony?' he mouthed.

Someone sniggered and pointed to the carpet on the floor. 'He's under there.'

'What?'

'Don't ask.'

Richard, in his attempt to 'restrain' Tony's big voice, had come up with the bizarre idea of getting him to lie on his back under a carpet. The result was an insecure lead singer and a rapidly deteriorating relationship between him and his producer. I was also taking out my frustration on Tony in minor ways that soon blew a sharp frost over our relationship. One day Tony just walked out. He was right to.

The playback of the album *Diamond* was in Air Studios and the record company gathered, hoping for some more of 'Chant No. 1'. During the 'difficult', esoteric second side there was some fidgeting and I knew, as I listened through their ears, that it was going to be a difficult sell and an uncomfortable 'after-party'.

We'd never sat down and decided where the album was going and I – in my fearful bedroom – was allowed to ramble. In my defence, the trilogy of 'Pharaoh', 'Innocence And Science' and 'Missionary' – an attempt at a concept complete with sound effects – has some strong ideas, especially the stalking funk of the first song, but the three were never realised with the panache they needed. One song on the album, though, bore the seeds of the future, only at that moment we were probably too immature to make it work. I loved it, but it would be the final straw in our relationship with Richard Burgess, and the tipping point of Spandau's career. Nevertheless, we had to put our faith in it as the next single. Although first, there was a photo-session to do.

I met David Bailey in New York that November with Dagger while Richard and I were out there cutting *Diamond*. The photographer, whose name had become an alternative noun for the profession, was famously cantankerous and didn't disappoint as we sat in the hotel bar.

'I loved that record of yours,' he said in his best Artful Dodger cockney while spinning the ice in his glass.

'Cheers, David. Which one?'

'What was it?' The ice stopped. 'Yeah, "Vienna".'

It was the same bugger that we met in his photo studio back in London.

'Oi, Lofty, move to your left.' Tony assumed correctly that he meant him and shuffled sideways. 'That's better, Sunflower.' He pointed at Steve. 'You all right, Blondie? You *can* smile, y'know.'

Steve was not going to smile after that. Bailey was rude and not funny. But the pictures certainly were when Dagger saw them. He phoned Bailey straight away.

'I'm sorry, David, but these pictures are shit. They're definitely not worth the money you've charged the record company.'

He chuckled. 'Why's that, then, Steve?'

'You know why. Tony's got a lamp stand coming out of his head in most of them and … Well, they just look like you've phoned them in.'

'All right, all right. Look, get the boys to come in again and I'll make them look good. Promise.'

On the second session there were no silly names and no light-bulb heads. He did it for free.

'So he should,' said Sunflower.

Four years later, during Bailey's rolling backstage photo-shoot for Live Aid, I reminded him of it.

He shot me the toothy grin I'd become familiar with. 'Yeah, well, you were a bunch o' pricks for all I knew. I had no idea you'd turn out to be any good.' He snapped a shot of us for posterity. 'Still think "Vienna" was your best song.'

From New York, Dagger, Richard and I flew to LA to meet the heads of Chrysalis America. With our newly cut album on my lap, I stared from the plane at the grid of glittering lights and the pools of lit turquoise dotted below us and felt thrilled that our journey had brought us to the Oz of entertainment. And then we were in a sleek stretch Cadillac driving up Sunset Strip – the name itself resonant of cool-cat dreams – with the giant Marlboro Man bravely smoking into the sky, the deco motels and diners all movie-familiar, and white fairy lights winking flirtatiously from the forecourt shrubbery of elegant hotels. Dagger surfed through the radio next to him, its fat FM sound filling the sexy darkness of the car with white America – REO Speedwagon, Journey, Rick Springfield. I poured myself another Jack Daniel's and Coke and delved for ice within the tiny spotlit bar in the door and thought this would be a town difficult to infiltrate but enjoyable to try. Dagger dialled away from a Styx song and suddenly a familiar sound filtered through the car's speakers. *It can't be. Is this some kind of trick?* The straining English vocal pierced my LA dream.

The DJ's rich FM timbre confirmed the nightmare. '*Two minutes later*! Oh yeah, I love those guys! That was Britain's finest, the amazing Duran Duran and "Girls On Film"!'

The dream deflated further at the record company the next morning. The West Coast-based joint-owner of the company, Terry Ellis (the phonetically-near-enough *alis* of Chrys-alis), was out playing tennis and therefore couldn't make the meeting. He was also currently at war with his London-based partner Chris Wright and we were about to get caught in the crossfire.

We played them some tracks from the new album and gave them the usual spin, but our words and music were as alien as wild birds in a room and found nowhere to land. Dagger was in no mood for excuses.

'But we heard our British rivals, Duran Duran.' I could hear the name sticking in his craw. 'On the radio. Yesterday. Someone must be interested!'

'Well, there is this small station based out in Pasadena that plays some of that stuff. Let me see if my secretary knows what it is. She likes that kinda music.'

'What's it called?' I asked.

'I'm not sure. Hey, Laura, what's the name of that weird station out in Pasadena that plays Brits?'

Her voice came from another room. 'Kay Rock.'

That 'weird station' would one day become one of the most success-ful in America, but in 1981 K-ROQ was a massively important bridge-head for an attempted invasion, an invasion that we couldn't join because at that moment we were busy fighting for our own professional lives on the beaches of home.

It was at the airport that we got hit. The band was on its way up to do a regional TV appearance in Manchester. The previous week our third single from the *Diamond* album, 'She Loved Like Diamond', had entered at forty-nine in the charts, too low to get *Top of the Pops*, and thus this trip to the north had become even more important. That morning the new chart position was due and we knew it would be make-or-break time for Spandau Ballet. A movement up and a *Pops* appearance – that would be all the oxygen needed to keep things going. We sat nervously at the gate while Dagger talked to the record company on the public pay-phone. He placed the receiver back on its hook, gathered his notebook and came back. He dropped into an empty chair in front of us. It was a simple three-word statement but we could read it in his face before he spoke.

'It's gone down.'

Back in Central London Chris Wright quietly told his team at Chrysalis that Spandau were dead. After two years and two albums the journey had come to an end. It felt far from glorious.

CHAPTER TWELVE

REMAKE/REMODEL

There were three suitors: an actor, an artist and a songwriter. All three bristled with jealousy, jostled for space and howled at her door, while her doting mother and father – Pat and Pat respectively – kept a polite yet attentive eye on proceedings.

I first met Clare at the BBC. A wee Celtic pixie with a scar on her cheek like a sickle moon. Her jaunty, Alice-in-Barrowland baby-tunes were skipping through the airwaves in 1981 and affecting hearts nationally, and one of them was mine. She'd just appeared in the Glaswegian youth movie (or 'fillum', as it's called on Sauchiehall Street) *Gregory's Girl*, and melted the heart of her gawky young star, John Gordon Sinclair, the thespian within our powerless triumvirate. The artist, a quick-witted textile designer with an eye for stylish trews, created record sleeves for her band in an effort to wrap himself around her. None of us, though, stood a chance.

Nevertheless, in 1982 I found endless excuses for jumping on and off planes and trains to sit in her parents' parlour in Glasgow and have tea and biscuits with her alongside my two equally piqued rivals and, of course, the vigilant Pats; or for meeting up with her and her band in the wistful Henley where they were recording. And yet all the time I remained faithful to my girlfriend Lee. Because this was different – this was courtly. And Clare's errant knights bonded in their frustration and, in order to keep an eye on each other, became friends.

There were three suitors: an actor, an artist and a songwriter. One acted for her; one painted for her; while the other had no idea he would end up writing a hit song.

On the plane back from Manchester, Dagger and I sat next to each other and looked for comfort in the slabs of prosthetic food, but not a crumb was to be found. I was embarrassed about, perhaps even responsible for, the position we were in. I'd written the song that couldn't chart. At the TV station it had been hard for me to look the other boys in the eye. *What are they thinking? Gary hasn't delivered?* I slugged at the free champagne. It occurred to me that it might be my last.

'Look, *Diamond* has just come out; it can't survive without another single from it.' Dagger wanted to talk about it. I was relying on him now. This could be his moment. He'd found the way through for us before: the door to Billy's; our event gigs; the record-breaking deal – all had been under his guidance. I hung on to his words, hoping that somewhere he'd have the cure for what I feared was now terminal. I let him continue. 'I'm worried it won't be enough just to release "Instinction". We need something else. A remix maybe.'

Remix was a business euphemism for SOS. But Dagger was right – the song had more pop in it than anything we'd ever done; although compared to what qualified as a great pop sound it fell a long way short. I rolled with it.

'Who could do it?'

We ordered two more champagnes and came up with two names. Andy Hill was the first on the table. He'd just reinvented the chirpy vocal group Bucks Fizz with a supersonic, pop-art production that was currently breezing through Britain's radios. The other was an old employer of Richard Burgess and the sound designer of a white-trash group called Dollar. Trevor Horn had moulded rhythmic yet theatrical backing tracks for the singing duo and understood the aural trick like no other. The rumour was he was about to produce Sheffield's answer to Spandau Ballet. But how would people react to us aligning ourselves with such outright pop?

'Do you remember what you said in the Janet Street-Porter film?' I looked at Dagger for the first time since that morning and suddenly felt lifted, undefeated. 'You can't be a cult band *and* sell millions of records, can you? What would you rather?'

I refilled my glass. He was right. It was time to look beyond Soho.

Trevor Horn stared down through his thick glasses at the joint he was building on his studio desk. In a spotlit corner Tony and I sat and silently rehearsed excuses as his engineer put the track through the sound system and its paces.

Trevor ran his tongue along the edge of the rolling paper and nodded to the beat. 'Good song.' It was nice to hear after all my recent self-loathing. 'It's just not produced.' He stared towards the speakers as if he could see the music in the air before him and how he might rearrange it. 'Yeah, we could make this work – couldn't we? But I'd love to re-record some of it.' He turned to us, letting the heavy smoke drift from his mouth. 'Would you mind singing it again, Tony?'

'No, I'd love to.'

Tony had suffered during the vocals on *Diamond* and now he was choosing to sing for this renowned studio perfectionist. The day after our airborne decision, Dagger had called Jill Sinclair, Trevor's manager and wife, and she'd immediately said yes on his behalf. Within the band there was a sudden sense of relief that a pop alchemist had come to save us, transform us even.

'I'd like to put some keyboards on it.' Trevor picked a thread of loose tobacco from his lip. 'If that's all right?'

In the impromptu band meeting in the baggage hall of Gatwick airport Martin had said: 'Whatever it takes. We have to have a hit.'

I held my hands out to Trevor. 'Whatever it takes,' I said.

Over the next week, Trevor tore 'Instinction' down and rebuilt it bar by bar. His orchestrator, Anne Dudley, with the bluestockinged look of a librarian, played some additional keys plus an elegant harp glissando; I did some extra vocals, guitar and piano; Steve did percussion; and Tony, standing upright this time, recorded his vocal in one take.

The final mixing of the tracks was astonishing to take part in. No computer subtly trimming the faders; instead we played the desk like an instrument – my hands, Tony's hands, Trevor's hands, all with a role, pushing and pulling to create the dynamics as we felt them. A live, adrenalin mix. In the end it was the same song as the one on the album, but the difference was about forty chart places.

During the makeover, Trevor revealed to me that every hit song had to have five tricks. The video, therefore, was the sixth, and this time Russell's brief was simple – no London club, no role-playing, no dwarfs; just us in a studio performing against a plain backdrop. And for the first time, we would be smiling. It was time for Spandau Ballet to make a *pop* video.

For the first time we wore no clothes designed by ex-Blitz kids, nor by any named designer either. Designer labels were not yet the thing for young West Enders – other than the sportswear made fashionable by football fans and soul boys. Gaultier and Yohji would not descend for another couple of years, so it was off to Lawrence Corner, the Army & Navy store in Camden. The clothes, for a reason now forgotten, had become early Alpinist/hunter chic; a sort of yodelling Elmer Fudd look. Where this originated from, I have no idea. Maybe it had something to do with my Scottish visits and the local penchant for woollen socks, haversacks and plaid shirts, although Bob had occasionally been known to present himself at Blitz as a 1920s Alpinist. *Why not?*

The final package was perfect, and not just for *Top of the Pops* but for punk's Antichrist – children's Saturday morning television, which at that time was *Saturday Superstore* and the truly anarchic *Tiswas*. There was a desire at the beginning of the eighties to make the single – and therefore pop music – credible again. Pop was 16 million people watching *TOTP* every Thursday night; pop was your nan knowing what was at number one; pop was power. And in any case, we liked it. Our generation had grown up believing in the credible art-school pop of Bolan and Bowie, and the dance-cool of Chic and Cameo. We were fascinated with the history of it, a history that gave us the Beatles, the Small Faces, the Kinks, Motown, and we'd watch the charts with the same tribal enthusiasm that we'd watch League Division One. After prog rock and punk's total rejection of it, the game of pop was once more, paradoxically, subversive.

As 'Instinction' hit Radio 1 and became Peter Powell's 'single of the week' and Simon Bates played the song twice, back to back, I met Richard in Soho. We went to the Beat Route and, arriving at the bar, he jumped in before I had a chance to offer my apologies. He understood, said he'd been distracted during the process and knew he hadn't got it quite right. I felt bad for him, and, impressed by his frankness, I wanted to be honest in return and admitted some of the album's difficulties were my fault. But he'd set the tone for the decade with 'Story', I told him, and 'Chant' was a dance classic that had broken new ground here and in the States. While we were talking, Steve Lewis spun 'Chant''s extended mix and the floor filled. We watched with some pride, finished our drinks and separated as friends.

As I climbed the stairs with the last few bars of our song fading behind me, it occurred to me that I was leaving more than just the club. I was leaving the town that made us.

Back in Glasgow, Clare played me Al Green and Marvin Gaye, old soul from my past that had now returned. The music posted itself through my heart and I knew that I had to reply. But I found it hard – hard to be truthful. So far everything was unspoken.

Since the mid-seventies, Bournemouth bank holiday weekend had been the chosen time and place for youth tribes of a dancing persuasion to converge. During those early years, Steve and I would head down in a friend's gold Capri, eight-track blaring Roy Ayres or Lonnie Liston Smith, and arrive at the gentle southern seaside town to pose, dance, pull and get wasted. The promenade lived up to its name and purpose as a catwalk for soul boys and casuals (northern and southern), all parading in their finest jelly shoes, coloured Smiths, high-waisters, baggies, skinny belts, winklepickers, mohair jumpers, Lacoste shirts, Hawaiian shirts, Woodhouse waistcoats, gold earrings, and the obligatory wedged hair. Blaring car triple-horns, neck-worn whistles and shoulder-carried boom-boxes added to this grand sensorial event.

And then the new decade brought New Romantics down in trains, coaches and XR3s to this coastal theatre of youth. Bournemouth filled with the captains and legionnaires of the new wave and they rode it all weekend. Here we'd meet the Cardiff lot, the Glasgow lot, the Manchester lot – everywhere had a sharp young club-runner and Dagger would swap numbers with them for later strategies. It seemed only right, therefore, given Spandau's now famous reference points, that we play there, and in '81 at the Exeter Bowl we put on the show everyone wanted to be seen at. Now, no longer new kids on the block and holding on to our promenade credibility by the skin of our leather pants, we were back as part of the *Diamond* tour, and this time there was competition.

It was inevitable that others would follow in our wake and fill the dance floor that we were exiting. Blue Rondo à la Turk was a multi-instrumental, Latin-influenced, zoot-suit-wearing crew designed by Chris Sullivan and starring himself, Christos Tolera and a northern soul boy called Mark Taylor. Managed by Graham Ball – who also worked for us in the Spandau office – they followed Dagger's blueprint and were about to do a bank job on Richard Branson and his Virgin label. Animal Nightlife was our ex-electrician and Beat Route DJ Steve Lewis's attempt at 'doing a Dagger'. A Latin-styled posse similar to Blue Rondo, they were fronted by Andy Polaris, the pretty mixed-race guy I'd seen slow-jiving on the floor of Billy's on my first visit there. Sade, having now discovered that she could sing, had a small smoochy-coochy band called Pride, while two Beat Route kids calling themselves Wham! and another band called Haircut 100,* who played a twee kind of nurs-ery funk, were now bursting into the playground. It was open season.

That weekend our show was sandwiched between Blue Rondo's and Animal Nightlife's, both attracting the kind of excitement and numbers that we had done only a year earlier. It should have been the homecoming for the prodigal sons, but instead we felt embarrassed by our pop success, by the screaming young girls, and envious of those fresh, hip boys still swinging their key-chains with the best of them. No one could feel part of something new and subversive with us any longer. Nevertheless, all of them desired to get on board the pop train, and so, with some silent sadness, we knew that this was our last time here together. This was a place where ordinary youth became special

---

* *Both had tried to get Dagger to manage them, but he'd refused owing to Spandau loyalty.*

for a weekend, stars of their own dance floor, lifted on to this seaside stage before returning to sell tellies, bleach hair, or whatever they did for a living. There was no room for real celebrity here. It was time for us to leave.

That bank holiday, every major Soho face that had strutted into my life over the last three years showed up, and on the final night, at a club called the Midnight Express, just above a chip shop, we all partied like it was the end of the world. The weekend had been a glorious swansong that no one on our particular stretch of promenade has ever forgotten.

By now, everywhere we went in Europe had a club, one that emulated the Steve Strange/Rusty Egan masterplan. The videos had filtered through as well as magazine imports, and radio and TV interviews that we'd given. New Romantics were everywhere and we were treated like ambassadors on our arrival in a city. One such club of serious NRs was in Lisbon. We'd first been there during a TV visit for the first album and saw how seriously they took their look. Now we were back in Portugal for two live shows. We were to start in Porto but on our arrival realised that our baggage had gone to Lagos, or some such random city. We'd flown in from Spain and were in our civvies for hot weather – shorts, T-shirts, sandals – not what we'd call stage wear. After the soundcheck we checked into our hotel and fretted about our bags. By seven o'clock it was obvious that they weren't coming and we were due on stage in an hour.

'What are we gonna do?' We were gathered in Martin and Steve's room. 'We can't go on stage like this,' I said. 'These are mad New Romantics. They'll lynch us.'

'*This* is what we can wear.' It was Martin thinking on his fashion feet as usual and pulling the white sheet off his bed. He stripped to his underpants and wrapped it around himself like a toga. By now Steve was in the process of doing the same to his sheet. That was it; the rest of us ran off to our rooms to gather our bedding and brought it back to the room. John started ripping up a pillowcase and made a headband; someone else made a neckerchief; another, an armband. It was fashion out of necessity and the flip-flops worked perfectly with our new ad hoc Romanesque look.

That night under the lights we were Daz-white and uniform, and took the breath away from all of the headband wearers in the audience. The following evening we played Lisbon, home of the hard-core fashionistas. This time our bags had arrived but word must have travelled even faster. Taking the stage in our regular clothes it was our turn for a sharp intake of breath. In front of us was a brilliantly white, sheet-wearing crowd.

She gave me a gift. I wanted to tell my two rivals but kept it a secret between us. It was a book. I read it as though she were reading it to me. It slipped beneath my skin and the words bubbled up inside, percolating through me.

I would send them back in song.

Regardless of the hits we'd already had, money wasn't flooding in and we all still lived at home. Not writing songs on the road, it was back to my bedroom, with my parents' television and my mother's brutish vacuum both in earshot. But this time I felt inspired. I knew what kind of an album I wanted to make. The freedom of not having to write just for Soho meant I could dive into that great big reservoir of pop, deep with melody and soul, and hopefully surface with the pearls I wanted. Where previously it had been about riffs and grooves, this time it would be about melody and chords.

As 'Instinction' placed us back in the top ten, and we reclaimed our stage on *TOTP*, I regained my confidence and started to write.

Strangely, my first attempt was to get right the kind of song I'd originally attempted with 'She Loved Like Diamond'. I loved the chord structures and emotionality of American Jewish music, the type that had travelled from eastern Europe and developed into movie themes and musicals. 'Gold' borrowed from those and suited the big, dramatic voice of Tony. I'd work on an idea and then call Martin in to play it to him. It was my young-brother whistle-test. He'd trot down from watching telly and then cringe, nod or 'wow' accordingly. He'd play along with his bass and I'd get a sense if I was going in the right direction or not. 'Gold' he loved, and more came quickly.

Dagger wanted to keep our ball rolling, and so Trevor came to my house. While Mum padded nervously around in the kitchen he sat on our beige vinyl sofa in the front room and I played my guitar and sang. His eyes swam inside his big lenses while he pawed at the songs falling out in front of him. Suddenly a hand came up and stopped me.

'That one. I like that one a lot. What's it called?'

'"Pleasure".' I'd become obsessed with the economy of one-word titles.

'Play it again.'

I dutifully sang the song once more while Trevor visibly started organising it into textures within his head. He stopped me and broke it down: softened the verse; pushed the chorus; lifted the end; all the time thinking about the dynamics, the five tricks.

'I'd like to work on that. It's great. Let's take it into rehearsals with Spandau.'

We were thrilled to be working with such a strong producer, one with a proven shiny-but-credible pop sound. He'd just finished producing the Sheffield band ABC, but now seemed refreshed by our musical ability. Or at least we thought he was. The rehearsal went well, Tony galvanised with confidence again, and we spent the day honing

'Pleasure' into what was to be the first single off of a Trevor Horn-produced Spandau Ballet album.

But just as Tony had found a producer he reacted well to, John was about to replace him under the studio grill. We began recording at George Martin's Air Studios in Oxford Street and, as is usual with recording, we started with the drums. John would have a 'click-track', set at the chosen speed for the number, play in his headphones and he'd go through the whole song over and over until we felt happy with it. On this occasion, though, Trevor was just not able to reach that point of satisfaction and our poor drummer thrashed himself into a sweating pulp. To the band it sounded as though the drums had reached their peak around lunchtime, but we all knew that Trevor was a perfection-ist and didn't want to question his studio ears. Gary Langan, his faith-ful engineer, endlessly spooled back the tape to hit the red button again. After ten hours we packed up for the day, convinced Trevor must by now have what he wanted.

Later that night I got a call. It was Trevor and my heart sank.

'The thing is, Gary, I really can't get into days of recording your drummer, I've just come off of a difficult album.'

'Trevor, I think John's a great drummer; he was just under a lot of pressure today.' I actually thought he had done a fantastic job, but it obviously hadn't been up to Trevor's expectations or standards. Or maybe Trevor was tired, having just finished an album, and was look-ing for a way out. Nevertheless I could hear in his voice that his mind was made up.

'Look, I'd be willing to programme the drums ... but maybe you should think about getting a new drummer.'

Wow! I was shocked. I heard myself saying that programming the drums would not just be psychologically wrong for our team spirit, but it would also undermine John as a player. As the words came out, I knew we were losing the opportunity of having Trevor Horn produce the record. 'John is every bit a part of this band as any one of us,' I pleaded. 'He has to be on the record.'

Trevor was sympathetic but gave me a flat bat. 'I understand, Gary, but I don't think I can do it otherwise.'

The next morning, a frantic Dagger called me. Trevor's manager had been on the phone to say that Trevor had been up all night worrying about it but he'd only continue the project if we fired John. We were devastated. It was out of the question that we fire him, not least because John had become my closest friend in the band. We sent our roadies to pick up the gear from Air Studios. The *Pleasure Project* was over.

We agreed not to tell John the true reason for Trevor's sudden departure and instead explained to him that Trevor was unable to fit in all of his commitments and so had decided to leave our production unfinished. But secretly John must have had his suspicions and I felt for him. Nevertheless it remained unspoken. We knew we had the best drummer in the world.

But the band needed a single to come quickly off the back of a hit, and so the job now for Dagger was to find a producer, and quickly, while I returned to my songwriting. And something different was percolating through.

The chord was G. The word was '*I*'. The word took four steps up and then settled down comfortably into an E. I did it again. And again. It became mesmeric. It grew into a C and I found myself singing, '*I know this much … I know this much …*' I wanted it to be Al Green; I wanted it to be Marvin; I wanted it to be about loving them; I wanted it to be a love song but felt inhibited, shy even, so I started to write about that very thing: the fear of revealing oneself, of saying in song what was true. '*Why do I find it hard …*' The heroine in the book she had given me was said to have '*seaside arms*'. I loved what that told me: freckles against sun-kissed flesh, sandy and youthful, a breeze stroking soft down. I put it in the song so she'd know it was about her, and then added *''cos I want the truth to be said'*. I went back to my rising and falling '*I*' and then, suddenly, '*I know this much … is true*'.

I gave it a key-change lift into the solo, a solo I knew would be for Steve and his new-found instrument the saxophone. Steve was by far the slickest musician in the band and the sax, an inspiration from the Beggar & Co. sessions, fell easily into his hands. As teenagers we'd listen endlessly to the blowing on Smokey and Stevie's hits, as well as, more recently, Evelyn Champagne King's sublime 'Shame' – with its silky sax breaks it had been on constant rotation for us since our cruising around Bournemouth during Easter weekend 1978. And so the sound of the sax felt very much like home and we loved the sweet, nostalgic voice it gave us. It was the sound of soul; it would be the sound of the new album.

And the songs had started to arrive quickly: 'Communication'; 'Code Of Love'; 'Heaven Is A Secret'; 'Lifeline'. Swimming around in that big pop pool, with some added heartfelt truth, the album wrote itself. The hard part was playing them to the band.

After the difficulties of the last few singles I felt the added pressure to come up with the goods, to keep us all in the game. I'd tell them – and I'm sure Martin would anyway – when I had enough songs to go into rehearsal, and rehearsal was the moment when I suffered the most anxiety. I had to reveal the songs to the men who relied so much upon them.

I stand at the mike, acoustic guitar in hand, and begin with a rambling verbal precis: its title; its lyric idea; its tempo; its feel; anything to keep me from actually beginning. In my head is how it could sound with the band playing, but as it's impossible to relay with just one instrument and a voice, I attempt to describe it. Often I'd get Martin to play along, especially if the bass riff was key to the song – as with

'Chant'; but this time it's not and I'm shooting on my own. They sit or stand, arms folded, waiting for what may or may not keep them in business for another year. But for me it's always the same experience: as if I were summoning the courage to tell someone for the first time that I loved them, desperately hoping that they felt the same way too. The unrequited song can be a devastating blow.

As I began offering what would eventually become the *True* album, there was real excitement, if not euphoria, and the band became thrilled at our new-found, soulful sound. We also had the addition of an old Owenian on keyboards. Just before the *Diamond* tour I'd bumped into Jess Bailey. He'd been through university and was back in London with a degree and nowhere to use it. Over a drink or two I suggested that he come on tour with us and he jumped at it. It was an augmentation that suited the sound of the show and the new songs even more, but most of all it helped heal my past through my present.

One afternoon we proudly played the songs to Dagger, and, buzzed by their commerciality, he had a smart idea as to who could produce them.

Jess hit the big, dirty church organ noise of 'Communication' for the song's final beat and the sound of a band slamming to a halt reverberated against the walls.

'God, I like that one too.' Tony Swain scratched at his neat black beard as though the answer to what song should be the next single might be nestling there. Tall, yet softly tempered, his presence in the rehearsal studio felt calming compared to the achingly hip Richard or the musical laboratory that was Trevor. Tony was like a schoolteacher you could call by his first name. The fair and slight Steve Jolley stood next to him. With arms tattooed and folded, head clipped to a No. 3 and Dr Marten boots set at ten-to-two, he gave the impression of being

– at some stage in his life – institutionalised; surname material. The two of them could not have been more different and yet they were a very successful unit.

'No, Tony. "Lifeline"'s the one. Absolutely.' For all of Steve Jolley's overt male symbolism his voice was as camp as a maiden aunt but his ears were as sharp as a switchblade.

One straight, one gay; one hirsute, one shaved; what brought them together was a love of soul, and the sale of about a million records. 'Body Talk' had been a Euro smash: breathy backing vocals, sultry instrumentation, and a kidney-melting synth bass that played irresistible footsy with you. Imagination was the band, but in reality it was all Swain and Jolley. As writers and producers, Tony made the cake and Steve laid on the icing.

I'd met them in a pub near their favourite studio, just off Church Street in Paddington. They were celebrating another hit, this time with a girl group of three ex-Blitz kids called Bananarama. We were a difficult decision for them: they had previously written all of their productions and Steve Jolley's job was not really in production but in the writing of lyrics and melody, something that was already taken care of on this job. Also we'd just come through a sticky patch and a strange experience with Britain's most talked-about producer. But our mood was sprightly, and over a pint we attempted to sell them the idea of making a blue-eyed soul album that utilised their white London sensibility for the genre. I could see they were nervous about the idea and so we struck a deal with them to just do the next single and see how things went.

They had come down to watch us play through the songs at Simon Napier-Bell's Nomis Studios in Shepherd's Bush. 'Pleasure' wasn't the one they landed on, though (probably because our enjoyment of it had been tainted by Trevor's rejection), and instead their ears were pricked by 'Communication' and what would in fact be their first choice, an up-tempo, more obvious pop sing-along called 'Lifeline'. With its standard-bearing reference to riding the '*Soul Train*', it would herald a new sound and a new style for the ever-evolving Spandau Ballet.

And in the end I was left with one stolen kiss in a hotel elevator. My courtly affair was over. But in my pocket was a bunch of songs that would lift Spandau Ballet as a band, and me as a writer, into places far beyond the streets of Soho, London or Glasgow.

CHAPTER THIRTEEN

LEAVING HOME

The tape hit the magnetic head and ran. Above the door a red light lit up. As the sound of the warm keyboard came through the speakers I started to chop away at the strings of my white Fender. It was an old soul guitar part that I'd borrowed from a hundred Motown records before, but it immediately lit up the groove of the track. I heard Tony's guide vocal soar and my own stacked-up voice sing the snaking '*I*' (now more an '*ahh*' – the sound of satisfaction) as the song swung into its chorus. Suddenly, goosebumps rose on my sunburnt skin.

Take your seaside arms …

At the end of 1982 I bought a flat. I was the first person in my family's known history to ever own a property. Dad came over and helped me put up some shelves. Actually, he didn't help me – he put them up while I stood back saying, 'Higher – no, lower.' I looked at him, his strong shoulder powering against the drill, a film of sweat forming on his forehead, and I couldn't help but feel guilty: here was a man who'd worked hard all his life; who'd virtually built the homes we'd lived in; who'd had a nervous breakdown in the process of trying to feed and clothe his beloved family; who'd done night shifts on Fleet Street to send us all on holidays; and then along I waltz, with a few tunes, a lot of playing (in the non-musical sense of the word) and no DIY sense, and I'm suddenly owning my own place.

Mum brought the tea in and Dad wiped his brow.

'I'll run up some nice nets for your windows,' she said, starting to put the hot cups down on a small cabinet.

'Not there, Mum! That's Tudor!' Flustered, she offered them to me. 'Actually, Mum, I thought I'd leave the windows with just shutters. No curtains. Nets can look a bit … y'know?'

'You *can't* have them bare, Gary, anyone can see in. People will think you're, well …'

It was more than a physical move away from home. Those aspirational yearnings that I'd been nurturing since my visit to the Landesmans' house all those years before were now fully fledged and allowed free flight. But as I placed art and books on the wall, church candles and interior magazines on the black enamelled coffee table, I felt a strong sense of denying everything my family was. I sat on my William Morris chair – *designed by the esteemed architect Philip Webb, I hasten to add –* and, with a glass of claret in my hand and something light and choral on the stereo, I realised I'd become middle-class.

It's hard to justify the kind of money that a pop star can make while his mother and father still live frugally in a council house. Sure, my brother and I would help them out, but here I'd get it wrong too. They didn't want, or need, that Wiener Werkstatte vase for their sideboard, nor, I'm sure, the 'original' William Morris tile I so patronisingly bestowed upon them and their mantelpiece; but my desire for higher things left me appearing like a snob. Or maybe I just was. Waves of pride and shame would alternately crash against me, especially when Martin and I parked our matching Porsches side by side outside our parents' home in a street full of rusting Fords. Were the locals proud of their prodigal sons or were we rubbing salt (Malvern, of course) into the wounds of a beleaguered working-class neighbourhood? Money left me a mass of neurotic contradictions, and, as much as I wanted a more cultured lifestyle and aspired to the other side of the Essex Road, I was still riven with guilt about it and the fear that I might be deserting my roots.

We were beginning to live in a time of fanatical meritocratic fantasies and the old boundaries were shifting, blurring. Suddenly a large group of zealous working-class kids with starched white shirts and red braces were making it big in finance as well as media, lording it loudly in wine bars across the south of the country. I'd seen this barber's-pole fashion statement before, with the red writing on the white butcher's coats of seventies football fans. It delivered the same statement as the red cross on the white bib, but these were financial crusaders, and those wide, red slashes vulgarly symbolised the blood they were willing to spill for their cause.

To the middle-class media these 'lads' were upstart crows, cawing about their winnings from newly claimed heights; to some they were a symbol of cultural change and class freedom, while others simply saw them as the personification of a callous new society of greed. Either way, the seemingly never-ending Winter of Discontent was finally defrosting and we were beginning to enjoy some of the warmth.

Compass Point Studios in Nassau had made perfect records. AC/DC's *Back In Black* – one of the biggest-selling albums of all time – had been wrought beneath its giant palm trees, and the Rolling Stones had lounged upon its lush lawns while finding *Emotional Rescue*. But the sound of Nassau, the one that we *so* desired, had been captured by artists such as Robert Palmer, Grace Jones, Talking Heads, Tom Tom Club and my early glam heroes, Roxy Music, with their XR3-cassette-player favourite, *Avalon*. Owned by Island Records' Chris Blackwell –

who'd employed in-house engineer and producer wunderkind Alex Sadkin, as well as Jamaican rhythm section Sly and Robbie, to work there – Compass Point Studios nestled on Love Beach in the north of New Providence island, and we were here to try and find some of its cool, Bahamian groove for our third album.

Billeted in the little clapperboard houses that edged the grounds and the beach, we felt a great sense of relief to be away from home and the hothouse of London, and we all needed the bonding that ensued. We swam together and waved at David Byrne and Tina Weymouth, who were mixing their new Talking Heads album in Studio 2; Steve would blow his sax around the pool while we tanned ourselves happily or pushed people in. The first song out of our suitcase and oiled up beneath the sunshine was 'Code Of Love', a soulful, reggae-tinged number that gorged itself on the chilled surroundings and set the tone in our search for the blue-eyed soul we wanted and the sound of a new Spandau.

'Lifeline' had dipped our toe in the water, but moreover had confirmed our place among the new pop royalty, one whose audience we felt no shame in embracing. If New Pop's edicts were issued by *The Face* then the empire's illuminated bible was *Smash Hits*. While the serious music press would get 100,000 readers a week max, *Smash Hits* and its new glossy rival, *No. 1*, would each sell half a million. At the beginning of the eighties it was virtually impossible to find anything about music in the national press, with thin, tucked-away columns appearing only once a week at most, but now the papers and the country were obsessed with the comings and goings, the parties and hangovers and the bending of genders that were being played out by pop's crowned heads. As the economy picked itself up and a new young princess batted her eyelids, New Pop's success seemed confirmation of a refreshed, more upwardly mobile Britain, and a soundtrack that only just drowned out the screaming girls.

We'd first noticed the phenomenon of the scream at the Liverpool Empire during the *Diamond* tour and 'Instinction''s chart success. Our support act was a young Scottish comedian I'd met with Clare called Peter Capaldi, and even he mustered a few screams from the audience – *don't get excited, they're just practising*, we told him. But the moment we took the stage it was unbelievable – we could barely hear ourselves playing as girls threw their lungs at us. Uncontrollable sobbing and the odd fainting added to the female pandemonium; a mass consciousness forged by a unison scream.

After the show we were collapsed in our third-floor dressing room when a young girl's head suddenly appeared at the window. *My God, she's climbed the drainpipe to get to us!* We quickly threw it open and hauled her into the room, but once in the presence of her quarry she found it impossible to talk. A picture of this brave assault on our dressing room belongs to David Johnson, who, armed with camera in the street below, captured the girl's swinging legs as she hung half out of the small window like Pooh in Rabbit's hole.

While she'd been in the street, standing with a crowd of girls, she'd screamed, but once inside the room she went utterly silent. It led Dagger to deduce a scream quotient, which, after some empirical observation on his part, was this: *it takes at least four girls to make a scream*. Apparently, in tests, any fewer than four and a certain self-consciousness mutes them, but once that golden number is reached all hell is unleashed.

And so, almost overnight, every arrival and departure from an auditorium meant us running the gauntlet of screaming, grabbing girls (unless, of course, there were three of them). The New Pop audience knew what their role was as much as we did, and they were determined to play their part with gusto.

We'd recorded the 'Lifeline' single in Paddington at Red Bus Studios and quickly fell into how things would work with our new producers. Tony Swain was also his own engineer and out of the two I became closer to him, especially at the mixing desk, discussing the sounds and arrangements while working alongside the other guys. Tony Hadley, on the other hand, found his confidence with Steve Jolley (as well as a gossipy smoking-pal, who'd sprinkle his deadpan remarks with some old-fashioned Soho gay-speak, or Polari, as it was known to fans of 'Julian and Sandy'). Steve became the sole producer of Tony's vocals and, after the last experience, I was happy to stay out of the room during those sessions. It was less intimidating for Tony and allowed Jolley to work on the vocal unhindered by the finicky songwriter who could only hear it one way – his way. They became a killer combination. Steve Jolley was steeped in soul love and knew how to soften Tony's voice without the use of Turkish rugs. It was about the approach and, most importantly, the story being told within the song.

Unfortunately the video for this particular story never quite matched the quality of the record. By now Russell Mulcahy had been swept away on Duran Duran's Learjet of fame. After proving with 'Musclebound' that he could conjure an epic, Duran's managers, the Berrow brothers – the same guys that had run the Rum Runner – had stolen him for their own purposes. And so, while Duran rode elephants in Sri Lanka, we shot 'Lifeline' in a hayloft somewhere in rural Britain. The chosen clothes for that video were also drab. We seemed to be caught in a moment of not knowing what to wear. The clothes worn at the Beat Route had become more low key as the sweat quotient of the club's frantically dancing clientele rose, and the main faces had started to leave and have their own chart success. In our new pop guise we didn't quite know what visual angle we were meant to take.

But with 'Lifeline' soon climbing the charts and reaching the top ten, we felt confident that our chart scare wasn't terminal and our revival had established Spandau as a force that wasn't about to slip away.

It was in this relaxed position that we found ourselves bonding around the pool in Compass Point that autumn, in what was to be a period of closeness like no other. We had a daft misogynistic saying at the time – *You can get a new bird, but you can't get new mates.* It was probably born out of our growing paranoia, because Tony was about to marry his girlfriend Leonie, and, as far as we were concerned, alter the chemistry of the group for ever.

It was perfectly normal that he should want to get married but we saw it as a slight against the band that somehow he would not be as committed to the cause; not be twenty-four-seven. Or maybe I was simply embarrassed at my own lack of commitment to Lee.

This much is true ...

The backing track stopped and, putting my Fender down, I rushed to the studio door.

'Get the others to come in, Nicky.'

Martin's heavyweight roadie found them by the pool and soon everybody was crammed into the studio, sweet with suncream.

'Play it back.'

We listened to the track, enraptured by its now sumptuous chorus, singing and swaying along with its 'Hey Jude'-like outro. I could see the faces of John, Tony, Martin, Steve and Dagger all alight with the realisation of what we had in front of us. With this song we'd found the sound of Nassau, and I'd found the sound of my soul.

Back at Red Bus the tracks were gradually being mixed. We'd come back from the Bahamas with seven songs of love and in the following few weeks Steve Jolley nurtured the best vocal recordings Tony had ever made. At the end of mixing 'True', Tony Swain felt dissatisfied with its introduction – an instrumental bass-line ramble that meandered up to the first verse. He had the ingenious idea of copying a chorus minus Tony's vocal and pasting that on to the front instead. It sold the song's key hook immediately, and who knows how many more records.

We had an allotted window of time to mix the tracks that had brought us to a final Sunday and the last song – 'Gold'. This final mix was turning into an all-nighter as Tony Swain, Johnny Keeble and I fought through the wee hours to get its delicate balance right. By nine o'clock the next morning we were bleary-eyed and cloth-eared but still all-hands-on-faders. It was like guiding a boat on a rough sea – one degree of misjudgement in a trim and the whole thing was tipping the wrong way and careering into the rocks.

'Shit, that was my fault that time. Sorry.'

'OK,' Tony sighed, 'once more.'

Outside the door hovered a distressed record producer, Steve Levine. It was now Monday morning and he was about to start his recording session but we were still involved with ours.

Tony Swain was always polite. 'Sorry, Steve, we're gonna need another pass on this. Is that OK?'

Just before ten o'clock the three of us moored 'Gold' successfully, and the version that would eventually be a hit all over the world had forever rearranged the particles of a slim reel of half-inch tape. I picked up my things and headed out of the studio.

In the corridor I found a piqued Boy George, all eyelashes and dread-locks. Of course, it was *his* band that Levine was coming into record.

'Get the fuck out, Spandau Ballet. This is my studio time you're wasting. I've got some *decent* music to record.'

Suddenly there just didn't seem enough room for everyone. We were all in the charts, and the old Blitz kids – including our glamorous cloakroom attendant – were as bitchy as ever with each other; albeit this time the stakes were a lot higher. Culture Club had lit up the pop parade with their soft-sell reggae, and George was suddenly competing with Princess Diana as the country's favourite pin-up. Our enemies from Birmingham were now well established and, what's more, both them and George had had a number one! Sheffield's hard-boiled electroids, the Human League, had obviously had successful therapy and were now crossing happily into the New Pop. They'd also had a huge number one with 'Don't You Want Me'. And even Soft Cell, who we'd written off in Crocs, had topped the charts.

Queuing up behind us all were New Pop bands like Blitz's own Jeremy Healy with his Haysi Fantayzee and Steve and Rusty's Visage, Basildon's Depeche Mode, McClaren's Bow Wow Wow, Sheffield's ABC, Haircut 100, Thompson Twins, Tears for Fears, Scritti Politti, OMD, Bananarama, Associates, Altered Images and a couple of suburban Beat Routers calling themselves Wham!. Not to mention the quickly-redressed-to-suit-the-*zeitgeist* bands like Classix Nouveaux and Modern Romance. All fought for their slot on *Top of the Pops* and a place in chart history.

But it was not enough to just *be* in the charts – as Dagger had said: 'On top is what counts'. After all, this was a league, a sport, and to win the championship was everything. And in 1983 that meant selling to at least 300,000 people.

The new album was exciting the record company. We'd flown in the heads of various European affiliate labels for a studio playback and the general consensus was that *True* the album – for that is what we'd decided to call it – was going to be a huge record. All ears were falling upon 'Gold' and the title track, but Dagger didn't want to go with a ballad next, and recommended another up-tempo first. 'Communication' got the band vote.

Why we didn't go straight for 'True' or 'Gold' as the next single, I'm not sure. Maybe we felt their success would be automatic and wanted to save them for later, during the album's release. But 'Communication' and its slow progress up the charts left us sweating again. Back then you had to sell a lot of singles to enter the top forty and our first week put us at number 41 and therefore its dire consequence – no *Top of the Pops*. The video was ready and waiting – a gritty *Sweeney*-esque film that starred Tony, a young Leslie Ash and a nasty villain played by the ex-boxing world champion and star of Wings' *Band On The Run* album cover, John Conteh. I relished making it with the director Chris Springhall, and greedily, as always, took a large role in the writing and directing. It therefore didn't bother me that I wasn't in it, but it did bother some members of the band that it was only Tony appearing. Martin was quietly seething that Tony had taken the plum acting role, but we were concerned that our singer's profile wasn't as high as it should have been, while Martin's swarthy image seemed to be posted everywhere. Also, unlike other bands where the lead singer dealt with most of the interviews, as the band's songwriter I did the largest share of them. And apart from group pictures, our other front covers to date had been Martin for *The Face*, Martin and me for the *NME*, me for *Record Mirror* and Steve Norman for *Smash Hits*. It was a trend that would continue but one that at that time we tried to buck. In fact it worked initially, giving Tony a solo cover for one of the weekly pop glossies with a still from the 'Communication' video.

Although the single eventually made it to number twelve in the UK, the problem was that radio DJs were all playing the album track 'True' instead, and sometimes all six minutes and thirty seconds of it. At the Chrysalis offices every room blared 'True'. Our friendly in-house press girl, Julia Marcus, even told us that she and a friend had boldly graffitied the toilet at Camden Palace with the Spandau dove and the word *True*. By public demand, 'True' would be our next single.

*

Taking it to the cradle of chic – St. Tropez, 1980. *Left to right:* Bob Elms, Steve, unknown, Tony, Simon Withers, Dagger, me and Graham Smith.

Martin, me and Steve play 'against the steely bulkhead' of HMS *Belfast*, 1980.

Above: Taking the Blitz to Birmingham for the Botanical Gardens gig, November 1980. *Left to right:* Christos Tolera, Chris Sullivan and Jeremy Healy.

Right: Spandau's young manager and visionary, Steve Dagger, circa. 1981.

Below: Backstage, preparing to go on at Cardiff's Casablanca club, 1980. Steve Strange is wearing the hat.

'A look as yet unseen on this great British institution'. Spandau wait to make their first appearance on *Top of the Pops*. BBC studios, November 1980.

A Thursday night at the Kemps' house. My brother snaps me during one of Spandau's *Top of the Pops* appearances, 1981.

Some of the Gang of Twenty One in New York, 1981. *Left to Right*: Steve, me, Tony, Richard James Burgess, John, Martin, Ollie O'Donnell, John 'Mole' Baker, Melissa Caplan, Bob Elms, Graham Smith, Sarah Lubel, Sade Adu, Dagger, Simon Withers.

Spandau and friends arriving in Ibiza in 1981 to play at the opening of the Ku club – and bring London club culture to the island.

Above: 'The New Pop audience knew what their role was as much as we did, and they were determined to play their part with gusto.' *True* tour, 1983.

Left: A brave assault upon our Liverpool Empire dressing room. *Diamond* tour, 1982.

Below: Martin and me with our parents during Martin's twenty-first birthday party at the Camden Palace, 1982.

Left: 'The familiar weight of wood and electronics'. *Parade* tour, 1985.

Below: 'Baroque 'n' roll, 1985.

Below: '*Through the Barricades – Across the Borders* was Spandau Ballet in its pomp.' Arena rock, 1986/87.

The Kemps flank Charlie Kray on the set of *The Krays*, 1989.

Being Ronnie.

The Kemp family at the premiere of *The Krays*, 1990.

Left: With my wife Lauren.

Below: Spandau play their first live appearance in nineteen years on *Friday Night With Jonathan Ross*, 2009.

Out of the three competitors in courtship, the artist deserved the most success with our courtee. But just like the other two suitors, he was left having to channel his ardour into his work. David Band had wit, charm and looks in equal measure, as well as the skill of coming up with simple, figurative graphics that would set a visual tone for the decade. Trained in textile design, he'd created the sleeves for Clare's Altered Images and Roddie Frame's Aztec Camera, and I loved his nursery-painting images. I'd asked him if he'd be interested in working with us on the sleeve of our new album and he came up with a design we all fell in love with – a strong yet simple felt-tip-penned silhouette of a man's head wearing a brimmed hat and facing a dove flying in purple rain. It was bright colours on white and gave us the logo of the flying bird, a bird that would accompany us on our biggest tour yet – Spandau Ballet Over Europe, a tour for which we needed a look. And after the fashion confusion of 'Lifeline' we decided to go back to the source of so many sartorial Soho statements.

The difficulty for us was we were now immersed only in Spandau Ballet. We were away from the familiar streets, and no longer the young Soho funslingers we once were. There was only one person to turn to – the man I'd first met monocled in spats while he was an impoverished student, the style guru from the Valleys; the prince of the dressing-up box, Chris Sullivan.

Chris's success with Blue Rondo had been sweet but sadly short and he was now more than willing to pass on a few fashion ideas à la mode to his old club chinas. We wanted to get back to a uniformity, the way we were during 'Chant No. 1'; it had to be the suit, which at that time nobody was doing. We all met in a little tailor's near Sullivan's flat in Kentish Town to be measured up. Chris displayed his elegant line drawings among the tape measures and the chalk, and we rifled through them to pick our favourites. He'd come up with the idea of the gambling gunslinger, a sort of Wyatt Earp meets City Boy; five Wild West-enders. And in good cowboy fashion, it was to brand us for ever.

So we hit the stage like Doc Holliday's gang ready to take another Tombstone. Spandau Ballet Over Britain had us flying the flag – resplendent with dove – throughout every major town. Being Spandau, we promoted it ourselves, but nevertheless, this was, for the first time, a 'proper' tour, with stage sets, backstage passes and branded merchandise. It was a tour to muscle with the best of them; a tour to prove we were the biggest band in Britain.

During our fall from grace with *Diamond* the common judgement from the serious rock press was that we were fashion-obsessed dandies who couldn't play and that we'd had our run on the fickle train of youth culture and been swiftly forced to alight. There was a certain amount of glee and told-you-so in their statements. Now they saw our new, successful, smiling version as irrefutable evidence that we were interested only in financial rewards and not musical credibility. One such article came from an *NME* writer called Paolo Hewitt. Paolo had been seconded to Bournemouth that Easter of 1983 to write a piece on us during our traditional bank holiday shows there, but after being sounded out and found out by Bob Elms we thought better of it and left him in the journalistic lurch. *No point doing an interview for an article that he's already written*, we thought. He wrote it anyway and the piece, predictably, slammed us.

A week later Martin and I were drinking at the Camden Palace, Steve and Rusty's new club in Camden High Street. London's glimmer twins had been asked to front the refurbished and renamed Music Machine, a second-division rock venue and a former Victorian theatre once immortalised in oils by Walter Sickert. It was to be London's answer to Danceteria and Britain's first multi-storey dancing house. Suddenly someone said that Paolo Hewitt was there. In the last few weeks Martin and I had read – and become obsessed with – John Pearson's book *The Profession of Violence*, a biography of the Kray twins. And so, with our feathers ruffled and oiled with booze, we decided to approach poor Paolo in a twin-pronged attack.

'What's your problem, you wanker? You don't even know us.'

'*What?*'

'Yeah, who do you think you are writing that bollocks in your shit paper? You're a Wellerite anyway,' one of us probably said, referring to a certain sullen type that followed the Jam and Paul Weller.

We had him pinned against the wall. Between us his beer can was raised pathetically as a shield. It was intimidating theatricals, born out of a need to prove our street credentials to a writer miffed by our snub and what he saw as our pop sell-out. There was a push, a shove, no more, but the following week, to our grim satisfaction, the verbal dust-up was reported in various gossip pages. You may wonder that if *Smash Hits* and *The Face* were where it was at, then why bother being so bloody angry with what the *NME* thought? But Fame can crown you with little horns; and its demonic twin, Celebrity, can goad you into vain paranoia and nonsense such as this. And maybe, even though I loved being one of the darlings of popular culture, part of me secretly wanted to be taken seriously, loved even, by the oracle of my youth.

Sheffield; Tuesday, 26 April 1983; 7.25 a.m. The phone had been ringing through the last few scenes of my dream. It sat squat upon the bedside cabinet, painfully close to my head. Its rude alarm upset the settled sediment of the hotel room that I shared with John. I reached my hand out of the covers and pulled the phone's receiver down towards me. It had been a late night.

'Hello.'

Dagger was on the other end. What he said had me leaping from the sheets to wake the prone drummer. Grabbing towels for decency and lifting a bottle of champagne from the minibar, we ran from the room and, approaching a shocked-looking maid, procured a pass key. With some stealth, I inched open the door to Tony's room, and after tiptoeing up to the sleeping giant, popped the cork and sprayed the hell out of him.

What John and I told Tony had the three of us jumping on the bed like kids.

'Tony, you fucker! We're number one!'

CHAPTER FOURTEEN

A BULLET FROM DISCO DANNY

'I've just played him the entire album in his office and he's gone *nuts*!'

'That's great, Steve. What's his—'

'At one point … Sorry, mate, go ahead.' The line from New York had a delay on it and Dagger had started talking before I'd finished.

'Don't worry. What were you gonna say, Steve?'

'It is amazing, though, isn't it – how clear it is. You could be just down the road. Anyway, at one point he jumps up and shouts *Take it to the bank*! It was hilarious. He's a Jewish bloke from Brooklyn. Priceless! They call him Disco Danny.'

Danny Glass was the new head of radio promotion at Chrysalis New York. He'd started as a DJ playing disco on his college radio station, but soon ended up on what it was then hip to call *the wheels of steel* at the club for the rich and fabulous, Regine's. Regine (real name, Regina Zylberberg) had invented the discotheque in Paris in 1958, when instead of a live band she'd played taped music for dancing. Or so legend has it. But now, at her New York place, it was Danny who'd tempt the likes of Jackie O and Andy Warhol from their ice buckets and on to the neon-lit, heart-shaped dance floor. Danny was flattered by his alliterative moniker. Danny wished he wasn't white.

'He wants to go black with it.'

'He wants to go *black?*'

'"True". The single. He's gonna take it exclusively to black radio – as a white-label of course, no pictures; he doesn't want to draw attention to the fact that you're not black – and then flip it, that's what he said, *flip it* into adult contemporary, or AC, and then, he hopes, into pop. With a bullet. He says you can forget college.'

'I can forget *college?*'

The line crackled. America was another world.

The week 'True' topped the charts in the UK we rolled into London like returning heroes. Dagger, still wanting to present us in an unconventional way, had come up with a triple-header of unusual venues for the city: the Royal Albert Hall, which hadn't been played by a rock band for years; the Royal Festival Hall (never before); and two nights at Sadler's Wells (the same). This last venue, apart from being a haven of refined classical arts, and having the pleasing irony of being one of the UK's foremost *ballet* venues, was also to be our real homecoming – not only was it situated in Islington, but it also sat a gob away from where our old school had once stood.

Our London shows began with us walking triumphantly on to the stage of the Festival Hall, but soon realising that not everyone wanted to give us the freedom of the city. About halfway through the show the crowd rushed to the front of the stage and the Festival Hall fire marshal lost his rag. For him this was a chance to swing his hose in the air and he wasted no time in threatening to pull the plug unless everyone in the audience sat down. Backstage he argued with Dagger and our tour manager. We then got a message from the wings to tell the audience to go back to their seats. Tony, being a reasonable sort of chap, obliged, but it infuriated me and I told the crowd to stay where they were. This was rock'n'roll after all. Our tour manager bore the brunt of my frustration and I collared him in the gap before the encore; I felt those horns of celebrity breaking through and I threw an aggressive stance.

'If you think I'm gonna tell them to sit down you can fuck off!' It suddenly became almost physical, and it might have done if it hadn't been for others coming between us. In the end, nobody sat down and the plug remained firmly in. Afterwards, my horns retracted and I apologised.

On the day 'True' had reached number one we played Nottingham and Steve Strange came up to celebrate with us. *If it hadn't been for Steve*, we all thought, and we'd given him a group hug. From his Tuesday night at that little basement club called Billy's so much had grown; so many should have been grateful; so many bitched. Now we were back home again in Islington, but this time as league leaders. And watching my oldest friend in the pack blow his sax on the Sadler's Wells stage, I thought about the times we'd sat for long hours as teenagers in his parents' home – just at the top of this very road – dreaming our school band into scenarios that we were told were nothing but fantasies. I watched John as he drove out the rhythm, and remembered when we'd drive in his car to the first service station off the M1 and visualise travelling the world; I looked over at Tony, standing in command of our audience, and wondered what would have happened if he hadn't worn that leather jacket to school; and then I walked across the stage to where my brother was causing such havoc among the female members of the audience and spoke into his ear: 'Can you believe it, Mart? We did it!'

After three weeks of us being at number one, *Top of the Pops* was to celebrate its 1,000th edition. Would we be the band to play out that all-important show? For that to happen, we needed to be at the top for a fourth week, but the Human League looked favourites with their highly anticipated post-*Dare* single, 'Keep Feeling Fascination'. Their record sales were sailing neck and neck with ours, but so confident was Richard

Branson, owner of the League's label Virgin, that he'd decided to throw a lavish post-show party at the Kensington Roof Gardens in honour of the history and importance of *TOTP*; but of course, him being a public-ity-loving beast, it would also elevate his own band's achievement. Tick ets and invites were sent out, but come the Tuesday morning, Spandau Ballet were still residing at the top of the charts. The next day we went in and recorded the special edition, playing around a huge birthday cake. That night, poor Richard had to suffer the indignity of the entire Chrysalis company – including the elusive Terry Ellis (obviously no tennis match to play that night) – as well as us, turning up to gloat and guzzle the Branson champagne.

Some, no matter how hard they scream, will always stay on the outside; others – and they always know who they are – can step through into the band's world without even having to knock. Patsy Kensit was one of those people. Gary Crowley introduced me to her. Gary was a TV presenter who'd followed us since the days of the Makers, and along with his girlfriend we went out as a foursome. Patsy was amazing to look at and fun too. She was born to cross the line. Anyway, with a face like hers there was no hiding. We started seeing quite a lot of each other, but my straight side, born from my fear of an uncontrollable world, couldn't finish with Lee. Patsy had a whiff of danger about her, while Lee was safety. Lee was never looking for the glamour, and I was never good at introducing her to it. Lee and I never spoke about children or marriage and, in any case, I was a self-obsessed faithless lover still living out his childhood. So why I tried to domesticate Lee and my relation-ship, I'm not quite sure. Maybe it was because I was having so much fun with Patsy – or creating muses like Clare – that out of fear I asked Lee to move into my flat. Lee represented my past; Lee loved me before fame; Lee was home.

But one or two of the screaming sorority found this too much to bear. It began with notes through the door and then left behind the windscreen wiper of Lee's car. They were always the same message: *To the Bitch, from Darkness – Beware!* A week later the same again, but this time spray-painted across her car window with the addition of *Ha! Ha! Ha!*. She was a timid girl and she'd nervously step from our flat in the morning, never sure what to expect. One day she opened the door and she was greeted by a dead rabbit on the step. Around its neck was an abusive threat of murder, again from Darkness. It was breaking point and we called the police. They were as concerned as we were, but before anything was done a sheep's head arrived. For the next few weeks we endured a policewoman sitting in our corridor from 5 a.m. onwards, and strangely, with the sight of a blue uniform, Darkness, whoever she was, vanished into the night.

The Camden Palace was buzzing with faces. In its top-floor VIP room Strange tried to concentrate on what Geldof was telling him while Paula intimidated Midge; George and Andrew, looking as though they'd just lost a fight with a tanning machine, compared notes with a polite Haircut 100 lad who I just couldn't name; and Spandau Ballet were in their regular place at the bar, getting rather beery.

'OK. It was like we'd won the league and all that was left was a home game where the result didn't matter. It was against … I dunno … Man United, but we thrashed them anyway. Well, *that* was Sadler's Wells.' Dagger was finding one of his much-loved analogies in a cool glass of chardonnay; it was usually sport or war that he compared great moments of his campaign in pop with. 'Now we have got a difficult away match to deal with – let's say … Ajax in the Fairs Cup.' He looked at us directly. 'But we will win this too.'

The answer was unanimous. '*Bring it on!*'

For all of their success in the UK, Europe had been slow to embrace the new British bands. They were cynical about their musical ability. Punk had never really happened there and Pink Floyd could commonly be found loitering on jukeboxes. The Rolling Stones were still the most popular band in France and, as they'd always been, bigger than the Beatles, whose most popular member – for some Gallic reason – was Ringo. *Awkward, nous?* How could I possibly begin to explain the cultural importance of the soul boy to a continent where the faded tour T-shirt and the snood were not only ubiquitous but seemingly compulsory.

Unable to book many shows, it was important for us to prove our playing credentials there; and so we booked ourselves into some of the live rock TV shows that were available. The first was to be at the Ahoy – an enormous velodrome in Rotterdam, and our first difficult away match. We were third on the bill beneath Peter Tosh and 10CC and felt way out of our depth. Conspicuously dressed in Sullivan's Western whistles, we nervously took the stage. It was a predictably dismissive audience and a long way from the screaming apoplexy and adoration we were used to in Britain. We certainly weren't expecting any third-floor-window visitations. Unless it was a lynch mob.

The first few numbers fell upon stoned ears as the crowd rolled spliffs and waited for their reliable heroes; but song by song their attention was stolen as we tried to deliver a show of evidence that this 'pop' band could rock with the best of them. An hour or so later, bathed in sweat, we held our instruments aloft to 10,000 Dutch rockers and listened to the hall reverberate with a unison chant: '*Spandau! Spandau!*'

Now, more confident, we travelled to Cologne, where a local young promoter had read some of our history and put us on at the city's botanical gardens. It was to be broadcast live and hopefully would give more proof to the hard-bitten rock stalwarts of Europe that we weren't just pretty clothes horses.

After the soundcheck we all spread out on one of the garden's grand lawns and bathed in the day's glorious sunshine. Across the gardens a small familiar figure seemed to be making its way up the slope. I recognised the long strides and blonde wedge of our peripatetic manager. Fresh in from a meeting in Paris, Dagger looked to be walking even quicker than usual. He was soon upon us and slightly breathless. 'I have some news.' As he stood backlit by the sun, it was as though Mercury had descended with some hot-off-the-cloud information. He hung out a theatrical pause, just long enough for no one to fill it, and then: 'Danny Glass called me from New York, just before I left. "True" has entered the American Hot 100. We are at number fifty-four. With a *bullet*!'

Doug D'Arcy and his marvellous Sheriff-of-Nottingham beard sat behind the desk at Chrysalis Records. Outside, Oxford Street continued.

'*Four singles?* We can't release four singles from the same album – can we? That's *half* the record, guys.' Doug was a good guy and our favoured man in the company. He had a way of tilting his head when listening which gave the impression that he was seasoning what he was receiving with just a little pinch of salt.

'Make the *whole* album singles. If they sell, they sell.' Dagger's response to Doug was excitable and involved some flapping of arms, but what we wanted was to put 'Gold' out. It was begging to be on the radio. We'd topped both album and singles charts simultaneously with *True*, with the single staying at number one for four consecutive weeks. 'It seems silly to stop here.'

Doug tilted his head.

'If that's OK with you, then, Doug,' I said, 'we need to think about mixing a twelve-inch version. I don't want to do a dance mix – something orchestral maybe. And of course, we need to make a video.'

'Mmm. A video …' Doug seemed to be coming round to the idea of a fourth release. 'Any thoughts on how it might look?'

In front of me a young, bikini clad model is pretending to be a flower growing from a pot. She holds her palms together above her head and from a crouched position writhes gradually upwards before spreading her arms wide.

'Very good, my dear. That was terrific,' says the veteran photographer Duffy, who sits beside me armed with pen, paper and no shame. The small video production office seems far too hot. I'm red faced and speechless while Duffy continues: 'Have you acted before?'

The flower drops her leaves and tells him she has. In fact she was a child actress, she says.

'OK. What's your full name?'

'It should be on my card. It's Sadie. Sadie Frost.'

'Well, Sadie, I'm Duffy and I'll be directing this video. You know we're shooting in Spain? Oh, and would you object to being painted gold?'

Duffy went mostly by his surname. It was a conceit that he, Bailey and Donovan had created for themselves during the sixties. Three working-class fashion photographers emulating the nomenclature of the former public schoolboy. Caine and Stamp also enjoyed this affectation. It came from aspiration. It came from wanting respect. It came from being the first of their class to drive Rollers and wear Savile Row. But Duffy – or Brian, as he was known to his friends – was the mildest mannered of them all and now preferred his antique-restoration hobby, which he ran from his Hampstead home.

'Which one did you like out of all the girls?'

I knew my favourite. She was small and boyish-looking, with an elfin charm that endeared her to both of us. 'I like the one called Sadie.'

The night I arrived in Andalusia I drank a glass or two of cold Jerez in the hotel courtyard with her. At seventeen she seemed to be itching with life and fidgeted endlessly upon a slatted metal seat while mosquitoes buzzed around the lights of a lazy central fountain. Sadie rapidly told me about her maverick family as though she were desperate to unburden herself – a Mancunian pug-nosed father who'd dragged his young family from squat to squat throughout the flower-power years; who'd terrified and lost friends by breaking into their homes while they were out and painting everything – including the carpets – red; who'd painted John Lennon's Rolls-Royce psychedelic (this time with permission) along with Paul McCartney's piano, and who'd dated his birth from an acid trip he'd once had. Her mother had run away to the circus at fifteen and Sadie had been born the year after. Then came her psychedelically named sister, Sunshine Tara Purple Velvet.

As she flapped at a mosquito her hair bobbed seductively across her face. She parted it with her little fingernail, sipped her drink rapidly and told me how at fifteen she'd returned from a modelling trip to Japan only to find that her mother had given her bedroom away to her baby sister. Her only choice was to leave home and live with her boyfriend, whom she was still living with. I registered this last bit of information with a coolness that belied my disappointment. The truth was I'd become fascinated with her, lured by her obvious sadness from the insanity that was her life. By the end of the shoot I would be smitten.

The following day the sun spanked off of the walls of the little *pueblo blanco* as Tony wandered its narrow streets, hot but in character. It was our first travel video, and an obvious answer to the epics-from-abroad that Duran was now making. A foreign location said something about you – it told people how much money your record company was willing to spend on you; it gave the impression that you were internationally famous and gave you a nice trip to boot. These videos were visual proof of Britain's expanding pop empire; modern postcards from the front.

All seemed to be going well. I was delivering my usual demands and ideas about proceedings while the subdued Duffy directed from the sidelines. After a hot morning's filming I was sitting with Tony at a table in a little square guzzling some bottled water when the producer came over to us. She looked nervous.

'Er, hi, guys. Listen, Duffy's got to go back to London.'

'When?'

'Now. In fact ... I think he's already gone.'

'*What?* You're joking. Why?'

'I'm not sure.' She was embarrassed. 'Look, I'm sorry.'

I knew it was me. Russell and the others had been au fait with the process of collaboration, but Duffy was an auteur photographer and having the talent's guitarist buzzing in his ear like an irritating Spanish fly had him running away. What was odd was that he never confronted me beforehand, and that up until that moment we'd all seemed to be getting on. Well, if he was quitting the game I wasn't going to let him take his ball home too.

'What do you want to do?' she said.

I felt a certain confidence, maybe even a thrill, that I could direct the rest myself. I was upset to have lost Duffy but the film needed to be finished. We knew what we wanted. 'We'll carry on.'

I spoke with the assistant director, a bullish cockney geezer, who was as shocked as I was at what appeared to be an unprofessional yet noiseless tantrum, and together we successfully completed the Spanish side of the shoot. Including painting the sylph-like Sadie golden.

The next morning I sat with her in the car to the airport. The thought that I'd first seen her emerging minus dignity from an imaginary pot had me squirming inside. She was certainly no wallflower. As she sat there talking I longed to reach over and touch her fragile, bronzed arm. I knew that I would want to see her once we were back in London. She gave me her number and said, 'Call me.' It would be three years before I'd meet her again.

As 'Gold' climbed the UK's top thirty, Danny Glass's plan was working Stateside, and we were not just *flipping* into pop radio via adult contemporary – Disco Danny was riding that Spandau bullet all the way up the American charts.

Video was the reason for British success in the US, and MTV built the pipeline that fed that continent with the UK's natural pop. What was apparent to Spandau Ballet as we crossed the USA on our first American tour was that wherever MTV was screened there were screams; as well as a far bigger audience. In those MTV towns, fashion among young people had suddenly become more UK-like, and gone were the flares, cap-sleeves and lumberjack shirts.

But nowhere was more excited about Spandau Ballet than LA. K-ROQ, that 'weird' station out in Pasadena with its star DJ, Richard Blade, had become a huge phenomenon and with it anything British that was under twenty-five-years old, with coloured hair and a synthesiser. The station had helped to springboard the Human League and Soft Cell into the school recess chats and eventually the charts, both having massive hits with 'Don't You Want Me' and 'Tainted Love' respectively. Along with Duran's 'Hungry Like The Wolf', George's 'Karma Chameleon' and Dexy's 'Come On Eileen', Spandau's 'True' – and its four weeks at number four in the US charts – was *Billboard* proof that this was more than some freak Limey incursion. LA, with its culture of surf's-up and good looks, understood the glamour of England's New Pop like no other city, and was starting to ride its incoming wave.

We were to play at the Wilton, a beautiful art deco theatre on Wilshire. We'd sold out three nights and added another LA gig for Thanksgiving at the Palace theatre, downtown. Before the run we decided to pay homage and visit K ROQ. Arriving at the station for our interview, we were shocked at how many girls there were outside. Our two minders slid out of the cars to clear our way through, but soon found their hair pulled, buttocks snatched and legs buckling.

'Could you stand— Ow! Come on, stand back.'

'Oh my *Gahh*d! I *love* his accent!'

'I've got his sunglasses!'

'There he is! Tony! I love you!'

'Maartiin!'

'Oh my *Gahh*d! Oh my *Gahh*d!'

Hysteria is an overused word for this sort of thing, but from behind the tinted glass of the limousine that's exactly what it looked like. I saw girls fighting, crying, screaming, their arms held out like some overplayed Greek Chorus; and then one girl was sick on another, who didn't care.

'I'm not getting out.' Martin was adamant; but suddenly a burly hand was reaching into our car and lifting him from his seat. I grabbed Martin's sleeve and went with him through a riptide of nubile legs and arms. We popped out on to the quiet air-conditioned shore of a foyer, the screams suddenly muted by the heavy plate door.

'Could you sign in here please?'

'*What?*'

'Fuck me – they got my chain.' Steve was already in but looking dazed and bewildered with a ripped shirtfront. Martin restyled his damaged quiff with his palms. Suddenly the airlock opened again and Tony was thrown in, accompanied by a sonic wave of screams. He'd skilfully managed to carry a cigarette through it all. I watched as girls threw themselves against the glass plate like Hitchcockian birds.

'Hi, guys, I'm Richard Blade. Thanks for coming in this morning. See you've had our Valley Girl welcome. The phone lines are going crazy, by the way. Someone wants to have your babies, Tony.'

'What do they want to do with them?'

Unfortunately, once in, we had to get out. By lunchtime we'd become virtual prisoners at the radio station, hunkered around a coffee machine while fanatical females crawled all over the building. It became impossible to leave without risking personal injury, and so finally the LA cops were called and turned up in Ray-Bans to manage a tonsorially undamaged exit.

From the sun of LA to the snows of Minneapolis, it became obvious to us that the MTV effect was everything for British groups. But although MTV was based in Manhattan, ironically, owing to some Tri-State cabling foible, New York was MTV-free. And so our audience at the Savoy Theatre that night were a neutered-but-arty Manhattan crowd, more reminiscent of our Underground gig a few years before than anything we'd experienced elsewhere. A large crowd wearing black polo-necks and deconstructed Yamamoto and Prada flapped through the theatre like a flock of blackbirds. But the most suave of them all was Danny.

'Spandau Ball*et*!' Dagger was with him, directing him backstage. And then Danny Glass snatched at his heart as though he'd been shot. '*My God*. I feel like I know you guys already.'

He *was* white. His voice *was* Jewish Brooklyn. But his clothes were most certainly black. And Danny was the man to thank for our American success, and we did. That weird little New Romantic band from the UK with 'no chance here' had landed itself straight into the American dream.

After the show we sat with him and celebrated our album's entry into the American top thirty. But Danny wasn't finished with us yet.

'Have you heard of a TV show we have over here called *Soul Train*?'

'Of course, Danny, it's famous. We were soul boys; we read about it in *Blues & Soul* all the time.'

'Then you know it's only *black* acts that play it. Well, I intend to get you guys on to that show.'

Danny was already reloading.

CHAPTER FIFTEEN

EMBRACING THE ENEMY

I know the most terrifying sound in the world. It is the sound of the telephone ringing in the middle of the night. Its noise jars you from sleep like a violent intruder; its alarm stabs at your heart; for with some certainty, it is a portent of tragedy.

Adrenalin was already flooding my veins as I lurched from sleep in automatic response. *Please don't let it be bad news.* There was little else it could be.

'Hello.'

'Gal.' It was my brother. 'It's Dad. He's had a heart attack.'

'*How? Where?*'

'At home. A few minutes ago. I was there. I saw it happen.'

Part of me wasn't quite loose from a dream and my free hand clutched at my scalp. 'Where is he?'

'Bart's Hospital. The ambulance took him with Mum. I'm going now.'

'OK, I'll see you there, Mart. Mart … is he gonna be all right?'

'I don't know. It was fucking horrible.'

At fifty-four my father was a not young man, but surely too young to die. Yet forty cigarettes a day was a number of greater significance. He'd come home from work on a Monday and I'd watch him spread the solidified dripping from Sunday's roast over half a loaf of sliced white bread and follow it with a chain of fags in front of the telly. Recently he'd made a humorous attempt to get fit. My parents were friendly with their neighbours and Saturday night was usually spent sampling each other's home-brewed beer or Dad's experimental-looking parsnip wine with some cheese and pickled onions; and often in fancy dress – a ritualistic ice-breaker that had had them laughing for a few years. It occurs to me now how absurd it all must have been – my brother and I dressed to go out looking like a Cossack and a *Star Trek* extra, saying goodbye to my parents who were dressed as Elvis and a ghoul! Anyway, one Saturday night my father insisted he and our two neighbours needed to lose some weight (my mother was perennially thin so didn't need to take part), and, after much tapping of tummies, a Sunday morning run was decided upon. To make it more efficient – but really to make it more of a laugh – my father insisted that they all wear bin-liners to help them sweat; he'd heard something about it on *TV-am*. The next morning, with a satirical starting whistle hanging from his neck, Dad took them off around the block like so much rubbish. They rustled hopelessly in the headwind. The attempted health assault upon their bodies ended unsuccessfully in fits of breathless giggles and became the perfect excuse for larger portions of roast potatoes and trifle that dinnertime.

The week before his heart attack I saw him jogging to get a newspaper. I watched him from the window as he set off. He secretly knew it was serious.

He was lit brightly in the chemical glare – a man reduced by pipes and wires and muted beneath a plastic mask. A needle pierced his arm and next to it I could see the familiar green tattoo of an anchor sunk beneath the thick dark hair. It was a mark that hinted at some other man – a younger, more devil-may-care person; the one that first combed Bryl-creem back through his Tony Curtis; the unknown one that existed before all of us.

Seeing Dad upon the bed I realised what else had brought him to this terrible place: overwork. I thought about the one time he had taken us to his print shop in the Angel. He'd put on a thin overcoat, the colour of brown wrapping paper, pulled from a narrow cupboard in the shop corridor. It transformed him; like the suit of a superhero. Escorting his two boys through his subterranean domain, he proudly introduced us to his workmates. Even to a small child the ceiling felt low, and the huge, noisy, paper-eating machines that they fought to keep under control created a nervous claustrophobia within me. But this place had a familiar smell, homely even. It smelt of Dad.

Being in his world, I remember how shocked I was when I heard him suddenly laugh and swear with a mate. It was only an innocuous *bloody*, but it was a word and a style of delivery that I'd never heard him use before. Like the tattoo, it was evidence of another man, someone other than the one I knew, and it made me feel temporarily disconnected.

Dad's daily workload was spent hauling reams of paper to the eating end of the machine, and then, when they were printed and ready, away from its spewing orifice. He filled ink reservoirs, set type, and then fed the hungry beasts some more. He worked every hour his bosses would allow. But the man's devotion to his family had almost broken his heart.

At home with Mum, nothing seemed to matter for a while, nothing other than looking after her. She sat quietly for most of the time Dad was in hospital and Martin and I comforted her with tea and small talk. But what she silently dwelt upon was the fact that her life had stopped moving along its upward trajectory that had sprung from her youthful dreams, and had now begun tipping itself downwards towards old age and infirmity. The photograph on the shelf of them smiling together suddenly seemed to be shocking in its naivety. I stared at it for clues. I was angry that my father's work had ignored his talents; I was sad that this great man must have felt such childlike fear; and, as always, I was guilty for what I did and who I'd become.

When Dad came home it was in the knowledge that he would have to return to hospital. He sat heavily in the chair that he'd almost died in a week before and told us that they wanted to break open his ribcage, deflate his lungs and stop his heart. His life would be fed for a few hours through a machine. He said they would take five good arteries out of his legs and use them to replace five bad ones in his chest. In my mind's eye I could see them throwing these broken threads into an incinerator. We were terrified and so was he. Somewhere inside he was scarred; it was a mark of the man he'd now become.

I took myself back to the withdrawn world of songwriting: the hotel room, the living room, the bedroom, wherever it was that might give me the necessary privacy to find new songs. The problem was the baggage that accompanied me into those spaces. With 'True' I'd created my own competition, setting a personal benchmark almost impossible to reach again. A hit song of that nature takes on a legend of its own: people's lives become personally involved in it; they fall in love and get married to it; and a hungry band wants more of it. That kind of iconic status needs time. But whatever I brought to the rehearsal table would only be judged by 'True'.

The solo songwriter stares into the blank page as if into the magic mirror on the wall, and waits to be spoken to, hopefully in flattering tones. Unfortunately it usually glares back mockingly, happy to reflect your ineptitude. The whole process of writing the next Spandau album was starting to depress me and I found numerous distractions in order to avoid it.

I was reading a book Steve had bought me for my birthday, a book on the life of Picasso by Roland Penrose. In it I learned how Picasso had worked with the great impresario Diaghilev for the Ballet Russe, designing the backdrops for the ballet *Parade*. It had music by Erik Satie and libretto by the great avant-garde poet (and, beautifully, I think, boxing manager) Jean Cocteau; Nijinsky choreographed. It reminded me of the multimedia group of creatives that had once surrounded our group. I called David Band and told him the idea. Being a huge fan of Picasso he was immediately inspired but also told me how his other great hero, Hockney, had recently painted the backdrops for a new version of *Parade*. I suddenly saw the album as a touring show. A musical pageant that would take us around the world. *Parade* would be our title and concept for both record and tour. It was the spark I needed.

Since writing the last album, we had become a live act; in fact, we were all beginning to prefer this louder version of ourselves. Where with the *True* album I'd only been concerned with the sound of the record, now the songs would be written for the stage, and this time those stages would be arenas.

And so Dad stopped smoking, stopped wearing fancy dress on a Saturday night and, along with my mother, said goodbye to the city he loved. My brother and I didn't want him returning to his paper-eating machines and, after much discussion, decided to help them into early retirement. Mum wasn't sure if this was what she wanted – leaving her circle of family; the streets she'd known since a child; the geometry of home – but Dad felt the possibilities of adventure coursing through his now free-flowing veins. And anyway, London was no longer a place for sentimentality – London wasn't his any more. His family and friends had been pushed out into the new towns of Hemel Hempstead, Luton and Basildon, or vanished on a boat with a cheap fare. London was a town of sinking estates and rising stars; tribalism and elitism; somewhere in the middle a generation was being squeezed. This rolling decade had become a juggernaut, proudly detaching itself from history until only the faint sound of ghosts could be heard singing from the bar of the Clarence.

As Thatcher culturally cleansed the council houses, we packed Mum and Dad's entire life's gatherings into a van and took them to live by the seaside.

I only hoped the phone wouldn't ring again in the middle of the night.

An overheard discussion between three schoolgirls in a supermarket in 1984:

> *Girl 1* So who are you?
> *Girl 2* I told you who she is, Jen. She's my little sister.
> *Girl 1* I don't mean that – I know who she *is*. I mean who *is* she?
>   Eh? Who do you like? What side are you on?
> *Girl 3* I don't know? Her side, I suppose.
> *Girl 1* Okay – 'Hungry Like The Wolf' or 'Gold'? Come on!
>   Simon or Tony? John Taylor or Martin Kemp?
> *Girl 2* She's not a Duranie, Jen! Leave her alone!
> *Girl 1* 'Cause if you are, you can't hang out with us today. We
>   *hate* Duranies more than anything.
> *Girl 2* But *you've* got all their records, you liar! Anyway, she's a
>   Spand, like us, ain't ya, Dawn? She likes Steve Norman.
> *Girl 3* Actually, I like Boy George.

By 1984 the dividing lines were clear: Duran had America while we had Europe; we had Australia while Duran had Japan; but Culture Club had the world. Then there was Wham! and the new kids on the charts, Frankie Goes to Hollywood, and of course, the greatest cross-continental British success for years, the old Blitz girl and member of the original Gang of Twenty-One, Sade. The House of Commons congratulated British music for the millions they were creating for the country in exports. Naturally competition between us all was fierce, and sometimes even a little bitter. Pop tribes within playgrounds was now an international phenomenon. But something was about to bring us all together.

With my first large cheque from the band – waved at me by Dagger across the bar of the Embassy club – I'd precociously purchased a chair designed by Philip Webb in about 1860 for the William Morris Company. My aspirational desire for design, especially that period of late Victorian British design, found me frequenting antique shops every-where, and I soon discovered the specific style that I was to fall in love with – the Aesthetic Movement. I lusted after certain pieces of furniture with the same breathless urgency that I'd once trawled shops while look-ing to find the right pair of trousers. My love of the Aesthetic Move-ment was fuelled by its exotic connections with Whistler, Wilde and the decadent period of the foppish 'velveteen ragamuffin', to quote Max Beerbohm, the group's commentator and the Bob Elms of that time. They seemed to me to be the designs of an impudent youth movement, set on outrage, hedonism and infamy. It all sounded excitingly familiar.

And this is why in October 1984 I'm standing in the window of an antique dealer's in the King's Road, looking at a hanging lamp. 'It's wonderful,' I'm saying to the toadying dealer, and: 'What's your best price?' when suddenly the window's being hammered from the outside. *Christ!* I jump back, toppling the suited owner off his dais and into an armoire. On the other side of the glass stands a fellow antique-chaser, the overly long and tousled Bob Geldof.

I'd first visited Bob's house in Camberwell on an invite from Paula for tea. It was an Aladdin's cave of found things and had been one of my early inspirations for how I'd like to surround myself. Paula, dressed in taffeta, flirted with me endlessly in Bob's absence but it was all teasing, and in any case, my friendship and respect for the Boomtown Rats' frontman had me coyly defending his honour from behind a fancy Edwardian teacup.

Geldof motions to me that he's coming in. I climb out of the window as a 'ding' announces his entrance through the door.

'Hey, Big Boy. Spending your fucking money again!' The peaceful interior recoiled in his presence. 'You should do the auctions like I do, it's cheaper than this fucking lot.' Geldof's head knocks a chandelier and he focuses down upon me. 'Did you see the BBC news last night? The Michael Burke report on the Ethiopian famine?'

'No.'

'*Jesus*. It's horrific. And *shameful*. I was in tears watching it. I can't tell you how fucking awful it was.'

He's seriously moved by it and I'm beginning to feel ashamed of where I've been found and of what, moments before, I'd lusted after. The cowering dealer seems to be quietly estimating the cost of Geldof's untimely appearance upon the scene.

'I'm wondering if we could do something,' Geldof continues, as if he were thinking on the spot, 'y'know, like a record? Make a record with everyone on it and donate all the money to the Ethiopian famine relief.'

I wasn't sure if it was a question or a statement.

'I'm gonna ask the Duran boys and Sting; everyone. Pop music is massive. We should use it to do something good. To help feed these poor people. Would you be up for it?'

He was certainly delivering a lot of pie-in-the-sky, I thought – not only did we all hate each other in this business but at any given time we were spread out around the globe. The logistics of coordinating these fearful egos, especially through their over-protective managers, would be impossible. *Pop stars save a country?*

'Yeah, I'd love to,' I said – I didn't want to be left behind if on the off-chance it actually happened. Geldof was a man who inspired attention and if anyone could do it, well … 'but we're off to Japan tomorrow for a few weeks and …'

'Great, I'll call you there. Get your office to send me your itinerary and any bollocks fake name you register yourself under these days, Kemp.' He went to leave. 'I've asked Midge already if he'd do the music and he's working on it.' And with that he left.

I turned to the dealer.

'Do you still want my best price?' he said.

'No, that's OK.'

A week later I get back to my hotel after our show in Osaka, a show where 5,000 Japanese teenage girls giggled and wriggled, to find a message at reception to phone Geldof. Up in my room I throw an armful of teddy bears aside and make the call.

'Bob, it's Gary.'

'*Big Boy!* It's on. Trevor Horn's gonna produce and he's letting us have his studio for free. Sting, Paul Weller, Boy George, George Michael, Duran, you lot. I'm trying to get Phil Collins and I'll ask my old mates U2. Oh, and the Quo boys are up for it – bring in a wider audience, y'know. Phonogram have agreed a huge fucking royalty of twenty-three per cent and I think I can get the vinyl donated from ICI. I want a Christmas number one, forget the other fucking shite out there.'

Some of that shite was ours. Our single 'Round and Round', along with Wham!'s on-the-nose-titled 'Last Christmas' and Frankie's 'The Power Of Love', were all in competition that winter.

'I've got the song and some lyrics already,' he said. 'It's called "Feed The World".'

'That's amazing, Bob.' I was stunned. He was making it happen. I still couldn't quite imagine it, though – *Paul Weller and George Michael around the same mike? Us and Duran? Boy George!* 'When are you recording?'

'We're looking at next Sunday at Sarm West. Can you do that? You lot *have* to be there.'

I knew we were flying to Germany from Japan, and the night before the recording we'd be doing a TV show there with our old adversaries from Birmingham. There'd be a hangover, but of course we'd do it. 'Definitely. Let me get Dagger to talk to your office.'

'Great. Oh, and Kemp – *Charles fucking Ryder*! You literary wanker!'

The *Parade* tour had been marching us through Europe. The band, wearing gaudy baroque-style ensembles of brocade jackets and military trews, performed in front of a huge David Band-painted figure of a man with a megaphone. He was part of the concept for the album, which had been released that July. On the album's sleeve was another David Band man, pointing westward into the distance. He was painted on a huge banner that hung from a vast art deco building. In the street below was a line of parading people: Chinese dragons, harlequins, majorettes and banner-holding miners; and for that last role we enlisted our fathers.

Stan Keeble, Pat Hadley, Tony Norman and Frank Kemp turned up like excitable schoolboys for the photo-shoot and gawped at the page-three glamour model Sam Fox, the TV presenter Sarah Green, and Patsy Kensit (now fronting her own band), all dressed revealingly as majorettes. David Band, in a homage to Hockney's *Parade*, played the harlequin. It wasn't quite the *Band On The Run* cover of celebrities, but it suited our purpose, and most of all the dads loved it. But my father looked worn out that morning. I could see he was still in fear of his heart and so was I. I worried that he felt diminished in front of the other fathers, all of whom still worked. He was a proud man with a strong work ethic, one that he'd passed on to me and Martin. He'd never been late for his job or called in sick in his life, but now he was taking tablets for a living. What he loved most of all, though, was his two sons' joint success with their group. That day, Frank Kemp, tired but ecstatic, lifted the union banner he'd been handed with pride, and claimed his rightful spot in our pop story.

We'd recorded the album in Munich under the supervision of Swain and Jolley. We settled into the bunker that was Musicland Studios. It was placed underneath the Arabella hotel in a particularly industrial-looking part of town, but it was considered one of the best-equipped studios in Europe. Here ELO had recorded 'Mr Blue Sky', and, more recently, Queen had made 'Radio Ga Ga'. In fact Freddie was in town tasting its nocturnal delights, and as an hors d'oeuvre to his evening, he'd often step out with us first; then it was 'Bye-bye, loves. Now I'm off to find my kind of place'.

Tony recorded with Steve Jolley in another studio, a method that had worked well for the band on *True*. It would at least stop me fretting and driving Tony insane over a particular nuance that he might give to the melody. It left Tony Swain and the rest of us to get on with the backing tracks. As with the previous album, we'd first rehearsed all the songs live back in England, and with their more guitar-orientated sound they were begging to be taken out on the road. Nine weeks after arriving we crawled pale-skinned from our Bavarian bunker brandishing the album *Parade* and its first single, 'Only When You Leave'. Within a few weeks it would be number three in the UK, all over European radio and heading for the top thirty in America.

Flying out of Japan there was only one thing we spoke about and it wasn't being part of Bob's Band Aid. We were to meet our opposition and spend an evening together with them. *Tommy's Pop Show* was a biannual event and huge in Germany; if you got it, you did it, and this

November it was to be Spandau Ballet and Duran Duran. Given our great media-driven rivalry and similar origins it was extraordinary that we hadn't met each other since the night we'd played Birmingham's Botanical Gardens and, on the floor of the promoter's flat, dismissed them. Now, putting music and chart successes aside, what we were all keen to prove was who could party the hardest. But our respective managements, seeing our horns appearing, were worried about the early start in the morning as both bands had to get back to London to record Geldof's charity single, and so after the show we were all grounded in the hotel bar. Nevertheless, there were things that could still be done there.

I guess the point of this post-show head-to-head was to stay up and stay standing. Unfortunately John Keeble, our star player, went bonkers on Jack Daniel's and was stretchered off in the first five minutes. 'The boy was overenthusiastic,' someone said respectfully, as one of our minders pulled him from the wreckage and away to his room. We could only watch gobsmacked: with no substitutes allowed on, we were already one man down and the Twiglets hadn't even arrived.

We were sort of pairing up now, sparring, like for like, pound for pound, mano-a-mano: I was enjoying some wry, arthouse natter with Nick; Tony and Simon discussed humidifiers; Steve and Andy talked at each other excitedly about music; while the two bass players – the so-called best-looking bass players of all time – sucked in their cheeks and sized each other up for the long haul.

We were all surrounded by minders, and all of us were surrounded by a velvet rope someone had found. Hotel guests on the outside of this privileged encampment watched with a certain morbid fascination as two of the most famous groups in the world got smashed, talked nonsense and, one by one, were removed for being too punchy for their own good. Occasionally one of us would want to use the loo, as bands do, which meant tactical discussions among the security as to who should stay or who should go. And then you're off. Now minders have a wonderful way of placing their hands not quite on you, as though they are touching a force field that surrounds you. With this they can pilot you through a crowd into any area or cubicle you wish to land in. It's amazing and it's commonly done with the artist's head lowered so as not to cause too much fuss and bother – or shame on his part.

I'd just returned from such a sojourn to find Nick earnestly telling Dagger something. 'We're gonna need make-up at the other end tomorrow. There'll be cameras everywhere.'

'Really? I never thought of that.' Dagger looked around at the remains of his band. 'Yeah, I guess you're right.'

'I know a girl who can do it,' said Nick, with a hint of authority. 'She can meet us at the airport. We'll split the costs if you like.'

People were sent off to find her number and phone her, but she was out.

'Forget the blusher, what we're gonna need, Nick, is security.' It was my turn to have the superior knowledge. 'My mum says it's been all over Radio 1 that we're flying in together.'

'No, you're right,' Nick conceded, but then topped me: 'Our office has organised something already.'

That something was the Metropolitan Police and the security services of Heathrow Airport. The next morning, while they waited at Heathrow, both bands boarded two private jets in Munich that would take them to make a record for a country of starving people.

'Faster! Can't you go faster? I can see their plane up ahead.'

'Shut up, Tone, I think I'm gonna be sick.'

Even airborne it was important to win.

Our arrival at Heathrow left us all a tad embarrassed. There, primed on the tarmac, were the Met, the airport security and the limos, but not only was there no make-up artist to greet us, there were no fans either.

The Duran lot climbed disappointedly into their pre-warmed cars.

'Race ya!'

'Oh, give it a rest.'

'Where is everyone? I thought this was gonna be something.'

Why *hadn't* anyone come to see Duran and Spandau turn up at the airport together? Had we suddenly gone out of fashion since leaving the country? And then it dawned on us – because they were all at Sarm Studios, waiting for the entire charts to turn up.

'Steve, this is all wrong. Why are we in a Queen's car for this? It doesn't look good.'

'I'm sorry, the record company sent them. It's what we usually have.'

As we approached the waiting crowds outside Sarm, it occurred to me that the black Daimler Princess we were riding in did not strike quite the right tone of humility for such an event as the recording of a song highlighting the starvation of a nation.

We pulled up and one of our minders opened the car door. Suddenly, as I climbed out, my embarrassment was multiplied. There, coming up the road with a rolled copy of the *Observer* placed ornamentally under his arm, looking for all the world as though he was casually walking to work, was Sting.

'Bollocks.'

'He's been dropped off by his limo driver around the corner, I betcha.'

'Trust him to get it right.'

'*Spandau! Spandau! Over here!*'

It was too late. Our ostentatious arrival was on record.

The Band Aid Story, shot that day, shows us standing outside the Basing Street studio looking ragged and a little too cocksure for the occasion. Martin raises a thumb to the waiting journalists and with a swagger tells them, 'We're back.'

Watching the documentary now it's surprising how many of us haven't quite got a handle on how to do sympathetic sincerity to camera; and apart from Geldof, there's a surprising lack of the muted enjoyment or earnest gravitas that you're used to seeing today. But this was the first, the dry run in how to do a socio-political pop record for charity; and anyway, we were all enjoying ourselves far too much for that.

Here I am on the floor playing the song acoustically with Weller and Geldof, a strange brew indeed, I remember thinking. And then it's Paula getting me to talk about my chance meeting with her man through a shop window, and I'm sounding far chirpier than I should. But it was all so thrilling – we knew we were making a piece of pop history.

Midge commanded his raggle-taggle band from the central position at the desk. Hymn sheet in hand, he spun round in his chair to face us. 'So who wants to go first?'

Silence descended upon the room.

'Well?'

'Oh, come on, then. I'll do it.' It was Tony. Midge gave him his lines and in he went. Through the speakers we heard him clearing half of Germany from his throat. I sat on my hands.

Tony was one-two-ing into his mike as George Michael arrived. The Wham! man looked shocked at the sheer wattage of fame sprawled out around the room. 'Shit. Have I got to do it in front of all this lot?'

George squeezed in at the back and Midge ran the tape. Tony delivered in two takes. A control room full of performers clapped and cheered and the rest of Spandau heartily slapped the back of our returning hero. Round one to us, we thought, but the quality around the mike that day was constant. And then Francis and Rick took their turn. The Quo boys had spent much of the day doing their Flanagan and Allen act outside the gents' toilets and by the time they were called in they were happily a little past their sing-by date.

'Man, they're out of tune.' Midge stopped the tape and the pair carried on regardless with their comedy routine.

Dagger leant across to me. 'Listen to them ... They're even out of tune when they talk!'

'Steve, isn't it? I'm Adam. From U2.'

The blond bass player was hovering over us.

'Hello, mate.' Dagger jumped up and shook his hand.

'I was gonna ask you ... Do your band get screamed at? I guess you do.'

'Er, yeah.'

'No, it's just that we're getting quite a few screams lately and, well, I was wondering how you deal with it.'

'Ah ... Well, first of all, let me tell you about the scream quotient.' And with that they went to the pub.

For a moment I sat alone, trying to freeze-frame this unique situation; to bottle it to memory. Scanning the room, it occurred to me how many here had sprung from that tiny club in Dean Street and from the scene that we'd helped to create five years earlier. Apart from us, there was Midge, the Bananarama girls and the boy Marilyn; then there was Duran, who'd led Birmingham's riposte, and George Michael, the Spandau fan who'd tried to hunt us down at Le Beat Route. Suddenly, in through the door walked the most famous of all Billy's veterans. Straight off Concorde, from a sell-out show at Madison Square Garden, it was the boy who'd once shouted over the banister that he could sing better than us; the bitchy, pilfering cloakroom attendant with the best put-down lines in London – Boy George. He threw some kisses, took the mike, and delivered like an angel.

This is the order of things. In the dark I follow the beam of a torch as it climbs ahead of me up a small set of steps. At the top I slip my arm through a hoisted guitar strap. I feel the familiar weight of wood and electronics hanging from my neck and make nervous adjustments to its settings. Across the black space a flight deck of LEDs glow, awaiting the imminent surge. Torch beams are scanning the stage and I peer through the smoke at the etched silhouettes of Steve and John as they're led to their lofty platforms. I watch as John climbs inside his kit like a tank commander strapping himself in for battle. At the far side I can just make out Martin settling into his bass guitar. Now I wait for Tony to step up behind me. Glancing over my shoulder into the blackness, I can see the glowing red tip of his cigarette as he takes a final hard tug and nervously expels. He's trying to focus on what is to come but already feeling the beat of the night rapid within his gut. Spandau Ballet is in position and ready to roll.

The anticipatory roar from the audience builds and I make a rapid mental rehearsal of my opening chords as the introductory tape moves to its dramatic climax. And now I'm caught up in the inevitability of the event unfolding, as suddenly, with a rush, I'm swept centre stage. However prepared, I'm astounded by the extreme assault upon the senses that this moment brings: the volume of the guitar that fires out as I slash down on to its strings; the intense brightness that simultaneously hits the stage, and the noise of a crowd that lifts its single voice in welcome for the arrival of the band they've come to see.

It's the first night of a record-breaking six consecutive sell-out shows at London's Wembley Arena, and Spandau are home for Christmas. I'm lifted high by 8,000 people and try to absorb their reaction. Looking out, I catch a glimpse of my parents and family standing in a box close to the stage. Huge grins of London pride light up their faces and I'm suddenly aware of how far I've come. And then something occurs to me: that the guitar, the *electric* guitar, is the single most powerful weapon that was ever given to the working class.

CHAPTER SIXTEEN

STARMEN

I hang dreamlike, high in a clear blue sky. Far below me an exaltation of people fold themselves into the old stadium that opens proudly in the sun; an oval of desire. Here, the focus of the world is being drawn. It is a day to change days; and with a tilt, I swoop down to join them.

If pop culture in the sixties was about dropping out of the establishment, and the seventies was about railing, kicking and screaming against it, then what was to be the overriding characteristic of our generation's decade? Looking back, the easy swipe has been to label us all Thatcher's children, conceived by the seed of greed. But the youthful desire for pop success could hardly be attributed to her. In any case, she must have hated what was happening. It was beginning to expose her heartlessness.

Geldof had confronted her about relinquishing the tax on the Band Aid record and popular demand had forced her into conceding it. Eighties pop was proving that democracy could be found mid-term just by buying a record. The voice of the country was being heard through its traditional medium – popular song. By the mid-eighties Thatcher had ridden roughshod over the unions – cynically labelling them 'the enemy within' – and a feeling of powerlessness in the country was becoming prevalent. Dad, with his begrudging vote for Labour, could hardly be called left wing, but he was still a union man. He believed in the power of the united voice to protect the worker; but Thatcher was in the process of muffling it. Now, in the summer of '85, at the apex of the decade, pop would unite the people of the country by delivering a new franchise, one found through their credit cards, chequebooks and tea caddies. All you had to do was pick up the phone, pledge, and you could change the world. It would also change the way they'd see themselves for ever.

America was not going to plan. 'Gold' had been a hit, although not as big as 'True', but 'Communication' and 'Only When You Leave' had fallen away early. Danny had been true to his word and got us that appearance on *Soul Train*, where we performed on a double bill with the Four Tops, but Danny wasn't the whole company, and anyway, his area was considered a little niche. While we were selling large amounts in Europe and the rest of the world, Chrysalis America were not pulling their weight. The spat between Wright and Ellis, the two company owners, was worsening and it seemed to us we were being affected like the children of a disintegrating marriage.

One afternoon in their London office Dagger threw down the gauntlet. 'Look, Chris, if you're so confident that the new album will go gold in America, then pay us in advance.'

It was an irresistible challenge if Chris were to retain his credibility with Dagger and, of course, himself. 'OK, then. I will.' It was to be a mistake on his part. On the third night of our American tour, while playing the Universal Amphitheatre in Los Angeles, Steve did his usual knee-slide across the stage to blow his sax, and blew his anterior cruciate ligament instead. Our American tour and World Parade were prematurely over.

Up until then we'd barnstormed our way through Europe (the last country to fall being Italy after we performed 'I Fly For You' at their famous San Remo TV festival and began a love affair between a country and a band), before heading off to spend five weeks in Australia, trashing house records and hotel suites. Australia encapsulated the Dagger-vision of Spandau as sun-seeking aspirationalists; hedonists in Speedos. *Bring in the journalists*, he thought. He flew Richard Blade down to Sydney to do daily reports for K-ROQ. We were getting a good base tan before arriving in our spiritual home of LA and two shows in front of 14,000 Los Angelenos. If the record company were not working it, then we would.

We were grabbing the dream of being rock stars by its horns and ticking the boxes of debauchery one after the other. We had grown men (minders) in tears with exhaustion (one even collapsed one night and was taken to hospital before being sent home and a fitter, younger version thrown into the fray); chemically extended post-show parties would roll themselves into mornings and airports and radio shows and photography studios and hotel check-ins and journalists and sound-checks and TV stations and record company execs before we'd finally remove sunglasses to take the stage and, lifted by the privileged thrill of it all, begin again.

But then suddenly we were a man down – a very important man down – and a tour of America that was to roll through into the Mediterranean during the height of summer was cancelled. Another band might have carried on regardless, temporarily substituting their fellow musician with someone else, but our loyalty to each other was famous, and so, without a second thought, we packed up and limped off. It would be a long recovery, and unfortunately we couldn't even go home.

Instead, we'd chosen to do a 'year out'. The painful irony of avoiding tax while complaining about one's government is not lost on me now, but what excited me then was the itinerant adventure of it all. We decided to unfold our rock'n'roll campaign furniture in Dublin. With its pale Georgian terraces there was something reminiscent of Islington about the Irish capital. It was also near enough if a quick fix of London were needed. We may have all been exhausted after over a year of non-stop work and play, but now, after four hit singles from *Parade*, I once more had a needy band at my heels.

Spandau Ballet were away from their home comforts and I knew I had to deliver some songs soon. Regardless of what I did, those thoughts of responsibility wouldn't leave me. They were there every time I played cricket with John in the backyard of our ironically named Stillorgan Road house; they were there while visiting the Cliffs of Moher with my parents; they were certainly there when drinking with Adam from U2 in the bars on Leeson Street. The fact that I was the only writer in the band was one that thrilled me and disturbed me in equal measure; it drove me forward one day and brought me to a grinding halt the next. In our early incarnations Steve had also written for the group, but since we'd achieved success, he'd stopped. He was hugely talented and I'm sure he could have developed his writing, but I clung proudly, and maybe even fearfully, to my post of delivering the band its material. Was I somehow exerting subconscious pressure upon Steve not to write? Avoiding his eye if the moment looked like it might arise? I certainly didn't encourage it. And maybe that's evidence enough. Maybe I was scared of what he might deliver, of being bettered, of even being usurped. My insecurity stoked my desire to control. But up until now that control had worked for us and it was to me that they looked once more. Between the cliffs and the Guinness, the fear and the bravado, I began again.

'It's gonna be the biggest concert of all time. It's easier to say who's not gonna to do it than who is.' Dagger hovered round our squalid kitchen as John and I diffused hangovers with our now traditional remedy of fish finger sandwiches.

'Duran?' John was still in his leather trousers from the night before. They would often double as pyjamas.

'They're doing the Philadelphia one. It's fifteen minutes for each artist. That's about … three or four songs, I would have thought.'

'Well, we've got to do "True".'

'Yeah. And I think you should do the new song you showed me yesterday. It could be a single, I think, and it's a brilliant chance to unveil it to the world.' As ideas go, Dagger had had some great ones; this, on the other hand, was not to be his best.

The band had set up shop in a decrepit, rat-infested disused theatre in Dun Laoghaire. There was no point going over old material, so it was there simply for when we had something new to work on. Roadies were flown in and equipment taken from storage; our keyboard player came over from London and ran up a bill in a hotel; all added to the pressure on what, and how much, I was to come up with. It seemed silly to have only one song for such a vast and expensive logistical operation, but at times my offerings were meagre. Dagger had come along the previous day and a song called 'Virgin' was the one he was excited about.

'I don't know when he writes them. He must do it when I go and get the coal,' said John, a mouthful of fish finger and Mother's Pride not stifling his wit.

'I was wondering,' Dagger continued, 'y'know, how it works here for you two.'

I could only write when alone. Having someone watch you while you try to write a song is like having someone watch you dress. You try on shirts, ties, shoes, discarding and keeping as you go along. Desperate to please, the room soon becomes a mess in the process. It's only when you're absolutely sure of the way you look that you step out; as though you'd casually pulled it all complete from your wardrobe.

'It works well,' I said. '*I'm* my biggest distraction.'

Dagger's taxi arrived and he grabbed his overnight bag. 'Anyway, did I say? Bob wants to call it Live Aid.'

Chuga chuga chuga … Drawing our heads into our shoulders we make that familiar little crouched run – pointless, but visually necessary when leaving any chopper – while enough hairspray to sear a hole in the ozone layer keeps the mullets perfectly intact. Live Aid is a mission to save a country and we've just been dropped in with military precision. Noel Edmonds has donated his helicopters to take the performers to and from Wembley and we've just shared ours with one of the Faces. Kenny Jones is here to play drums for the Who, and I'm thrilled at being on the same bill. Too thrilled. *When's Pete coming, Kenny? How's Rog, Kenny? Whatcha gonna do, Kenny?* He looked happy to get off.

Backstage, a cordon of Winnebagos, managers and minders try to defend their stars, who seem far happier in the open air, hugging and air-kissing each other, their lanyards swinging congenially in the sun. Choppers drop in freshly laminated artists, assistants and hangers-on every few minutes. Shades, carefully fashioned stubble, Day-Glo jackets (with *Miami Vice*-style half-mast sleeves), flapping silk shirts and career-shortening shoulder pads proliferate and roam in packs. Janice Long – the ordinary lass of Radio 1 – is pulling some of them towards her microphone, which is replete with red foam knob in an attempt to make it chummy. As soon as they're in front of it their voices change: 'Well, it's really important that we all remember what today's about, Janice.' 'Of course. Will you be doing your new single?'

A band of guardsmen in red tunics polish their brass horns, while PAs with Filofaxes and runners with clipboards race around with great purpose, regardless of any mission. A baggy horde of roadies in shorts – the sappers and foot soldiers of this pop army – wheel around skittish flight cases that are stencilled with the names of the famous. Mind your backs, please, all life is here. It's reminiscent of the opening scene from *The Battle of the Somme*, but without the horses and fear.

The Hard Rock Cafe, a rock-themed burger bar, has set up shop to water and feed this mob and Spandau Ballet quickly make their way into its greasy comfort.

'Oi! Look, it's Bowie.'

It was the Starman himself, and he was standing at the bar pretending to be an ordinary person. *If we can sparkle we may land tonight* – the phrase suddenly glimmered into my mind and I remembered that evening in Islington when an adolescent boy's life felt transformed. And suddenly I could visualise my journey from then to here: this man was the reason I was about to take the stage in front of most of the world.

He was with a group of people (stars are never alone) and looked sensational in a slim, pastel suit – Tommy Nutter, I presumed, or some such cool cutter. I drifted from the others and made my move. 'David? Hi. It's Gary Kemp.'

His eyes flicked round at me. 'Hi.' And then returned to the guy he was with.

OK, maybe he doesn't know who I am; thinks I'm nobody; I'll qualify it: 'From Spandau Ballet …?'

His eyes flicked to me again; a faint grin, maybe an imperceptible nod, and then his friend spoke and I'd lost him.

I mumbled something about having a good one, and walked backwards while nodding like some creepy courtier, and that was that. I was humbled. Disappointed. Humiliated even. After all these years … But why should he talk to me? This was *Ziggy Stardust*, for Christ sake! *Aladdin Sane*! *The Thin White Duke*! *My God!* Who did I think I was!

'What did he say?' Tony was eating potato skins.

'Oh, y'know – *Good luck*.'

Our tour manager arrived. 'Here you are. We're on at two, immediately after Ultravox – ooh, gimme one of those, Tone.'

I saw Bowie being ushered away. His force field was on.

The tour manager spotted him. 'He must be off to the line-up. They're all meeting Charles and Di.'

'What about us?'

'No. It's just the nobs. Y'know, Sting, Geldof, Elton … Freddie.'

'George Michael's doing it, y'know.' My brother had inside knowledge.

'*George Michael?*'

'If he's doing it we should be.'

'She's a Duranie, anyway. It's well known.'

'I thought she liked Dire Straits.'

'Are they in the line-up too?'

'George couldn't even get in the Beat Route and now he's in the line-up!'

'You should've got us in the line-up!'

Our tour manager had had enough. 'Look, it doesn't matter who's in the fucking line-up!' He stuffed his potato skin into his mouth to tell us it was over and left the tent.

There were two stages, one behind the other, and they'd revolve between acts. At 1.45 p.m. we were called. Pumped, we walked escorted towards the stage, me in shades and *Flaming June* shirt. Our roadies and Adam Ant's swapped gear on the back stage while we hovered near the steps, enjoying the familiar, self-regarding vanity of the moment. Just before 2 p.m. Ultravox exited, a green light came on and the revolve happened. Then the mid-Atlantic voice of a Radio 1 DJ came over the speakers: 'And now, will you welcome onstage here at Wembley … Spandau Ballet!' And they did. In truth, they were cheering themselves. The whole world was cheering what it was doing.

Fifteen minutes later I fell from the stage dripping with sweat, expecting my usual towel, glass of something, a helping hand. Instead we were so much debris, literally moved aside for the next delivery of pop.

'Shall we get a drink, then?'

I went up through the stadium and found Mum and Dad in their seats near the royal box.

'Hello, boy. You were brilliant. Well done.'

'Thanks, Dad.'

'Shame, though – Charles and Di left just before you came on.'

'Oh. Right.'

Pete knew me. We went back to before his collapse in a Club for Heroes cubicle. Steve Strange had probably introduced us and he was hungry for new sounds. I'd been a fan since *Live At Leeds*, and seen the Who with Martin once at Charlton and twice at Hammersmith Odeon, but they'd first entered my consciousness when the bishop mentioned them in my parents' front room the evening I'd decided what I wanted to be.

Pete could see I was excited – they hadn't played together for eight years. 'Look, follow us and you can watch us from the side of the stage.'

I hung tightly behind his light blue jean shirt and saw him walk on and become someone else – someone more familiar. It was even more thrilling than being onstage myself. But then suddenly there was a tap on my shoulder. Oh well, that was it – someone removing me from the stage for not being famous enough; for not being worthy. I turned round. There was a man standing behind me who looked like Paul McCartney. My vision wobbled momentarily.

'Hey, Gary. Just wanted to say that I thought you lot were *fab* earlier.' His voice was Paul McCartney's. And there was a woman who looked like Linda, next to him, smiling and agreeing with what he'd said. He jabbed his thumb up in front of me.

'Thank you. Thank you … *Paul*.' I played it cool and turned back to the stage just as Pete hit the opening power chord of 'Won't Get Fooled Again'. He knows who I am! *Paul McCartney knows who I am and actually stopped what he was doing to watch us play!* I was in a rock-'n'roll sandwich somewhere in music heaven. I'd been recognised and complimented by the most famous pop star alive while standing at the side of the stage on an invite from a hero – St Pete at the gate. I only wished my beloved Bowie had been there to see it.

But what was this all about, this craving for recognition? Was it about being recognised for one's talent or simply being recognised? Being seen as part of an elite or just having your own existence confirmed? It's all of the above, I guess. No matter how successful one is, we first fell in love with this business as fans; and that is exactly what we still are. The famous will befriend the famous because they can. How thrilling to have each other over for dinner and some mutual mastur-bation of the ego, even though the only thing you might have in common is your celebrity. But it's not only admiration you're after, it's affirmation: I am famous therefore I am. Being invited, or having your invite accepted, confirms that you can cut the mustard at the captain's table, dine above the salt, slip behind life's velvet rope, ushered through without even as much as a lanyard; a permanent name on the guest list of life. Unfortunately, this world has inner sanctums within inner sanc-tums, and threading your way through the temple of celebrity while holding on to your trousers of self-respect is nigh on impossible. That burning desire to belong is probably only a sheep's head away from my girlfriend's old nemesis, Darkness.

So let's cut to the show's finale, the big 'Feed The World' sing-along, and the chance to hang out onstage – *equally* – with the greats of pop. Even there the hustle and bustle of standing next to and with the right person is apparent, McCartney and Geldof being the magnets, the messianic glimmer twins of the evening. Here's George Michael, not hiding his light at all, setting himself up centre stage by the Irish one. Then there's Bono, squeezing in. He's become a near-solo artist for the day, changing the entire shape of his band's career simply by choosing to dance with a girl in the crowd. Freddie's up close and personal too, his band having created what will now become a Queen renaissance. They'd made the best choice of all of the artists who performed that day, cramming as many hits as possible into their allotted time.

And as for us? Well, we're a little squeezed out right now, trapped behind Macca's piano and a few session players stage right. *We just didn't get to the front in time.* Once the race was on, if you were slow but still wanted the middle, you ran the risk of ending up looking like a fairground head, bobbing up and down at the back. We wanted the front of stage, but unfortunately, by the time we arrived, that meant being out of shot and out of any reflected glory. *How fast those big stars are!* But maybe, just maybe, it wasn't lack of speed we suffered from but something else: not feeling worthy enough. Subconsciously we held back; eternal fans who knew their place.

Now I can see Bob is looking for someone – it's Tony. His line in the song is coming up. But then it's too late, and it's every man for himself around the microphones.

It's a reflection of our whole day really. Our choice of doing a new song had been a mistake: given the number of hits we had to choose from we could have blown the world away that afternoon, but our desire to promote a new album had dropped us back with the also-rans. Of course, what was achieved on 13 July 1985 was much more than just an opportunity to give celebrities a chance to enjoy each other's presence. Yes, obviously it was sublime charity, a passionate hymn of hope, all driven by Bob and his belief in what was right, but it was also more than raising money to save lives. On that day ordinary people saw that their actions could affect the world and change government policy. It was a genie released into the air for ever. Power to the people had finally arrived, and it had happened, surprisingly, in the eighties.

Flying back to Ireland the next morning I couldn't think about the highs of the day before, because I knew I had to get back to writing an album. Fortunately, John's coal-buying trips must have been frequent and long, because a group of new songs were slowly starting to present themselves. But I was still missing that *killer* song, the song that the album would be defined by. I needed something to inspire me. As it turned out, I'd also need a record company.

CHAPTER SEVENTEEN

BARRICADES

Kidso was a Belfast boy whose Falls Road accent revealed his alle-giances. I'd met this ardent Celtic fan – christened Thomas Reilly – during my courtly friendship with Clare Grogan. Small, dark and fit for the street, he'd worked with Altered Images as part of their road crew, but later, in 1983, he joined us on our UK tour, helping, rather successfully, to sell merchandise. We soon became very fond of him. He was a good guy whose optimistic temperament encouraged others to fold their proverbial wings around him. Sadly, he was about to be given a pair of his own.

One hot, sunny evening, Kidso was walking home bare chested through the streets of West Belfast, when he and a few friends were stopped by an army patrol. After giving his name and details he walked away. In one hand was his takeout, in the other his T-shirt. A few seconds later he was dead, shot in the back by a young private who would later become the first British soldier convicted of murder while serving in Northern Ireland. Kidso was twenty-three.

For a band used to touring Western cities, Belfast came as a shock. The observation towers that loomed like giant beasts of war flagged up the city's difference as soon as you arrived. And then there were the army trucks, cruising nervously through the old streets, the tanks, the RUC's bullet-proof vans, and the general visibility of weaponry, all of which told of a city under occupation, a city that in 1983 I found impossible to imagine as part of the cosy, tea-and-toast Britain I thought I knew.

We'd arrive at the famous Europa Hotel and pass through the sandbags and security before checking in. It was known as the most bombed hotel in the world, and the staff seemed to be as proud of this as they were of the stars on a plaque in reception. We were terrified. During our first trip there, Martin, Tony and I had to leave the hotel early one morning to be taken to the local radio station for an interview. Driving through the quiet streets, we were pulled over by an RUC van. Our local driver told us to stay where we were as three officers jumped out. One stood back and pointed his automatic rifle at our car. The driver wound his window down and explained the innocent journey we were making. They peered in the back and then waved us on. It left me with a little more understanding of some of the everyday tensions within this place.

That night, the audience did their best to let those go. We soon learned that Belfast was the best audience – *crowd!* – in Britain, and the King's Hall became our favourite venue to play.

Kidso's death shocked us all. The crude reality of the outside world hardly ever broke through our cocoon of celebrity, but here we were, made fully aware that there were things more important, more dangerous, than running the gauntlet of screaming fans. On the day of his funeral our wreath lay among a few others from the world of pop: the Jam, Depeche Mode, Bananarama, and, of course, wee Clare.

The following year we were back in Belfast for the *Parade* tour and I'm introduced to Jim Reilly. He's a drummer – he'd played in the punk band Stiff Little Fingers – but he's also Kidso's brother and he came along to meet us at the King's Hall. Somehow he and I decided that he'd walk me down the Falls Road the next day, for a little insight into how he and his family lived.

What affected me most as we walked were the so-called 'peace lines' that blocked the streets branching off that Catholic thorough-fare. On the other side I saw people walking, dressed in a similar style, fellow citizens, no different from the people I found myself with on this side, but, cordoned off by the barricades, they could have been on another continent.

We carried on walking until the shops ended. We turned off the main road and into the quiet of Milltown Cemetery. Jim wound me through the broken angels, headstones and dying flowers until finally I was kneeling down looking at a simple cross. On it was pinned a small picture. It's Kidso. And he's exactly how I remember him – glad to be alive.

A few months later, living in Dublin, I'm doing my history, and Ulick O'Connor's *The Troubles* lodges upon my bedside table. One night, while reading, I find myself thinking of that day, of Kidso, of the barricades and the divided people. *What do I know? I'm a privileged pop star.* But what I did know, as I closed the book, was how affected I was by it all.

About two in the morning I wake, and lying beneath the covers find lines forming in my head. They come in images, voices, a constantly moving loom of nouns and verbs that draw themselves together and then fall apart, only to quickly rearrange themselves. In all my time of writing songs I'd never leapt, cliché-like, from the bed in search of a pen, but now I am. It's a love song – that's what I know best; no: that's how best to tell it – a Romeo and Juliet tale set somewhere divided, somewhere torn, somewhere made for a tragic assignation. Belfast.

It came in one sitting; a surprise delivery of lyrics and music. By morning, I was ready to play it to the band.

In London, Dagger was preparing for battle. He pleaded with Chris Wright to license us to a bigger label in the US but he wouldn't do it;

it would have put a knife clean through his company. 'Well, Chris, then I'm afraid we'll have to try and leave the label.'

Dagger rang me in Dublin and explained how he wanted to threaten them with incompetence and was taking legal advice on whether we could get out of our contract with Chrysalis.

'But we're in the middle of writing an album, Steve. Do we stay on hold until this is resolved? It might take a year.'

'Look, Gary, you carry on. We'll fund our own recording. We'll make our own album and then sell it to the highest bidder.'

We wanted to move on from Swain and Jolley, we wanted a bigger, meatier sound, one more suitable to the arenas we were now playing. An engineer cum co-producer was what we were after and Gary Langan was our first choice. He'd been Trevor's engineer for years and had worked with us on the fateful *Pleasure Project*. He'd also co-produced a B-side with us during that time. His ear was great, as they say, and he loved playing the music loud in the control room. We would go back to Munich and record one track to see how things went. If it worked, we'd take on the album with him. But first we had to fly back to London for a little event.

A procession of black limos stretches itself down Oxford Street, red brake lights flaring in the damp night air. Inside one of these reflective shells sit our five heroes, feeling more than a little impotent. People shout at us through the windows, aiming cameras that flash pointlessly at the glass. It's like a safari in reverse. I can see our regular fans, toting autograph books, posters of us from photo-shoots we'd rather forget and the odd picture disc (impossible to write on). They hurl hopes of trysts across the barricades: 'Come outside after, Tone! It's Terri's birthday! She'd love it!' Then there are the rival fans: 'It's them! It's Simon! Aahhh! Oh no, it's Spandau.'

Unfortunately, we've been stuck beside a group of these antagonists for the last five minutes and they're making our slow progression as uncomfortable as they can for us. An elderly couple, obviously caught out on an evening's window shopping, gaze into our car to see if it might be anyone they'd heard of – a Brucie or a Tarby; the man shrugs at his wife. Oh, and here's the student tourist – *Jesus!* – leaning over the barrier in a generic Puffa, pushing people's pens and cameras into their faces with his elbows, screaming at anything and everything because this is how they do it in his town. *Oh God, he's burnt someone with his cigarette!* Behind them all, a furtive-looking chap in a dark raincoat and earpiece peers above the crowd like a periscope. He's obviously looking for any active anti-monarchists. It occurs to me that he could try our limo – there are a few in here. But we're not waving any republican flags this evening. Oh no. Charles and Di are having a thank-you party for all the artists who've helped with the Prince's Trust. It's at Air Studios and we've been invited to meet with them, hang out even. *Honk your horn, driver!*

We'd met Charles the previous year in Edinburgh. Our show there was for the Prince's charity and he'd come along to bear witness to it as well as receive a cheque from us. We met him just before we went onstage (luckily no longer dressed like Jacobites but in a more royalist-looking brocade) and I felt a twinge of embarrassment that our music might upset his delicately trained ear. He sat near Dagger during the show and confirmed my thoughts with his only comment: 'They do have a lot of energy.' He was aged thirty-six at the time.

But everybody wanted to meet Diana, ever since she'd first worn those New Romantic knickerbockers and, for a brief moment, became the people's Topshop royal. Above our heads helicopters and marksmen look for the worst-case scenario as our car finally lurches the few extra feet we need for our minder to leap from his front seat and release us into the clamour. We hop on to the pavement, straighten our Yamamotos, and make our way up to the studio's entrance, smiling and waving and looking so fine. Making our final waves to the crowd, we turn into the doorway, but I hit locked glass. Before I can say anything the rest of the band pile in behind me like the carriages of a derailed train.

'Where are we?'

'Is this it?'

It was dark behind the glass and I peered in. 'It's a fucking shoe shop!'

Realising we'd walked into the wrong place we had no choice but to shuffle back out into the street. The crowd opposite had seen it all. Obviously there were some who were mocking – 'Ha ha! Spandau Ballet just walked into Dolcis!' – some who were helpful – 'It's the next one along, guys!' – and some who were not – 'Wankers.'

We did the waving thing again but it was too late to recover and our smiles were a little rictus as we finally found the correct door. A royalist with an earpiece caught my eye and chuckled knowingly. Dagger blamed the minders – they'd obviously lost control of our force field.

The first person to hear it was John. He threw himself casually across the sofa while I, being nervous, stood more formally by the fireplace. You hear songs differently through the ears of others, and with 'Through The Barricades' I could sense John's goosebumps from early on as he shifted and manoeuvred through its dynamics, ending up sitting forward on the sofa, as if he were trying to lean into the song. Structurally, it was like nothing I'd ever written – not the safe havens of verse, bridge and chorus that I usually clung to, but more of a three-act piece. Sure, hiding in there somewhere was Bowie with 'Five Years' or 'Life On Mars', but it owed more to my early prog rock records – a touch of Jethro Tull's *Thick As A Brick* maybe – as well as adolescent trips to folk clubs. It was climactic and dramatic, and all in all I began to have a relationship with it like no other song I'd ever written. When you sang it, you felt its power. I was like Gollum and his Ring – this was *my precious*.

But for me, it was a dangerous relationship to have, as I was about to give the song to Tony.

The road crew swung into action, the keyboard player was roused from accumulating his room-service bill and I stood in the circle of trust and presented the song. As the band began to find their way through it, I made reasoned excuses to Tony as to why I should sing it just one more time – 'Have a listen to how the middle section goes' – 'Just read the lyrics for now until you get the vibe'– 'Let me show you again'. I had to let the song go, but with 'Barricades' a dangerous desire to own it started to form within me.

Dublin was full of musicians, and we spent days with Frankie Goes to Hollywood and Def Leppard, who were both living there. I even helped out with some backing vocals on the Leppard's song, *Rocket*. And for John and me, there was another stage outing to be done before we flew off to Germany. Elton arrived in town and invited the two of us to play with him onstage. We pleasurably thrashed out 'Saturday Night's Alright For Fighting' and Marvin Gaye's 'Can I Get A Witness'. That night, playing guitar with Davey Johnstone, I remembered how I'd once begged my mother, as she washed up at the sink, to give me £1.99 so that I could buy Elton's new album. Back from Pop Inn, *Don't Shoot Me, I'm Only The Piano Player* stayed for days on our record player until I'd learnt all of Bernie Taupin's lyrics. That night, from across the stage, Elton gave me a smile as I helped out with the familiar backing vocals.

John and I repeated our guest performance the following evening, then back in London, a few days later, we joined Elton again onstage at Wembley Arena. The thrill of being onstage was a good reminder to get our album done and get back to what we enjoyed doing the most. But extricating ourselves from the loving clutches of Chrysalis, and then going through the process of finding a new relationship, would take quite a while. That Christmas, our office received the usual gift from the record company. Dagger was in a particularly foul mood that afternoon, and had no time for condescending cases of emollient wine. He told his secretary to send it back.

'Hang on, Jackie, before you do that.' Dagger scribbled on a Post-it note and slapped it on top of the box. The two words were unambiguous in sentiment – *Piss Off*.

That Christmas also brought an opportunity for me to give 'Barricades' its maiden outing, in a show at the Dominion Theatre in London. Put together by Pete Townshend, the Snowball Review was a fund-raiser for a women's domestic violence charity and I chose to unveil 'Barricades' alone on stage that night. What made it even more mouth-drying was the fact that the rest of Spandau chose to come along and watch. How did Tony feel as I stood alone presenting a new song that was meant for him? Did he see it as a statement of intent? I wasn't sure how I saw it myself, but the song was already finding its voice through my delivery, and, perhaps only subconsciously, I was presenting a challenge. It was the first time any of us had ever stepped outside of the group since the school music room ten years before.

Working in Germany in the wintery new year of 1986, we got off to a great start with the song 'Fight For Ourselves' and rubber-stamped Langan through into continuing the co-production of the whole album with us. But Tony'd lost the mentor he had in Steve Jolley, and I was back on his case, worrying him about his vocal performances. And especially 'Through The Barricades'.

For Tony, it must have brought back all the fear he felt back under that Turkish rug. 'Look, Gary. I know the fucking sentiment behind the song! All right? You've explained it enough times!' I'd been stopping Tony after every line. I could see him frustrated behind the glass, watching the tape-op spooling back yet again, but I gnawed away at any loose nuance. A few days earlier I'd played the guitar part, and then, at my suggestion, put on a guide vocal myself. It was meant to be a template for other overdubs but was more a flag of ownership stuck in the track. It only led to more pressure on Tony to deliver.

Langan turned the talkback button to off so Tony couldn't hear what we were saying. 'Look, Gary, why don't we start again tomorrow on this? But maybe I should do it my own with Tony.' He was right. I had to let it go. The following day, while I took a walk around town, Tony gave the most incredible vocal he'd ever sung, and claimed the song not only for himself, but for the whole band. It would be the best piece of music we would ever make.

As I move back through this decade one question is beginning to circle above me: where did the end start? Certainly it would have gone unnoticed in 1986, so much good stuff was happening. We were famously 'five mates', 'the Angel Boys', closer than any other band, drinking pals on a permanent world bender and having the time of our lives. But at some time, something must have started imperceptibly to alter things, a mutation of a single cell, unnoticed at first, but with our fate contained within it. Where can I find the first fissure, the first footfall of the trouble that was about to arrive? Somewhere beneath our calm surface a tremor must have occurred, but locating where and when isn't easy. Maybe it was 'Barricades' and my sudden yearning not to part with the song? It certainly was a foretaste of the future. But no, I think it's here, in Chateau Miraval Studios, Provence, where two young wannabe film producers are arriving, and the end may be about to begin.

Dominic Anciano had produced four videos for us, two of which had been in the postcards-from-the-front style, with one filmed in Hong Kong and the other in the swamplands of New Orleans. We'd first met him when he did some animation for the 'True' video, a disastrous stickman that soon found himself, courtesy of the band, lying on the editing-room floor. Dom was a witty, cockney geezer with a great deal of intelligence and flair and we enjoyed his ribald humour. His invite from us to come to the French studio where we were mixing the album was so we could play him the potential singles – 'Fight For Ourselves' and 'Barricades' – and discuss their possible video scenarios. But Ray Burdis had accompanied him for another reason.

We last saw Ray as a child coming down the school stairs in the title sequence of my film debut, *Junket 89*. He was an Anna Scher boy who'd gone on to have a successful career in acting with roles in *Scum* and *Gandhi*, and was currently starring in the BBC sitcom *Three Up, Two Down*. Now Ray had dreams of film production, and, along with the highly creative Anciano, knew what film he wanted to make.

The idea of Martin and I starring in a movie about the Kray twins, London's notorious gangsters of the fifties and sixties, had first been mooted by Dagger in 1981. The *Soul Boys of the Western World NME* cover – a sulky-looking picture of the two of us in fifties-style clothing – had prompted the notion in his head. He'd been reading their seminal biography, *The Profession of Violence* by John Pearson, and passed the book on to me during the *Diamond* tour, believing the aspirational desire, obsession with style and skill with publicity that the twins had might hold some resonance with Spandau's own pair of brothers. As we'd been child actors, Dagger thought that Martin and I were perfect for the roles if a film was ever made. I read the book while imagining myself in the movie. Which one of the twins I should play if it happened seemed obvious, and not only to me.

'We see *you* as Ronnie, and Martin as Reggie,' said Ray. We were sitting at the long trestle table in a shaded area just outside the studio, overlooking Chateau Miraval's own vineyard. It had been the idyllic setting for long lunches during those weeks spent putting the album into its final shape, but now it was Dom, Ray, Dagger, Martin and me who were soaking up the last rays of the evening sun with a few bottles of the studio's own red.

'It's funny you should say that,' I said, 'I've always thought it should be that way round,'

'What? You playing the raving mad, homosexual sociopath?'

'Thanks, Dom.'

Although they were twins, Ronnie appeared to be the older of the two. He was definitely the one in charge. Reggie, on the other hand, was the cuter, more sensitive one – a slam-dunk for Martin.

'We've been in touch with the twins,' said Ray, a little too flippantly.

'*Have you?*'

'Yeah. Unfortunately Roger Daltrey has already got the rights to the book,' Ray continued. 'He's had them for a while, so we think we might be able to get them from him, especially if the twins like the idea of you two playing them. That's if you want to.'

Martin and I had been playing it a little cool, I suppose, probably because it felt disloyal to be discussing a project outside of the band while drinking their booze. And then Dom dropped his hook. 'Paul and Mark McGann are interested in doing it.'

'Really?' I slugged back my wine without tasting it. I was suddenly horrified at the thought of missing this opportunity.

'Don't be daft. Of course Gary and Martin should play them!' It was Dagger, flying to our support. 'They understand what would have motivated the Krays more than any other actors would!'

'What do you mean, Steve?'

'Yeah, Steve, what are you implying?' Dom giggled and threw an olive into his mouth.

'No, no. What they have in common,' continued Dagger, beginning his familiar run-up to something succinct and tasty with a little pause, 'is that they're both working-class lads who desire the same thing.'

'What's that, then?'

'The Good Life.'

The last ray of sun glinted orange through my wine as I looked out over the vineyards and hills of Provence, and felt that familiar prick of guilt. 'I'd better get inside,' I said, 'and see how the others are getting on.'

CBS had all the swagger of a powerful record company and Dagger and Brian Carr realised how much their corporate ego wanted us. EMI had Duran so CBS wanted Spandau, and after flying down to Munich to listen to what we'd been recording they wanted us even more. In true Dagger style the offer they made was ratcheted up and up until it was breaking all records. Chrysalis had decided not to get into a mud-slinging fight in court and allowed us to find another label, albeit with the promise of some kind of transfer fee to be negotiated on signing. So on a sunny day in Paris, at the lavish Charles V Hotel, we met CBS to sign the contract. There were some backwards-and-forwardings as Brian Carr and their business affairs man battled it out over some minor points, but then the pen went to paper and we finally had a label to release our album on. It was a huge deal financially – Dagger certainly had brought home the CBS bacon – but would they succeed for us in America the way we knew Chrysalis just couldn't? We certainly felt the album – which we'd titled *Through The Barricades* – was strong enough. The one place we didn't want them to sell records, though, was in South Africa, and we managed to get a clause in our contract stating that. And right then, South Africa was very much on my mind. That, and a meeting with someone from my past.

He'd called my house in Dublin. It had been fifteen years but his voice was as familiar as my own. Trevor Huddleston was the bishop; the man who'd panicked my mother into rapid cushion-plumping and over-egged consonants. He was the man who, during an unforgettable appearance by Rod and the Faces on TV, had placed a cassette recorder in my hands in exchange for a promise: to write more songs.

He'd phoned to ask if I would like to play at an anti-apartheid concert on Clapham Common. He was now leading the anti-apartheid movement along with Desmond Tutu and was part of the organisation for this event. Of course I would play – it would be another chance to perform 'Barricades', as well as a way of meeting my great mentor.

This was to be my third solo outing with this particular song. Towards the end of 1985 I'd given my support to a group that singer/songwriter Billy Bragg was organising with Paul Weller and the Style Council. Red Wedge was designed to focus the attention of the young upon the policies of the Labour Party in hope that their vote would win them the next election. In early '86 I went up to Manchester and performed 'Barricades' as a proud guest on the tour. Johnny Marr from the Smiths was also there and while the Style Council played their set, Johnny, Billy and I routined the finale, 'Move On Up', in a dressing room.

One of Paul Weller's roadies came in. 'Er, Paul says don't play too loud as Style Council audiences don't like loud guitar.' We were a little surprised as we thought we were at a Red Wedge gig, not a Style Council one. But later onstage, during the Curtis Mayfield song, Paul himself flew over to the three of us, who were posing madly with our guitars, and told us to turn down. We felt like naughty schoolboys caught giggling at the back, but it was a little ironic given our brothers-in-arms cause. Some musicians are more equal than others, I guess. Sadly, yet unsurprisingly, Neil Kinnock lost the '87 election and I hope our loud guitar playing wasn't to blame in some way.

Artists Against Apartheid was an organisation formed by the Specials' Jerry Dammers and Oliver Tambo's son, Dali. It grew out of the Rock Against Racism movement of the mid-seventies and served to put more pressure upon the abhorrent government of South Africa. Clapham Common and the concert were the destination of a march that would start in Trafalgar Square. My neighbour, Sade, would be performing, as well as a Culture Club-less Boy George.

I was shocked to see George when he took the stage that day in front of over 100,000 people. His face was theatrically covered in flour, but it only seemed to emphasis his pallor, a thoroughly desanguinated face. By now George had gone the way of many of my Blitz contemporaries – sadly including Steve Strange – who'd chosen heroin as a means to greater extremes of play and outrage. Luckily it had been a drug too far for me, and it was therefore difficult to judge other people's motivations for taking it, but standing on the side of the stage that sunny afternoon, I was sure this would be the last time I'd ever see George. It occurred to me that the mirror we'd all held up to that beautiful moment in British youth culture was beginning to crack.

Coming offstage after my performance, I saw the man I'd come for, his lofty frame elevated above the crowd mingling in the artist area; his elegant composure – a fine weapon in the job of peace – setting him apart; and I remembered him all those years before, standing conspicuously in his liturgical vestments outside our shabby front door, being heckled by the little street-rakers of Rotherfield Street.

'Trevor?'

'Gary! I'm thrilled you're here. Thank you.'

I wanted to embrace him but instead hugged my guitar.

'You sang wonderfully.' Fifteen years earlier he'd heard me singing in that dusty school hall, singing about Easter and being alone.

'It's all been because of you,' I said. 'I have to say that what you did for me changed my life.'

'Well … I've followed your career avidly. As I have someone else's here today as well. I may have told you – you probably don't remember

– before I met you I'd given the gift of a trumpet to a young African boy. Well, I'm thrilled to say that he's also here today.'

A breeze prickled the hairs on my arms. I *did* remember, but now I couldn't speak. I was waiting for him to say the name.

'It's Hugh Masekela.'

It was extraordinary. Hugh Masekela was a huge name in jazz. I was in awe of Trevor's vision – the two seeds of encouragement that he'd planted had not only come to fruition but we'd also grown to embrace the very movement he held so dear. Had we become who we were because of him, or had he chosen us because he saw something familiar? Someone found Hugh Masekela among the caravans and tents behind the stage, and then took a picture of the three of us standing together. Trevor stood proudly smiling between his two protégés, his long arms wrapped broadly around us. His gifts had been returned.

I'm staring at what looks like a puppet theatre covering about four square feet of the floor. A black curtain hangs at the front from a miniature lighting truss above it. As the lights in the room are dimmed, Prokofiev's 'Dance Of The Knights' from *Romeo and Juliet* begins to play and the curtain slowly rises, allowing smoke and blue light to pour out from underneath. Gradually, a stage set behind is revealed. The music climaxes and suddenly the first song on our new album plays, distorted through the boogie-box on the floor. The stage lights up to reveal Martin, Tony and me as little cardboard cut-outs. Behind 'me' stands 'Steve' on what looks like the half-body of a Dalek, while 'John' sits behind tiny drums on a similar riser in the middle. Our cut-out versions remain disturbingly still, regardless of the music and lighting changes that go on around them. We smile at our motionless, six-inch selves, and try to envisage how this will look in the arenas and stadiums of Europe, while our designer, Patrick Woodroffe, jumps through the show's acts until he reaches the beginning of the finale. Now the lights die down on the little figures as the portentous string introduction rises and my delicate acoustic guitar arpeggio begins its melancholic run.

A single spot lights me. I'm standing onstage in Belfast's King's Hall, focusing upon the fretboard of my acoustic guitar and trying desperately not to fluff the opening. I've dreaded this moment: bringing 'Through The Barricades' to Belfast, its spiritual home. What will the people here think of a pop star from London writing about their struggle? I feel exposed in the light, and my discomfort is only slightly relieved when Tony starts to sing. Another spotlight slowly reveals Steve, who's now playing alto sax behind me – just as we'd seen in Patrick's microcosm – and we build into the final verse of the song's opening section. Soon it will crash into its middle eight, and I slip the spotlight and wander to the side of the stage. In the musical pause I swap acoustic for electric with my guitar tech. And then John counts in the band …

As I slam into my guitar, the kabuki-style backdrop falls, revealing banks of white aircraft lights that blaze out into the auditorium, lighting everybody in that Belfast hall.

'*Oh, turn around and I'll be there …*'

Before me is a reaction I'd never expected. Everywhere people are standing, arms held high above their heads. To achieve intimacy with a huge crowd is the most thrilling thing for everyone involved, and at this point all 6,000 of us are as one. And then, just in front of me, I spot a teenage boy on the shoulders of his friend. The hoisted boy is punching the air, his face screwed with emotion while he sings every lyric from the bottom of his heart. I look out into the crowd and think about Kidso.

Through The Barricades – Across The Borders was Spandau Ballet in its pomp, the moment when all our stars aligned and burst their light upon the stages of Europe. With 'Barricades' a hit single, the UK tour saw us play to more people there than we'd ever done before. In Madrid we received the keys to the city, presented to us by the mayor in Franco's palace, and then played as the only artists on the bill to our biggest audience ever – over 100,000 in the town's Casa de Campo. Our final show was in front of 50,000 in a park in Treviso, and it brought the number of tickets sold on that tour to almost a million. As fireworks exploded in the night sky, we ran from the stage and threw ourselves into the windowless getaway van. High on the mutual adrenalin of the moment, we hugged and roared excitedly as sirens blazed us back through the city.

We had no idea that everything was about to break.

CHAPTER EIGHTEEN

FALLING

'*Kids would rather go out to a club than see a band … There's more energy and friction … You're the entertainment in a club.*' That was me, talking to *Creem* magazine's Annene Kaye in LA during our injury-stricken American tour of '85. It was a stance I saw as provocatively anti-rock'n'roll and threatening to its monolithic media. It was a line that I'd said many times since 1980. The interviews to promote the first album had all been about not touring and instead issuing 12-inch mixes to sympathetic clubs – 'there, the crowd are the stars', I would say. But those wheels of steel we'd set in motion in the early eighties were now picking up such speed they were about to railroad New Pop off its highly polished tracks. To take another analogy, the monster was about to kill its maker.

In the summer of 1987 a DJ called Danny Rampling was holidaying in the super-hip island of Ibiza. Here, along with Paul Oakenfold and a few other DJ friends, he discovered the Balearic beats that would inspire him. On his return to London, Danny began promoting his own club, Shoom, based around what he'd heard in Ibiza, while Paul started his Spectrum nights at Heaven along similar grooves. They plugged their Roland 303s into a desire to dance and that growing need to be one's own star, the celebrity of the dance floor. One more ingredient and it would have its own name. The drug I'd sampled on my first trip to New York had been rebranded with the more does-what-it-says-on-the-tin label of Ecstasy. With that little tab thrown into the mix, Acid House was born.

It was the first youth movement since the one we'd helped to form, and suddenly, we were yesterday's men. *The Face*, our bible up till that point, was now throwing its focus upon these new clubs, ones that included the growing '*Mad*chester' scene at the Hacienda, and their own superstar DJ, Mike Pickering. By the following year it would be enormous and the summer of 1988 would become known as *The Summer of Love*. For me, that phrase couldn't have been more appropriate.

Coming back to London after the tour, Tony and I give a performance of 'Through The Barricades' at Wembley Arena on behalf of the Prince's Trust. We get to play with the 'house band' that includes Eric Clapton, Midge Ure and Phil Collins. Tony and I end the evening performing 'With A Little Help From My Friends' with George and Ringo. Given what was about to happen, the title couldn't have been more ironic.

I continued my tour partying at London's new clubs. There was Oliver Peyton's RAW and City of Angels, Quiet Storm with Davina McCall on the door, and Robert Perino's Crazy Larry's with 'wild child' majorettes Amanda de Cadenet and Emma Ridley on the dance floor, underage girls flaunting chrome belt buckles that spelled 'Fuck'. The bars were all slamming tequila and cokespeak, while the clothes were as ripped and torn as the personalities within them. Even though I was in the process of moving into a new house in Highgate with Lee, I'd be out without her most nights. Like Britain's youth, I too was looking for something new.

October, and I find myself at Nick Fry's Café de Paris. There has to be more than my passionless relationship keeping me in the West End and away from Lee; maybe it's a pathetic effort to find my clubland glory days again, wanting to be part of the London night and its freshly whetted edge, but it's late, and once more the drinking's been tough.

I spot her from the bar. She's sitting on a chair near the dance floor, hugging her knees up to her chin, her pale, round face smudged with mascara, raw with tears. It's the girl I'd first seen growing from an imaginary flowerpot. The previous year I'd met her for the first time since that week in Spain – by chance she'd been cast in the video of 'Fight For Ourselves' and screen-kissed Steve. But now Sadie and I are talking. I help her with her tears. I'm not thinking about going home.

I'd seen her only the week before. Standing outside my new house, she and a girlfriend jog by me on their way to the park. A flirty 'Hi!' and then a few days later the two of them are knocking on our door and Lee is serving us all tea. Within a fortnight, a big storm will come and fell the ancient trees upon the heath, and in the aftermath I'll walk with Lee and tell her that it's over. It was as though I'd told her the paper hadn't been delivered that morning. It had come to an end for her too. Of course, I didn't say that it was due to the flowerpot girl I'd been visiting in West Hampstead and nights feeling new again, nights spent sipping Earl Grey tea and listening to Van Morrison and burning ylang-ylang. Nights not thinking about the band.

How strange *that* was.

Lee went back to Highbury and Sadie came to Highgate. Everything was happening so fast that I wondered why I hadn't done it before. It was as though time were running out and I had to move quickly to save myself, move how she moved, move at the speed of love. Watching her, I was reminded of one of those toy cars, the kind that hit walls and spin off in other directions.

If Lee had satisfied my conservative side then Sadie represented the sense of danger that I lacked – a devilish alter ego to balance my natural cautiousness. I wanted to hold her hand and have her pull me into those wild places I'd never dare go before. My parents were shocked by the changes, but this was for me, not others. It was about time I indulged myself, lost it a little. I'd cared too much for far too long. It was the ride I'd never dared take, and I didn't care where it would end. Part of it was born out of wanting to be free; part of it, I'm sure, was born out of anger.

She was the catalyst for something that had been brewing inside me for a while, a frustration with the endless cycle of touring and writing. During the last tour I'd withdrawn myself more and more: not connecting with my brother like I used to, and rarely socialising with Tony and Steve. Even my regular calls to Dagger had dried up. I lived in fear of being found out as a charlatan, that Steve would come along one day and blow me out of the musical water and everyone would have me sussed for the fake that I was. If it hadn't been for Steve I would never have been here, and yet I'd forgotten how to communicate with him, thank him, embrace him. I'd become tired of pouring myself into the band. A rest might have been the answer. I chose love and destruction.

And then suddenly I had the urge to write again. More than ever. 'Crashed Into Love' came first, then they all came falling out. 'Big Feeling'; 'Be Free With Your Love'; 'Empty Spaces'; they all rolled off my tongue. I called Toby, our keyboard player. He had the latest computerised recording technology. It gave me the ability to make demos with drum samples that could sound like the real thing. We set up in the rehearsal studio usually reserved for the whole band, and the two of us spent days arranging and recording, tweaking and mixing, until I had a set of demos that almost covered a whole album. Now all I had to do was play them to the others. Whether unconscious or wilful, I must have understood that it was a huge mistake.

The demo cassette delivered itself like a letter bomb. It was a fait accompli of arrangements that destroyed the rest of the band's organic input in a flash. But I guarded the tapes like a loyal pit bull – *herein lies my love*. John was hurt the most. Understandably. The programmed drums had removed his input. And yet, in my strange, faithless behaviour, I even tried to persuade him that we should use the programmed drums instead. Was I the same man who'd once protected our drummer at the expense of losing the great Trevor Horn as producer? It was as though I were at war with our philosophy. It was as though I were at war with the band.

In St Lucia I write MARRY ME in the sand, and she agrees before a bright wave comes and sucks it smooth. But back home, under grey Soho skies, our decision crashes heavily. Sitting with the band and friends at a birthday dinner for Gary Langan, Sadie and I happily announce our engagement. Steve stands and hugs me, but some of the band's partners seem less than congratulatory. Lee had been part of their group; her rejection and Sadie's arrival rocks them. One girlfriend bursts into tears – she was about to proudly announce *their* forthcoming union, she tells me. I don't know what to say, or why the fact that I'm getting married should upset her so much, but she flies to the toilets. Sadie goes to find her and becomes trapped there by a group of them, informing her what a foolish idea it is, given my historic lack of commitment to anything other than myself. A boil has been lanced and the pus is now unstoppable. We're all caught in this private room with poor Gary Langan's birthday cake hovering in the doorway. We try to move on but the drama has already snuffed the celebrations out. The next day I phone my mother, and for the first time since being a child, I cry.

Six weeks later I'm standing outside the little Saxon church of St Peter's in Stanton Lacy, waiting to get married. She'll wear an A-line wedding dress cut above her knees and pose coquettishly in sunglasses, as impudent as ever, even on her wedding day. As Martin stands by me, I watch the rest of the band arrive with their partners in a streamlined coach that Dagger has arranged. I watch it jolt to a halt on the gravelled path of the church, and realise that my heart is now elsewhere.

Becoming Ronnie didn't help. I was suddenly looking in two directions outside of the group. More importantly, the process was beginning to infringe upon the band's business. Martin and I were back with Anna Scher and Charles Verrall to do workshops for *The Krays*, which occasionally meant having to be absent from the recording studio during the making of the album. Anciano and Burdis had secured the rights from Roger Daltrey and the film was all ready to happen, although a date to start filming – as well as a director – had still not been decided upon. The workshops were a chance for Martin and I to bond again. Something had slipped away from us over the last few years since leaving home and buying Mum and Dad their house in Poole, but here was a project where we *had* to explore our brotherly connection. We may have been refinding our love, but it was helping to split the band into two camps, and Dagger was trying to hold us all together.

He wanted us to get away from London, to record in LA and hopefully connect with CBS America. He was haunted by the lack of interest shown by them towards the *Barricades* album, which was ironic, given America was the reason we'd joined them in the first place. 'It's my fault, Steve,' I told him one day. 'I keep changing our style. I should have just written 'True' over and over again.' *America likes to bracket you. That's how their radio works.* I'd heard it enough times. But because of Sadie, and my need to be around for the movie's preparation, I'd pitched to stay in London to record, and Olympic Studios in Barnes become our dysfunctional home in that summer of '88.

For the rest of the band, the movie must have felt as though we were being unfaithful towards them. For my part, I felt they were being unfair, given all the commitment to the band I'd shown over the years. Self-preservation was suddenly everything. I called Dagger and told him that I wanted to be individually credited for production on the new album as I'd done so much work on the demos. I'd always spent a great deal of time in the studio and the band had had joint production credits with Swain and Jolley as well as with Gary Langan, but this time I wanted some personal recognition. I knew this would be our final album and I didn't care what the others thought. I felt as though I'd been taken for granted for far too long and I was angry. As little trenches were already opening up, Dagger tried to persuade me otherwise, but I was determined. The blue touchpaper had been fizzing for a while; I wanted to blow some more heat into it.

Around this time, I made another decision. Since the early eighties I'd had my own publishing company. It collected the money I earned as the songwriter for Spandau Ballet. Brian Carr had recommended the autonomy and Dagger successfully ran it from his office. I wanted my company to contribute towards the running costs of the band. To me, it seemed a fair thing to do, and so I did it on a year-by-year basis. Now, with the end looming, I chose to stop that contribution. I told Dagger and Martin. Dagger told the others. There was no confrontation about it, but it was a decision that would have a very slow-burning fuse indeed, and more destructive firepower than anything I could possibly imagine.

The door of Broadmoor Hospital closed like an airlock. The air I breathed seemed rank, poisonous even, heavy with the carbon dioxide of killers. I was inside Britain's infamous high-security psychiatric prison and on my way to meet one of its most celebrated inmates. The building's Victorian Gothic design, oppressive even for the sanest mind, seemed steeped in the malevolence of some of the darkest crimes ever committed. Here, somewhere around me, resided the child-killer Ian Brady, the Yorkshire Ripper, Peter Sutcliffe, and the man I'd come to see, the leader of a fraternal duo that once held London in its grip of fear – Ronnie Kray.

The Kray twins threatened, they hurt, they killed, and they evaded the police and justice for nearly fifteen years. Eventually the conspiracy of silence crumbled and in 1969 they were imprisoned for a minimum of thirty years for the murders of George Cornell and Jack 'The Hat' McVitie.

I was here to find something in Ronnie that would help me portray him in the movie of his life: a voice, a speed, a weight. Philip Ridley, a new writer – living coincidently in Bethnal Green, the heartland of the Krays – had delivered a script that would hopefully play out the story as a heightened, Grand Guignol telling of the twins' lives; a stylised East End opera.

Ronnie was wearing a sky-blue seersucker suit when we met. In Broadmoor they're not prisoners but *patients*, allowed to wear their own clothes and meet visitors in the large canteen that acts as a social hub. He held his arm high to shake my hand and welcomed me to a little table that he'd chosen for our meet. I felt his grip and noticed the large gold cufflink-containing a diamond-encrusted R. He looked thin within his shirt collar; gaunt; surprisingly, an old man; no longer the large bulldog powerhouse once known as the Colonel. Legend has him sitting alone in his East End apartment, playing with his pet boa constrictor and listening to recordings of Winston Churchill's speeches, firing himself up for murder. Now he was politely ordering a non-alcoholic lager from a nervous-looking inmate and offering me a seat.

He noticed my earring. He had probably been informed that I'd played in a pop band for the last ten years and, I thought, maybe he was worried that I wouldn't cut the mustard. 'You won't wear that when you play me, will you?' His voice was unusually high, even a little camp, in an old-fashioned way. Ronnie was openly homosexual

at a time when it added to his list of misdemeanours. It was a contra-
dictory twist to his macho status that would have unsettled his enemies
even more.

'No, Ronnie. I'll take it out when I'm you.'

I wasn't nervous, although Ronnie had the disconcerting habit of
looking directly into your eyes without ever glancing away. I felt that I
had to look back, hold his stare, gain his blessing. I wanted to understand him. I needed to empathise.

After some small talk and a few sips of the watery beer I asked him
if he'd ever felt competitive with his twin Reggie during their heyday.

He looked shocked. 'Never! Never. We were a team.'

Maybe I'd gone too far too soon, but I didn't believe him. I already
knew too much about him. He tasted his beer and I noticed his cufflinks
again. 'I like those.'

'Look.' He opened his jacket and proudly revealed a monogram on
his shirt breast: a blue RK with a small crown embroidered on top. *I'll
use that*, I thought.

'How is it for you in here, Ronnie?'

'It's OK. Lots of nice people. We all get on.' And then he said something that was obviously on his mind. 'It's important to me that my
mum doesn't swear.' He meant in the film.

Ronnie was famously devoted to his mother. When she died, the
Krays were allowed out to her funeral, and stood handcuffed to freak-
ishly tall prison officers, chosen in an effort to literally belittle the twins
in front of the media frenzy.

'I never heard her swear in my life,' he said gently.

Ronnie came from a theatrical version of the past. His clothes and
style, his ethics and morals, his London, had all been in contradiction
to the counterculture of the sixties. His was a nostalgic version of Good
Old England where men dressed as men and women listened; where

the social order within this lowest of classes was a microcosm of ancient feudalism; there, Ronnie was King.

'Can I ask you – how did it feel when you killed George Cornell?'

On 9 March 1966, Ronnie had walked into a packed pub on the Whitechapel Road called the Blind Beggar, unloaded a 9mm Mauser into a petty gangster's sweaty forehead and sauntered out. It took more than a year for anyone to admit to seeing it happen.

'I didn't feel anything. I'd fucking do it again if I could.' Ronnie was leaning across the small institutional table, staring straight into my eyes. 'I walked in, and I saw him sitting on a stool by the bar. I went up to him and he said, "Hello, Ron." I pulled out my gun and shot him through the head. I remember he fell forwards, which surprised me – and blood was coming out. I went straight home and told my brothers what had happened and gave Reggie my clothes to burn. I had a bath and we sat and listened to the news on the radio, and it came on that Cornell had been killed and I thought thank fuck for that.' I thought he meant that if Cornell had still been alive he might have told the police who'd tried to kill him; but Ronnie continued: 'Because if he wasn't ... I'd have to go back and do him again.'

There was a moment's silence and we sipped some beer from the thin cans. I was in the position of trying not to judge him with my own ethics. I needed to understand what made him angry. Or sad.

'Do you regret it, Ronnie?'

'*No*,' he fired back. 'I'd do it again if I could.'

I'd meant did he regret everything, all of it, not just the public assassination of another gangster. A look of softness crossed his grey, hatched face. 'I do regret hurting my mum.'

We shifted our gaze. The space between us had suddenly become uncomfortably close.

'I'm sorry,' he said quietly, 'I get a bit dehydrated. It's the medicine they give me.' And then suddenly it was over. 'I've gotta go. It was nice to meet you.'

Through his glasses his eyes looked rheumy. He stood to leave. The area was now full of visitors and inmates. In a far corner sat a man. I was sure it was him.

'What about the Yorkshire Ripper, Ronnie? How's he treated here?' Peter Sutcliffe had serially murdered thirteen women.

'He's all right. We have to get on in here.'

I watched Ronnie leave, straight-backed and proud, but shrinking in his suit. He'd obviously dressed for our meeting. It was impressive.

The obsequious inmate who'd served us earlier returned and put the bill on the table. It was for £100!

'I'm sorry, we only had *two beers*,' I said.

'Hope you don't mind, but Ronnie put a few fags on there.'

I paid the money. I was desperate to get some air.

Somehow, through all the bitterness, we managed to finish the album. 'Raw' was to be the first single. A return to 'Chant'-style funk with a swamp-infested, malevolent beat that in our opinion would take Spandau Ballet straight back to the dance floor. It wasn't to be. By then Rampling's Acid was burning through the UK clubs, and we weren't even warm. We should have read the signs earlier. Shooting the single's cover in a deserted market, I'd made a comment on what Tony was wearing, suggesting that it wasn't right for the picture. Instead of the support I expected from the others, I got Steve flying at me. I bit back. It wasn't about Tony's clothes at all, it was about everything. We were sick of each other. Or maybe they were just sick of me.

Then I got the call from Dagger that I'd long dreaded.

'Gary. Steve wants you to go to his house.'

'Why?'

'He's got a song he wants to play to you.'

'What, he's written a song?' I heard the panic in my voice and tried to rein it in.

'That's right.'

'But we've already finished the album.'

'Just go and listen to it.' Dagger was worn out with it all, I could tell. 'Give him a call.'

So this was to be the moment when I'd be revealed as a hoax. Song-writing was a con trick, and Steve had worked out how to play it. Maybe he would even play it better. Reluctantly I made the call.

Steve had moved into a house farther up my road and yet I hadn't been to visit him once, such was my growing fear. As I gathered myself to leave I thought of the times in his parents' Bourne Estate flat, listening to Stevie Wonder and playing songs together on guitar; of seeing the Sex Pistols and dreaming of making a band of our own. We were the inseparable centre of group operations. All changed because of my para-noia. I remembered those days, yet still couldn't shake off my anxiety, couldn't connect those two boys with the men we now were. My fear hung heavily on me as I pulled myself up the hill to his house.

We sat awkwardly together in his living room and I listened to the taped demo. Steve seemed equally nervous. 'I just want your blessing, Gary.' When he put it that way I felt crushed, ridiculous. It pointed me out as the pompous fool that I was.

'It's good, Steve. Let's do it.'

In the end, the album, which we entitled *Heart Like A Sky*, had a quality that was unmistakably Spandau Ballet, but it lacked our unani-mous belief, and in 1989, it lacked relevance. Outside, the decade we'd helped to create was in its final death throes; but I was already planning my escape.

CHAPTER NINETEEN

BEING RONNIE

I knew the story. Even the so-called truth. And as for the legend? Well, that was everywhere.

'You know how they got their superpowers, don't ya?'

Martin and I were sitting in the back of a black cab and being driven over Waterloo Bridge. Since it had been announced that the Kemp brothers – '*two preening pop stars*' – were about to play the Kray twins in a film, everyone, especially cabbies, wanted to inform us with titbits of their Kray knowledge. I'd started to dread it. Once you were in the back, the glass partition dividing you would slide open and a corner of a mouth would appear through it.

I caught the driver's eye in his rear-view mirror. 'No, I don't know. How did they get their *superpowers*?'

'Their mother used to get them to drink the juice the greens was boiled in.' He didn't laugh. He was serious. He slid the partition closed as though we were in a confession box. He'd delivered his part of the legend.

Over the next few months, random people would offer up more clues: greengrocers would give you a morsel along with your spuds; solo drinkers in bars would surprise you sotto voce while not even glancing up from the head of their pint; at Highbury stadium, some-

one coming back to his seat holding Wagon Wheels and a hot choco-
late might offer another sweetener your way. But cabbies had the real
meat and potatoes of the legend. No other profession seemed to know
them as well as they did.

'I drove the twins once.'

'No, really?'

'They sat right where you are now. Shall I tell you what happened?'
He was going to anyway. 'I was coming up to a T-junction and Ronnie
tells me to turn right. Then Reggie says, "No, it ain't, Ron, it's
left." Then they're shouting at me – "Right!" – "Left!" – "Right!" –
"Left!" I didn't know what to do. I ended up driving straight into the
fucking wall.'

Since my experience meeting Ronnie in Broadmoor, I had continued
my research into his life elsewhere. I needed to find him. One afternoon
Martin and I drove to an estate of high-rise blocks in Bethnal Green to
meet their Aunt May, who was to be played in the movie by Charlotte
Cornwell. As Martin drove his Porsche into the estate, a police car came
up behind us, lights flashing. We stopped and got out of the car. I was
armed with a huge bunch of flowers that we'd bought on the way.

One of the two coppers was already on the pavement. He looked
surprised. 'It's the Kemp brothers, innit?'

'Yes.'

'What you doing round here?'

'We've come to see an aunt of the Krays. She lives here somewhere
– Aunt May?'

'Ah right. Yes, 'course. Do you know where she is? We'll show you
if you like.' He pulled their car in front of ours and escorted us to her
block. We parked up and thanked them.

'Give her our best, will you.' There was deference in his voice. It
seemed that the legend still held weight in these parts.

We took the piss-stained lift up to her flat. Charlie, the twins' brother and now 'technical adviser' on the movie, answered the door. He had bright eyes, a nicotine grin and a leathered face. On top of his head sat a twisted whip of lively grey hair. He took us through. Inside, Aunt May sat aged and smiling in her armchair, and for a moment, I thought of Nan, puffing herself away all those years ago, out of time and lost in that soulless high-rise they'd dumped her in. To the side of the old Kray, a broad picture window looked out over what would have once been her nephews' grand domain. Somewhere out there was Vallance Road, where their family house had stood, untouched by the fearful developers who'd demolished the rest of the buildings around it. Or so the legend tells us.

Charlie escorted the bouquet off to the kitchen and May directed us to a glass cabinet in the corner of the room. In it she'd built a little shrine to the twins. A picture of them wearing sharp Italian suits, walking their old East End, dominated the case, while in front of it, on a glass shelf, she'd placed two Ronson lighters, a cigarette case and a plastic comb – saintly relics from another world. Apart from the fact that the twins were 'little terrors but lovely boys', we didn't learn very much about them; but it was a connection with a cockney past that we'd come for, a past that had long since gone. Aunt May was one of the last standing. Outside, the Bengali community had replaced the Jews, while the twins' tribe had mostly gone downriver to Essex. Or prison.

May was holding a photograph album. She opened its padded cover and delicately slid the crisp tissue paper aside. The landscape pages were studded with black-and-white pictures of the twins with their family and friends. Lots of beery smiles in clubs and pubs. Women in sequins and pearls, men in heavy suits and ties, all smoking happily. But there was something strange. Two or three of the photographs had the empty shapes of what looked to be people neatly cut from them.

'Why are some pictures like that, May?'

'Because they, darling, was horrible people.' Terrible villains they must have been too, to be purged in such a Stalinesque fashion by the old bird. And so exquisitely jigsawed.

'Really?'

'Oh yeah, horrible. They were the sods who turned Queen's evidence against our boys.'

It was a kind of East End voodoo, cut out like little paper juju dolls. God only knows what she'd done with them afterwards.

Ray Birdis arrived, and after introducing himself to May, made a short speech. 'Aunt May – because we're portraying you as a character in the film, I've a duty, as producer, to give you this one pound coin in payment.' He held it up towards her with a smile.

'Ooh, lovely! Here, put it in me knickers!' And she waved her skirt at him playfully, giving us a hint of what a game young girl she once must have been. They were getting more than a pound each, though. Controversy would surround the film later when it was revealed that the family had received payment for giving their 'blessing' to the film. It certainly gave them a financial incentive for the movie to be made. At that time, Martin and I were a long way off playing the twins – I would eventually put on a stone in weight for the part – and looked the delicate flowers that we were, earrings included; but as we both thanked Aunt May for the tea and stood to leave, Charlie suddenly recoiled in his chair.

'My God,' he said, putting a hand up to shield his eyes, 'for a minute, I thought it was me own two brothers standing there!' He needn't have worried – we were going to make the film.

For the movie's boxing scenes Martin and I trained with ex-world champion John H. Stracey, at the Henry Cooper gym, a hardman's paradise above a pub on the Old Kent Road. The old cockney actor Johnny Shannon was here most days. He'd sit heavily on a stool and watch the young fighters do their work, including a great prospect called Lennox Lewis. Johnny was one of those actors who'd always play villains, including a thug in my early movie *Hide and Seek*, although when I mentioned it to him, he seemed to have no memory of the film at all. I concluded that years of playing gangsters had left Johnny with an automatic response of denial and alibi whenever anyone claimed to have seen him somewhere.

Martin and I sparred with each other under John H. Stracey's rigorous supervision. The minute clock on the wall counted down the rounds as we jabbed and hooked until a bell rang and John called time. But that wasn't time enough for the two brothers. Both of us, riled by each other's over-exuberance in the ring, slammed on while the ex-world champion tried to break us up. During difficult days on the road, we'd often ended up at each other's throats. We were an outlet for relieving pressure within the band, one that would heal itself up as quickly as it had opened. It just so happened that, at this time, we had a lot we wanted to throw our fists at. Of course, we were breaking the Marquess of Queensberry's famously treasured rules, so the boxing faithful within the gym stopped what they were doing to stare, open mouthed, at the anarchy in the ring.

'It's all right,' John explained to them, 'it's all right – they're brothers.'

Oh, they're brothers – it's understandable, then, was the general shrug of opinion as normality returned. There were some things Martin and I didn't have to learn about being the twins.

I pushed weights and ate boxes of Mars Bars and eventually they dyed my hair black. Philip Ridley's vision was darkly stylised. He saw them as a pair of murderous crows, mobbing any rivals who dared to challenge their power; black hair, black suits, black ties. Later, while living in Hollywood, I worked with Quentin Tarantino. He told me that before shooting *Reservoir Dogs*, he'd handed all his crew tapes of *The Krays*, saying that this was how he wanted his movie to look. Philip Ridley and *The Krays* are to thank for that particular piece of cinematic iconography.

Principal photography began on 14 September. It should have been a terrifying prospect, so many people had opinions as to what the Kray brothers were like and therefore how we should play them. But Martin and I calmed our fears by accepting that *we* would be the ones who decided who the Krays were in this film; after all, very few people actually knew what they were like anyway. Well, very few people except for the crowd of extras that had been conscripted in for the boxing scene. Mostly members of the old firm that Charlie had brought down – Wilf Pine, Joey Pyle, Lenny McLean – plus various satellite villains who had helped their cause from afar. They all huddled on to the set, awaiting the arrival of the 'twins'.

'Oi, Martin. You doing the twitch?' It was one of the satellites. He and a friend had caught us leaving our trailer.

'The twitch? What twitch.'

They were both dressed in the extras' wardrobe of fifties suits and trilbies. 'Oh no.' The man turned to his friend. 'He doesn't know about the twitch, Paul.' Paul, whoever he was, rolled his eyes in exasperation. So much for these two, he was probably thinking. The man explained it slowly to Martin: 'Reggie had a twitch.'

'Did he?'

'Yeah. Famous.'

'Show him,' said Paul, nudging his friend.

The man prepared himself for what was obviously his party piece, and then suddenly flicked his head to the left while momentarily tensing the muscles in his face. Paul nodded sagely, affirming his friend's skill in imitating the apparently famous twitch.

'Right.' Martin remained calm. 'No, I'm sorry, mate, I'm not doing the twitch. I've never heard of it.' The two experts looked disappointed as we headed on set.

We're shooting the scene in the ring. It's exhausting as we circle one another again and again while punching out our rehearsed choreography. Sugar-blood streams from our nostrils as we receive and lay on punch after punch. But it's an even tougher scene for Martin: every time he comes round to face the authority on Reggie's facial affliction, he can see them both looking up at him, twitching for all they're worth, desperate to get Martin to join in.

And then I spot someone who looks familiar. A white-haired, russet-faced man in his sixties. He's wearing a white three-piece suit with an open collar, and a matching coat draped over his shoulders. He's standing at the edge of the boxing tent and I'm not sure if he's in costume or not. He seems to be looking furiously at me. Then I realise who he is – the twins' great nemesis during the sixties and head controller of everything villainous south of the Thames, Charlie Richardson. He's obviously disgusted that a film is being made about the twins rather than him, and has arrived to show his revulsion to all present. Fortunately for me, he decides to express himself by walking out.

The disused station of Aldwych, near the Strand, was where a scene set in the London Underground during the Blitz was to be filmed, and I invited my parents along to watch. They'd driven up that morning from Poole in their new, blue Ford Escort that I'd recently bought for them, and Dad was more than a little excited at seeing a 'proper film' being made and, hopefully, a glimpse into his past. He'd worn a jacket and tie, while Mum had put on some best clothes for the day. I took them down the steep steps of the station, with its familiar cream brick tiling, and into the warm zephyrs of the platform. We passed the camera crew, negotiated our way through the paraphernalia of movie-making, and suddenly, before us, was the 1940s – the posters, the bedding, the mothers cradling babies, the elderly trying to sleep beneath issued blankets, the children with gas masks, frightened of the noise above. But it was all too close to reality for Mum. Her delicate fair skin quivered around her mouth, and for the first time I saw how much pain the war had been for her. She couldn't talk. She was struggling to hold back the tears. In her head the sound of bombing still reverberated. She wanted to go. As I walked her back up I realised that somewhere, way below the surface of her daily life, a little girl's story lay buried. It was a story that I would never manage to fully uncover.

During the filming I seemed to lose who I was when not Ronnie, suffering feelings of insecurity that often left me dark and depressed. Sadie arranged a surprise thirtieth birthday party for me and I sulked my way through it in a cap, self-conscious of the black hair that would fall around my face like a Mary Quant bob. But in my dressing room the following morning, as I combed the Brylcreem in and donned one of the suits tailored for me, I felt fantastic, galvanised. Ronnie lived in the detail: the black heart of the tiny Windsor knot; the permanently visible, three-quarters of an inch of white cuff, like the end of a magician's wand; the timely lift of the trouser leg when sitting, revealing a narrow ring of flesh above the sock; the single jacket button, fastened only when standing or walking; the vigorous *tap-tap-tap* of the cigarette end upon the top of the silver cigarette case, and the flip-top Ronson lighter, with its pebble-smooth body and masculine whiff of fuel. An armoury of style that told the world who he was. I'd sit and shine my shoes – *his shoes* – spitting on them and buffing them with long, dramatic swipes, just as I'd seen my father do when I was a child, and the smell of the black Cherry Blossom polish would take me back to our cramped Islington kitchen, to the sounds outside emanating from the Clarence, and to a past that had once belonged to men like Ronnie.

*

While Martin and I were being the Krays the rest of the band were waiting for us to become two-fifths of Spandau Ballet again. As far as they
were concerned the film had disrupted preparations for the forthcoming tour and was probably costing them money. It had also put the
album release back several times. Dagger hadn't wanted the record to
come out until after we'd finished shooting the movie, but owing to
the film's financing problems, that date kept shifting. In the end it was
released just as Martin and I were donning fifties suits for the camera.
We were therefore unavailable for initial publicity, and a TV appearance
somewhere in Europe had Spandau miming with two unknowns impersonating Martin and me on bass and guitar.

I understood how awful this must have been for the other three,
but it still hurt when Martin and I walked back into rehearsals only two
days after finishing the movie, and no one expressed any interest in what
we'd done over the past eight weeks. For me, the saddest loss of all was
my friendship with John. We'd been room-buddies, housemates, and
confidants. His wry, intellectual wit had made him master of badinage
on tour, and he'd lift my spirits on the more difficult days. Now, as the
tour rolled itself out, we found ourselves permanently at different ends
of the bus. I'd sit at the front with Martin, and find my escape in books,
while John, Tony and Steve claimed the TV room at the back. Martin
often tried to bridge the gap but invariably found himself rebuffed.
Nights, usually spent in hotel bars or clubs, would have me going to bed
early, afraid that alcohol would loosen tongues and end in confrontation. Even Steve, normally the head of comedy and entertainment,
inverted his usually spirited personality for the tour. We were all hiding,
protecting ourselves in case of an explosion. For Dagger, it manifested
itself physically. While he tried desperately to hold everything together,
his body decided that it had had enough. One day it suddenly crashed
and he found himself trapped hopelessly in a hospital bed, with a system
that desperately needed some peace and quiet.

In Barcelona things became too much for me. After the show, our Spanish promoter came backstage and swaggeringly said that he'd arranged a party for us, one that would go on till tomorrow morning. I thought it a little ridiculous given that we had to leave the hotel at 9 a.m. to drive to Madrid. I told him we'd go if he agreed to fly us up there instead of expecting us to travel by coach.

He suddenly darkened. 'If you'd written some hit songs and a better album it might have been possible, but I'm not making any money with you here this time!' I couldn't believe what I was hearing, but he continued. 'I built this band in Spain and now you're fucking letting me down!'

I grabbed him by his pathetic indoor scarf and rushed him against the dressing-room wall. Jabbing a finger near his face, I let rip. 'You cunt! What the fuck are you talking about! Our album's gold here!'

The band pulled me off, but it was too late. I was damaged. He'd spoken words that others in the room wanted to say, and we all knew it.

It couldn't have all been my fault. As the new decade began, change was everywhere. In Berlin I rented a small hammer and chisel and helped hundreds to knock bits of the Berlin Wall down; in a hotel room in Italy, I saw Nelson Mandela walking free in South Africa; and in Britain, Thatcher was on the eve of her own self-destruction. For Spandau Ballet, 1990 also seemed like a sell-by date, and the present like a new club we couldn't get into. But one night in January, just as we were about to go on stage in Brussels, my future suddenly revealed itself through a different door.

'Gary. Your wife's on the production office phone.'

'*Really?*' I was concerned. Why would she be calling me at this time? As I went, I felt the band's silence upon my back.

In a little office with old posters of smiling jazz players, I picked up the receiver that was lying on the desk.

'Hi, Sade, what's up?'

'I've got good news and bad news.'

'Give me the bad news.'

'I crashed the car.'

'What happened? Are you all right?'

'It doesn't matter – I'm OK. But listen – let me tell you the good news.'

For some reason it never occurred to me that getting married would mean having babies. I'd been far too interested in making songs to think about children. But at the age of thirty, and with my new tunes no longer in such demand, it seemed like the perfect moment. I looked up. The jazz players on the wall were still smiling.

News of a baby lightened everyone's mood and Sadie flew out to join us all in Rome. We indulged in the beauties of the city and hunted Caravaggio everywhere. Tony's wife arrived and we all ate alfresco together, happy to momentarily forget our troubles and celebrate our continuing success in this most wonderful country.

But Britain brought a different story. It felt cold and unwelcoming as we ground our way around its cities. In London we played the new arena, built in the cold financial heart of the eighties dream – Docklands. Tony's sore throat, plus our own growing feeling of cultural dislocation, kept us and the audience under par during a difficult first half in which we played the less-than-successful new album. Things warmed up, though, during the final half's more familiar numbers, and our usual London party had Geldof, John Taylor and Paul Young, plus family and friends, celebrating what was probably no more than a one-goal victory.

Our final show of the tour was in Edinburgh. And, as if to highlight our internal combustion, nothing went to plan. The keyboards detuned themselves, forcing us to restart a few numbers; 'True''s synthesised bass line transformed itself into a full horn section, and the roadies played their usual end-of-tour pranks – while performing our last number, a hail of ping-pong balls, hilarious from the wings, fell on grim faces.

And with that it was over. In a lyric book I have from the time, scribbled by a set-list of the night, is a note I made: *Played the last bar of 'Chant' and said our goodnights. Will it be the last time?*

It certainly would be years.

On Thursday, 26 April 1990, *The Krays* premiered in London at the Odeon Leicester Square. Sadie, now with bulge, squeezed into an Anthony Price number, while I donned a dinner suit, stitched by his own fair hands. That afternoon, fascinated by the newly televised House of Commons, I was shocked to see a London MP stand and ask Geoffrey Howe, the Home Secretary, if he was aware that a film based on the Krays' lives was to be released and that the Krays themselves would be profiting from it. The MP then asked Howe for an injunction to be put on the film. Howe replied in his pompous, public school voice that he was fully aware of the situation and would look into it. Oh, how their celebrity still rankled the establishment.

Dad, who'd come up with Mum for the premiere, watched it with me. 'That's good, innit?' he said, pointing his tea mug at Howe. 'Bit of extra publicity.'

Fabulous, I thought.

Around London, some cabbies had advertisements for the movie painted upon their taxis, while double-decker buses also carried the image of my brother and me as Reggie and Ronnie. The Krays legend had emblazoned itself on two other great historic icons of London. Below us the movie tagline read *Bonded by Blood*. It wasn't far wrong.

That night, one hundred black cabs were drafted in to take the guests to Leicester Square. The front three, carrying us and our families, were pristine sixties models, and delivered us to the front of the cinema, which was now mobbed by a huge crowd, all hoping to get a glimpse of pop stars, actors and gangsters. They weren't disappointed. On the steps of the Odeon someone approached me. In the movie there's a rather gruesome scene where I, as Ronnie, put a sword sideways through the mouth of another gangster, leaving him with what's known in the trade as a 'Chelsea Smile'.

'Gary. Pleased to meet you. D'you know that's me in the film? The sword? Ronnie did it to *me*.' It was a man in his sixties. He was smiling, and from the corners of his mouth ran the evidence he seemed most proud of.

Peter Medak had recruited some great British actors to support us in *The Krays*: Billie Whitelaw, Susan Fleetwood, Tom Bell and Steven Berkoff, to name but a few. Bolstered by the Krays' enduring legend, it all added up to a film that would become the most successful British movie for over twenty years. But something tainted that heady, spring evening for me: Tony and John had decided not to come. It was a statement by absence. I understood, but still it hurt. We were already beginning to go our separate ways.

CHAPTER TWENTY

A BIGGER SPLASH

I 'm driving on Sunset, top down, and running lines from a script in my head. The Marlboro Man is still smoking as I pass beneath him and head west to a meeting with one of Hollywood's biggest movie stars.

As much as LA's East Coast counterpart fascinated me, New York, with its galleries, phallic architecture and slick, urban scene, never felt dissimilar enough to London for my taste; and on a bad day, the city could swallow you whole. But in LA my glass was always half full, and usually with a plump olive floating in it. It managed to give me a sense of hope, even when failing, which, in the end, is what most people in the movie business do here.

But when LA's got a crush on you, it's the greatest town in the world. It might all be fake tan for the mind, but it left me with an inner glow at a time when I needed it. It also had a notable pop story. Be it in the cocaine canyons with the Mamas & the Papas, Little Feat, Crosby Stills Nash and Young, or by its crashing ocean, with the doo-wop of the Beach Boys and their attendant natty surf culture, where you could catch the perfect wave and ride it straight around the world, LA's rock stories had forever fascinated me. Over the years English bands had laced the town with a cocktail of outrages – scandalous anecdotes that had fired the loins of all swashbuckling descendants worthy of their place onstage – and made LA their own. But Hollywood was the real pull, and at the beginning of the new decade Sadie and I, accompanied by Finlay, our new baby boy, flew out to dip our toe into its big, blue pool.

Sadie was to meet the movie maestro Francis Ford Coppola, for the part of Lucy in his new production, *Bram Stoker's Dracula*. A few days earlier, in London, her agent enquired if she could 'put something down on tape' to send out to the casting director in LA. These auditions by proxy never worked. I suggested that she would have more chance of getting the part if we got on a plane to LA so that she could do the audition face to face. Within a week or so my theory had paid dividends and we were excitedly looking around West Hollywood for a home while she prepared to be Coppola's vampirical ingénue. A glass-fronted bungalow with a kidney-shaped swimming pool stood on top of Crescent Heights, overlooking the city like a thumbs-up. We took it. All I had to do was try and get a job too.

I'd found an agent in the US after Bob and Harvey Weinstein had helped to give *The Krays* some success there, and he'd put me up for a role the week we moved in. *The Bodyguard* was a slick script by Lawrence Kasdan – who'd been Oscar nominated for *The Big Chill* – and Kevin Costner's first film as producer and star since his enormous success with *Dances with Wolves*. It was about the music biz and centred on a pop diva called Rachel Marron, who was to be played by the singer Whitney Houston in her first acting role. Under a death threat from an obsessive fan, Rachel calls in an ex-presidential Secret Service bodyguard in the shape of Costner's character, Frank Farmer, and goes through a series of hate/love/hate/love relationships with him. I was up for the part of her spin-doctor, Sy Spector, an oily PR man who bathed himself in her reflected glory while hissing at any encroaching male threats. Well, that's how I saw him anyway. I'd met this sort of slick media player many times before and felt that I had a good fix on who Sy was. At least it impressed the casting director on my first reading. It took another audition in front of Costner's co-producer and director, the Englishman Mick Jackson, before finally getting to level three – meeting the man himself.

And so I arrive at Costner's ranch-style offices and, parking up, take one last look at the notes I've scribbled in the margins of the script. I know I'm close but I have to do well with Costner in order to nail it. In the reception I try to ignore the cute, LA'ed receptionist as well as the snappy *Variety* headlines beaming up from the side table, and instead attempt to concentrate on what's to come. There's no point running lines in my head, I know them too well, so I simply try to be Sy, which gives me the excuse to pick up *Variety* and let my eyes wander over to the receptionist – *well, it's what he would have done!* But the smiling casting director is now upon me with her clipboard and Polaroid camera and she's politely asking me to follow her through.

'How are you today?' she sings.

I was fine until you asked me that. What do you think? – I'm bloody terrified. 'I'm OK, thanks.' *Think Sy.* But as we walk down the corridor I'm confronted by a large photo of Costner holding his two Oscars. It's been strategically placed above his office door at the end, to remind people, just before they enter, of their place in his particular Hollywood food chain. She knocks while opening the door.

Inside, Kevin is deep in a sofa, hands behind his head with legs crossed on a wooden coffee table in front of him. He's wearing what look to be a pair of black-and-white pony-skin cowboy boots. *Don't stare at them!*

'Hey, Gary, how ya doing.' He leaps up and grabs my hand. He's tall but I like the way it makes me – as Sy – feel physically diminished. It helps. Sy's a long way from Ronnie, and my Englishness feels suddenly yet suitably uptight next to his thumbs-in-belt cowboy manner. We go through the ritual small talk and I discover his surprising knowledge of

English 'soccer'. I say yes to a coffee – this usually puts doing the scenes off for a few more minutes – but he's up already and waving his script pages at me. 'Fancy running some?'

It's an odd sensation auditioning. You know that the other people in the room are seeing if you fit their conception of the part – not if you can act! Although that does help – and in the preliminary chat you're trying to gauge what that conception is. You're acting as soon as you walk through the door because if you're too unlike the character from the moment they meet you then they've written you off before you've started.

'We see him as a kind of ... typical English guy.'

I cross my legs and sit a little more upright.

'But ... relaxed in difficult situations.'

I uncross my legs and slouch a little more sideways.

We're running the scene but Kevin's pied boots keep looming large in my periphery. They are purposely trying to put me off. I'm beginning to lose my concentration when Kevin suddenly snaps out of being the eponymous bodyguard. 'You know, Gary, I gotta tell ya something...'

Bollocks! It's not what they want. It was those boots of his!

'... I absolutely love your song "True".'

Now I'm really uncomfortable – I'm trying to be Sy Spector but I'm being pulled backwards into my old world. I thank him anyway; flattered, of course.

'Fact,' he gives me a shy smile, 'my wife and I like to call it *our* song. It reminds us of when we first met.' His Midwestern intonation and hokey compliment make me feel a little warm. And then something funny pops into my head – my plumber, a random taxi driver, some bloke in the supermarket, *and* now Kevin Costner have all said the same thing to me. People were getting married to that song. And, judging by Kevin's backslap, I was getting a part in his movie.

'True' was everywhere during that summer of '91, albeit in the shape of another tune. A young, black R&B act from New York, calling themselves PM Dawn, loved the song as well. They'd sampled it and blended it with a sexy, mellifluous melody of their own. What they needed now was to get permission to use it, and one afternoon they went into the downtown offices of their record label and played it to the owner of the company.

'Ha! You're joking! I know these blokes!' It was John Baker, known to us all as Mole, and one of the original Gang of Twenty-One. A Londoner, John had once worked for Rough Trade Records, selling singles and albums out of the back of a van, but now, at the age of thirty, and permanently settled in New York, he'd set up a label of his own and called it G-Street. He'd even started smoking cigars.

For all his whiteness, Mole was now a homey. 'Don't worry, man, this tune is *da bomb*! I'll get permission for it. I know the exact guy to ask.' And with that, he phoned Dagger.

Samples, or interpolations as they are known in the industry, were rare in those days, but Mole and Dagger soon came to a financial arrangement that pleased both of them, and as I filmed *The Bodyguard*, PM Dawn's 'Set Adrift On Memory Bliss' was suddenly the hottest thing on radio that summer.

It was a long shoot – four months – and an intriguing glimpse of a Hollywood movie-making machine in motion. During it, a crew member was killed when a mobile lighting rig went out of control and smashed into him. Out of respect we were given the rest of the afternoon off. The following day he'd been reduced to a small cut-out photograph of his head stuck on a white mug that was being passed around for donations to his family. These things happen; hey, the machine has to keep rolling.

Friends were all questioning me about Whitney's acting ability, but her famously immaculate timing in singing seemed to translate itself perfectly to her delivery nous as an actress, and in the scenes I was involved in she looked very comfortable. In any case, sitting next to her in the make-up trailer listening to her singing gospel at six in the morning was one of those sublime moments that life only occasionally delivers. From then on, as far as I was concerned, she could do no wrong.

Tony, Dagger and John were in town. With Martin and me acting, and an unspoken acceptance that the band would not be working, at least for the foreseeable future, Dagger had helped Tony sign a deal with EMI to record his first solo album. He was accompanied by John, whom he'd asked to play drums. Now, confident of our lives outside of the band, it was easier for us to meet again. I went over to the studio where they were recording and listened to his album in progress. It was a highly polished, West Coast affair, and listening in that darkened control room I felt my musical sap rising, pushed by a pulse of envy that they were making music without me, decent music, with guitar licks I could only dream of playing. Tony had obviously learnt the writing trick, and even John was finding it easy with an impressive composition of his own called 'Riverside'. I felt paranoid again – they had my songwriting thing sussed.

The last time we'd been in a studio together had been just after coming off of the *Heart Like A Sky* tour, and was a gruelling experience that we'd all chosen to forget. I'd been in no mood to write another Spandau album and Dagger knew it. We all wanted to step away from the band and take stock. Dagger was rightly worried that we'd not do another album together ever again, and, hoping for the best but planning for the worst, he called to tell me that if we went into the studio we'd trigger a payment from CBS for the advance on the next album. I suggested we find a song to cover rather than face each other in a musical confrontation of personal interests. Two songs were suggested: the Walker Brothers' 'You've Lost That Loving Feeling' (which had already been covered by the Human League) and Simon and Garfunkel's 'The Boxer'. 'The Boxer' was decided upon and I'd suggested that the composer and arranger Michael Kamen produce it.

I'd met Michael when he'd written the score for *The Krays*. He was a gentle bear of a man, but recording 'The Boxer' was an uncomfortable experience for him. The band weren't all on talking terms and, for him, there must have been no sense of recording a band – Martin already hankered for a future in acting and was certainly not dreaming of hit records and world tours, while I just wanted to go home as soon as possible each night. The final product was, not surprisingly, bland, with nothing about it that might suddenly reverse Spandau's limp exit from grace. We collected the CBS cheque but kept 'The Boxer' on the shelf, never to be released. It was the first time we'd ever done anything cynically, but by now there was little pride left. At the end of the recording there was no group meeting, no plans, no farewell, just a deceitful see-you-later, as I slipped out of the studio, and out of the band.

Now Tony and I needed to show one another that we were successfully existing in our respective new places, and the day after visiting him at his LA studio – and hopefully helping to patch up some of our ill-feelings towards one another – he reciprocated by coming to see me on the set of *The Bodyguard*. An estate in Beverly Hills was being used as Rachel's mansion, and Tony and I hovered around the lavish trestle table of food – known strangely as craft services – and, surrounded by pink bougainvillea and sunshine, we small-talked. I introduced him to Kevin and Whitney and felt pleased that some of our past problems were now seeming a little less consequential.

Someone called me to the set and, knocking back his coffee, Tony mumbled that he should be getting back to the studio. As a make-up girl flicked a brush across my face we said our goodbyes. I shook his hand and watched his tall frame leave down the lush path. I had no idea that it would be the last time we'd speak to each other for eighteen years.

That October, Sadie threw me a birthday party at our hilltop house. I was thirty-one. Paul McGann DJed while Gary Oldman and Winona Ryder danced; Richard E. Grant chatted with Harry Dean Stanton and Ben Kingsley and Tim Roth gatecrashed. I stepped out to the pool area that overlooked the twinkling matrix of the city and sucked on the straw of a cocktail. Sadie and I had just finished two of the biggest movies in Hollywood, PM Dawn had done something that Spandau could never achieve and taken me as a songwriter to number one in the *Billboard* charts, and Gandhi was in my house – albeit uninvited. Things couldn't get much better, I thought.

And I was right. The following year Sadie and I would be forced to give up the house, move down the hill, and no one would gatecrash my birthday party. *The Bodyguard* would become a huge hit but actors are everywhere in Hollywood and I was just another. Things would become increasingly hard, not just finding work, but keeping our relationship afloat. I'd gone from being in complete control of my artistic life to sitting in waiting rooms learning my lines next to other contenders, and that's if I was lucky enough to be offered the chance in the first place. I couldn't have been easy to live with. Often scripts would arrive – as did one called *Reservoir Dogs* – and I'd excitedly call my agent only to be told the part had gone. I'd moved from writing my own words to hoping I'd be allowed to speak those of others. I would shoot *Killing Zoe* with Tarantino producing, but it would only be a cult success; and then I'd turn down the part of the baddie in a movie called *The Mask* (with a new star, Jim Carrie) in order to play the lead in a Hungarian arthouse movie that would bomb. LA doesn't like rejection, and its crush on me was soon to be over. And with it, my marriage to Sadie.

Coming back to Britain, devastated, barely holding my head above the emotional waters that were flooding my life, I got a call from Steve. He told me he wanted to do another Spandau album, but seemed prepared for my response. I didn't want to do it and I told him so. He was angry and fumed at me – I owed him this, he said; after all these years he felt I had a responsibility to him and the band. I didn't want to do it, though. I couldn't. I put the phone down on him. Now Steve, the most important of them all, the boy with whom I'd begun everything, would leave my life. What I didn't know then was that I wouldn't hear his voice again until he took the stand against me, nearly a decade later, in Court 59 of the Royal Courts of Justice, and made the oath to tell the whole truth, and nothing but.

LONDON, 30 APRIL 1999

I an Mill's wig sits snug within his briefcase as he shakes my hand on the steps of the court. It's over. The day seems bright after the shadows of the grand hall. Mr Justice Park had heard all he needed to and the final box-file had been closed and trolleyed off to somewhere musty and dark. For nearly six weeks the case had ground on through the ups and downs of Spandau Ballet's story and left us all emotionally confused. Everything we'd ever achieved now seemed tainted, having been dragged through this Kafkaesque experience of pompous wigs and antiquated language, with all its accompanying accusations and ramifications. It had been absurd to watch the merry toe-tapping of the judge while a little CD player perched on his huge desk played our music. He'd flatteringly told us how much he liked what he'd heard, and both sides rapidly calculated if this was a good thing for them or not. *What signs was he giving?* We'd stare at him for any nuance that might offer us a hint as to the way he was leaning. We looked for any crumb of hope, praying that he wouldn't sweep them, and us, from his desk.

Throughout the trial, and leading up to it, I'd comforted myself with one thought: none of us was lying. I had to believe this; the alternative was too horrific to consider. I had a particular memory of events and so did they. Our story was a series of subjective ones, ones that altered themselves with time and influence, and where you happened to have stood upon the stage over the last twenty-three years. That's why so many witnesses were called, all with their own versions, so that Park could somehow mine truth from repetition. And now, after a few weeks of painful limbo, we'd been called back to the court and told the judgement he'd arrived at.

My decision in 1987 to stop the payments from my publishing company to the band's company had brought us all, twelve years on, crashing into court. Tony, Steve and John had said that I'd promised to pay them for ever; Dagger and I said differently. The final outcome was a public display of all our dirty washing. None of us was leaving the court feeling good about ourselves.

Ian, his white barrister bands flapping gaily in the breeze, leads me down the steps with a hop – he seems lighter in victory – and ushers me towards the waiting media that stand between me and home. I blather some statement about the rights of songwriters being upheld but I'm desperate to get away. Of course I was relieved – for three years an accusing finger had been pointed at me – but most of all I was deeply ashamed that it had come to this: a proud band and a group of friends, smashed and broken on the steps of the Royal Court. It was irredeemable now. Surely.

I panic as I lose Dagger but then he's pushing me into a taxi and the flashbulbs are bursting against the glass. The cab's radio is on and the reporter is coming live from somewhere just behind me on the pavement. I turn and look through the rear window for a man with a mike. There are a few. The one on the radio is saying how Gary Kemp has won the case brought against him by his three band mates. *Won? That's a joke!* What have I won, for Christ's sake! It feels like a mess.

Dagger's next to me and suggests going into Soho for a drink. The weather's announcing spring and everyone's pouring out of work early and into the old square mile of fun – the place where it all began, where it all started, so different now. Here, in 1979, if you wore make-up or outlandish clothes you'd have to hide from the bigots that patrolled the place. Now, no longer the furtive haunt of clandestine tribes, Old Compton Street is London's very own Boys' Town and alive with open-air dining and open air-kissing. Transvestites don't even get stared at any more, so common is their drag. The place seems full with diners sucking on lobster claws or twirling angel-hair pasta, slurping Kir Royales or necking Mexican beers. It's an urban promenade, a symbol of something good the eighties left behind.

We pass 69 Dean Street and I glance at the step where once I met a Cossack with a quiff and paid £2 to change my life, and it occurs to me that these narrow Georgian streets are a palimpsest of ghosts, endlessly playing out their stories of hope; every corner impressed with the strata of Soho lives. But then the taxi pulls up and we're outside the Groucho Club with Dagger paying the fare. Here I'd done a lot of personal damage over the years but today would be a sedate drink. I sign in and immediately people are coming up and congratulating me as though the judgement were an award I'd just received. I'm given a glass of champagne and a backslap. After one or two of these I've got to get out. Somewhere, in another bar, three old friends are drinking for other reasons and I feel diminished by the thought. I'm also aware that this whole thing has taken its toll on Dagger. He'd believed in this band more than anyone and now it was crushed. I thank him for everything and leave. He's OK – he's already got one foot in the night.

I move against the tide that floods in as I walk out of Soho and to the corner of Charing Cross Road. I grab an *Evening Standard* and a taxi by the Palace Theatre and, flicking through the paper, see a picture of me standing outside the court. I can't read it – I've had enough. I leave it on the back seat.

I'm happy to get back home. Since Sadie left I've lived alone in Highgate. I've grown to enjoy it. I can keep things under control this way, ordered. Finlay stays with me more often than not and that I love. We've even started to climb mountains together, making weekend trips to the Lakes, building a one-to-one relationship that gives me more joy than anything I've ever done before. I've a piano upstairs that I've been bashing on – trying to write a musical with my good friend Guy! There's even a possibility we may get it on at the National. Now that would be something.

I make myself a pot of camomile and phone Martin, as I had done every day during the trial. I begin to tell him about the morning while idly picking up the remote and switching on the kitchen TV. It's six o'clock. On the news is what looks surprisingly like Soho, but it's in chaos.

'Mart, can I call you back?'

There are people lying in the road with blood on their faces; people being stretchered, rushed to ambulances; sirens, police, paramedics everywhere. It is Soho, it is! There's the Admiral Duncan pub, or at least what looks like it. Is this now? The reporter is interviewing some-one. A man is saying how he was in the pub when the bomb went off. A bomb in Soho! It's a gay pub. It's because they're gay.

Soho, our great emblem of multicultural, liberal London, and the geographical and social heartland of my own story, has been hit by the bomb of a bigot, its tolerance punished in one limb-shearing flash. And just when they all thought it was safe. Suddenly I remember Dagger's still there and call his number. He's all right, he says; he's going home. The fun was over. None of us had anything more to celebrate.

INTO HISTORY

The final metal clasp pops open and the wooden front drops away from the long flight-case that stands as tall as a man in front of me. For the last nineteen years, since 1990's last show, it has remained closed, like some rock'n'roll sepulchre. Inside, the familiar silver board of customised effects and amps that had once stood with its LEDs flashing at my side of the stage reveals itself. The humorously dated Dymo Tape labels still boldly indicate what each knob is for, while the chinagraph markings indicate where I'd once decided were the best positions for them. My guitar tech pops a smaller case and opens its hinged door. Inside is my cream Stratocaster guitar, my number one for all Spandau shows. He removes it from its foam bed, tunes it at his workstation and, finished, hoists its strap up for me to step into. I notice the little mother-of-pearl dove on the guitar's upper body – the Spandau symbol, still flying after all these years – as I slip my arm through the strap and feel the familiar weight of wood and electronics hanging from my neck.

On one of the slim handles that run down the large effects unit I spot a little toy doll that's clinging to it with gripping hands. It's the furry, troll-like thing with smiling face that had once been thrown up on to the stage by a devoted young fan during the height of our success. Usually they were discarded, but on that night my guitar tech picked him up and clipped him there. He'd soon become our mascot, and a superstitious ritual developed of saying hello to 'Rackman' before every soundcheck. As I cross to my pedal board and stomp on the lit mute button, I smile – it seems that for the last two decades he's been cling-ing on for dear life, waiting for this moment to come.

The legacy of Disco Danny's decision to 'go black with it' meant that since the band's demise 'True' had enjoyed numerous interpretations through the music of American R&B acts. PM Dawn started it, and then came Teddy Riley, Queen Penn, Shades, Back Street Boys, Nelly, Black Eyed Peas, Lloyd and Lil Wayne, with Spandau's version being played almost four million times on American radio alone. International artists had pillaged the catalogue for riffs and melodies over the years, and even indie bands had started to cover some of our earlier material. Spandau songs found their way on to American movies too, including *16 Candles*, *Charlie's Angels*, *The Wedding Singer* and *50 First Dates*. TV shows like *Spin City*, *The Simpsons* and *Ugly Betty* had incorporated them, and of course, there were the many commercials that used Span-dau songs to sell their products, ranging from phones to knickers. One day, my son, Finlay, tuning the radio of a stolen car he was driving in the computer game *Grand Theft Auto*, found 'Gold' playing. Backstage at Wembley a couple of years ago, I asked the rap star Nelly why he'd used 'True' as the backing track for his latest single. He said it was one of his favourite songs growing up. A bunch of white kids from Islington getting played in the hood! *Da bomb*, as Mole would have said.

  For many years I tried to escape it, outrun the shadow of Spandau Ballet that loomed large wherever I went. I made solo records, films, plays, musicals, but any mention that I got in the press would always refer to me as *Spandau Ballet's Gary Kemp*. I was infuriated by it – I hadn't played in the group for years but it still seemed to be my full name. I was branded by what I'd done. It was impossible to escape. It didn't occur to me that I should feel pride in it, because to me the band's name brought back too many bad memories; memories of fight-ing, and especially memories of litigation.

And then in 2004 I was asked to remix the live film of the *Through The Barricades* show that had been shot at the NEC Arena in Birmingham during that heady Christmas of 1986. Sony, who owned the film, wanted to release a surround-sound mix and restore the images. I took on the project with Gary Langan and we set ourselves up at Metropolis Studios in Chiswick. There, on the large screen in front of me, were the five of us strutting our stuff upon the stage, and enjoying every minute of being in Spandau Ballet. But there was a sadness about it too. Smiling and laughing with each other, we were blind to the crisis that awaited us just up ahead.

What I was watching was not how I remembered it, though. The playing was louder, more dynamic, more full of ideas and energy. It didn't just make me want to get back onstage, it made me want to feel that power of sound around me once more; to make that noise that can lift an arena full of people; to embrace that camaraderie that we so obviously once had. It made me want to be in Spandau Ballet again.

I called my brother and begged him to come over and have a look at the film. I dimmed the lights and turned up the volume. He was equally surprised. I told him that I thought we'd be mad not to try and make it work again. We'd created something that most people could only dream about; why on earth had I been in denial for so long? Over the years I'd bumped into Roger Daltrey a few times and he'd always told me the same thing: 'Patch up your differences and get back onstage. Do you think me and Pete always get on? You've got the licence to do it – the name that you made.'

I was convinced that if Tony, Steve and John saw the film they would want the same thing I did. Martin was in contact with Steve, who now lived in Ibiza with his family. 'Get in touch with him, Martin. Find out if he'd let me go down and see him.'

It was more than just wanting to be back onstage with Spandau. Since the court case I'd had endless dreams about meeting Tony, Steve and John. In some of them they dismissed me, but in most we shook hands and re-formed our friendship. I needed closure. The idea of not being able to meet up and talk together about the most powerful experience of our lives was dreadful. None of my friends had any idea what that experience had been like. There was no one apart from my brother to remember it with.

Martin called Steve and he agreed to meet up, and with the DVD in my bag, I flew to Ibiza. Lauren came with me. After seven years of avoiding love I'd met this beautiful, intelligent woman and my defences had collapsed in days. I'd never felt more comfortable living with someone before, and within two years we were married and being blessed beneath a chuppah, surrounded by family and friends in a sunny garden in Gloucestershire. Now, as I dreamt of re-forming my past, she carried our future in her belly.

She dropped me at the top of a dusty lane with the promise that she'd collect me when I called. I could see Steve waiting for me, nervously pacing around in the restaurant's corralled outer area. He looked lean and tanned, but the tension in his face was obvious. Not knowing what was to come, I felt the same. I walked through and presumptuously hugged him. I could feel his shoulders flex. It was an awkward moment that I immediately regretted.

Sitting outside in the sun, he ordered in perfect Spanish and then expelled whatever he needed to at me. I stayed calm. I felt a different person to the one who'd slammed the phone down during our last conversation – not fearfully trying to control everything any more; I'd proved myself and failed at the same time; I was in a secure marriage with a beautiful son and a child on the way; everything now could only be a bonus. After a glass of wine Steve's face softened, and as we ate our fish and tortilla we begun to find some of the old jokes, and dream, like we'd done once before, about the two of us making a band.

The problem was Tony and John weren't having the same dream. We screened the finished film at a hotel in the West End. Dagger, Steve, Martin and I went along. It was the closest I'd ever been to sitting in a Spandau concert, but unfortunately, like most fans, I never got to meet Tony and John afterwards. I would have to wait another three years for that to happen.

At the end of 2007, Steve phoned me to say that he'd had a call from John. John had told him that there was a will to do it and wondered how we should go about moving things forward. It wouldn't be as simple as the five of us getting together and pressing go – there were now separate managements and people were only half peeking out of their emotional trenches. Steve gave me John's number, and after staring at it for a long time on my phone, I nervously made the call. It was odd how familiar his voice sounded. I felt a comfort in its tone, and I was immediately caught up in a nostalgia for the experiences we'd shared together. I suggested that we meet.

The Christmas drinkers were flirting hard at the bar of Soho House as I waited for him. Would our talk be uncomfortable? Would I have to deal with an emptying of baggage that he may have dragged with him all these years? He arrived wrapped for the cold and, to my relief, we immediately embraced. He seemed relaxed and ordered a beer and I took a red wine and we sat on a sofa together. He told me that we couldn't change the past but we *were* in control of our future. Better than that, he revealed that he and Tony had been talking more and more about trying to make Spandau work again. I could see how much it meant to him. It always did.

After a few glasses and some planning, we left and walked back up Greek Street. We passed the building where Le Beat Route had once been, a place where we'd made something good, and I felt the old excitement returning. I was healing my dream. There was only Tony to meet now.

As the following year began to move through its seasons, the politics of trying to re-form the band were proving more and more difficult. Just when I'd think there was a clear, unhindered vision, the view would rapidly became stormy again. On many occasions, John and I, like war-weary heralds, returned to Soho House and tried to solve the problems and resume talks. But my mind was becoming preoccupied with other things. Lauren was pregnant again, and my parents were becoming increasingly sick.

They loved living in Poole. They'd used the beaches and the cliffs to walk on, and the local club to socialise in, but Mum's health seemed to be declining and they were getting out less and less. Her body ached and she was constantly short of breath, and the poor woman was scared that in her mid-seventies she was turning into her own mother. They'd found the twin crises of my brother's brain tumours and my court case exhausting, but their love for us had kept us all strong throughout. Now the problems all seemed to be theirs. On top of my mother's debilitation, Dad had developed a mysterious knee problem. Initially the doctors couldn't find the answer to it, but it was eventually diagnosed as some sort of infection. And then one night he threw up blood into the sink. My mother collapsed with shock and somehow my father managed to call a neighbour, who called an ambulance. In hospital, they couldn't find any clear reason for it other than the possibility that he'd had a bad reaction to some antibiotics he was taking. But on leaving hospital he started to rapidly lose weight. They tested him but came up with little explanation as to why it was happening. This constantly mobile, hands-on kind of guy was now becoming increasingly chair-bound, and reduced to shopping on the internet.

Back in London, I was pressing for something – to meet Tony. He'd met with Martin and all seemed positive, but, understandably, he was wary of seeing me. I felt that the only way through was to make a personal connection rather than the second-party conversation we seemed to be having. And then, through John, I got the message – a lunchtime meeting at a pub in Highgate; all three of us.

I was grateful for John's support as he and I sat in the watery October sunshine that flooded the pub's forecourt and waited for the singer. I was scared – I wanted it to go well; I wanted us both to feel comfortable with the situation; I wanted closure.

And then he arrived. The sun was behind him and I felt small in the shadow of this big man. We shook hands and happily put off serious talk by ordering some lunch and discussing local parking problems. But at the table, Tony had a short statement that he wanted to make, something that felt rehearsed but that he needed to do. I listened, made a tidy reply in my own defence, and then watched as he raised his glass to mine and said, 'That's it.'

That's it. The war was over. All we had to do now was plan the peace.

But just before Christmas, the phone rang in the early hours. It was Dad – Mum had collapsed and couldn't breathe properly. They rushed her to hospital and Martin and I flew to her side. She'd had a heart attack. Her second, as it turned out.

In the hospital bed, she seemed healthier than she'd recently looked at home, struggling to do simple things. But inside she was broken. They said she could go home for Christmas but had to return in the new year to have a heart valve repaired and three arteries replaced.

To cheer her up I brought in my little boy, Milo, and with him some good news. 'Mum, the whole band met up for the first time the other day.'

'Oh, I am pleased. How was it?'

'Amazing. It couldn't have gone better. It's going to happen. Get yourself well, Mum; I want you to be in London next year to watch us play.'

'Please God. I want to hold that baby too when it comes.' I could tell what she was thinking.

'You will,' I said.

No one, though, was more excited than Dad. Not only had he run Martin's fan club for the last few years, he was the biggest fan of them all. It was giving our parents something to aim at.

Not being able to get out, they found Christmas hard – all toys and gifts bought through the Net or newspaper offers. They'd always felt so nervous about giving me anything – their arty son with his 'fussy' tastes – and I'd accept whatever it was with thanks and kisses, but was left feeling pompous and painfully aware of my high-minded opinion about the 'something for the house' they'd obviously hunted hard to find. This year it was towels and they were perfect. I still wrap myself warmly in them.

Things for the band were moving at a fast rate now, with offers of tours coming in, but with an announcement in the planning we were still no more than a talking shop, and all of us felt that we couldn't get up in front of the world's press without first proving ourselves musically again. But with my mother going into hospital for her operation, and my father waiting on knee surgery, Martin and I found it difficult to put a date to any rehearsals. The band had to bear with us for a while, at least until we'd seen our mother through.

On 6 January, Martin drove Mum from Poole to the Spire Hospital in Southampton where she would have the bypass operation the next day. She was scared. That night, as Mum prayed that she would survive the ordeal, we were told by her surgeons that she would probably need a long recovery and could be on a ventilator for up to four weeks. We had no choice.

But the following day, within a few hours of the operation, Mum was sitting up in bed and talking. I drove down to Southampton, stopping at a butcher's to pick up a chicken on the way, my plan being to stay with Dad that night and cook him a good meal. I met Martin and Dad by Mum's bedside. She looked frail but strong enough to chat fondly about the imminent birth of my new baby. Dad, sitting in the wheelchair Martin had found for him at reception, looked lost in the clothes that he was, disturbingly, shrinking in, but he was clearly happy that his dear wife had survived a difficult operation and was in much better shape than predicted. He was also relieved to have finally received a date for an operation on his infected knee.

Martin had to get back and said his goodbyes, then Dad lifted himself painfully out of the wheelchair and kissed his wife. 'Goodbye, sweetheart,' he said. 'See you tomorrow.' I'd never heard him call her sweetheart before and I realised how relieved he was that the two of them could finally see some end to their troubles. Nothing had diminished for these two lovers except their physicality. Here, still, were the same two souls that had once danced and fallen in love to Bill Haley and the Comets. Time had simply made everything a lot harder for them.

Dad and I drove back to Poole with him quizzing me about the band and telling me how successful he felt it could be. We attempted to make plans for how best my parents could get around their immediate difficulties and tried to focus positively on the forthcoming spring, when they would, hopefully, start to see some green shoots of health. But I was immensely stressed about the whole situation; trying to balance work with care for my family was an act that had left me with many sleepless nights and exhausting days.

I parked up in their little close, but even the short walk from the car to their house had my father leaning heavily on his NHS stick, flinching at every step. I couldn't wait to get my old dad back. Just six months earlier he'd driven down to London for Milo's fourth birthday, as healthy as I'd ever seen him, but now he seemed to be falling in on himself, subsiding rapidly into the physical clichés of age. I wanted to stop it; to straighten his back; to reset him into the man we'd been used to.

While I prepared the chicken and vegetables, he made calls to neighbours, friends and family, telling them how well Eileen was. I could hear his voice from the living room, chirpier and more relaxed than I'd heard it in months. I brought in the meal and we sat together on the sofa, eating and watching TV. He started to become distracted and picked at his dinner the best he could – food was always pounced upon by Dad, but recently he had to force himself to eat. He did his best with it and we laughed at a British comedy about a London couple living away from their city. And then he said something about his ear 'wooshing' and being worried about getting a cold. As he rubbed at it I noticed how loose and crinkled the mottled brown skin on his hand had become and I wanted to touch it, heal it somehow. I gave him a pat on the back instead and some positive thoughts about the future. But suddenly he was very cold and dragged himself up to fiddle with the thermostat in the hall. Coming back, Dad fell exhausted into a chair and I could tell the TV was of no interest to him. It was roasting in the room but he was still cold. Obviously concerned about the rushing blood in his ear, he got up again, saying he needed to use the toilet. I watched him struggle on his knee through the door, supporting himself with the door frame and stick as he went. My dad; my childhood hero; reduced to a stooping invalid. I hated seeing it.

I stared at the TV, not really watching what was on it, and then something occurred to me. I tried batting it away but it rapidly returned. Maybe it was because he seemed to be taking some time, but the thought that Dad had collapsed in the toilet appeared again in my head.

I went out into the hall. Oddly, he hadn't shut the toilet door fully and I could see his stick propped against the sink.

'Dad, are you OK?'

'Yeah, I'm all right. I'm just trying to clear my head.'

His voice sounded odd, spongy, almost without consonants. I felt a cold rush across my skin and a shortening of my breath. *Is it my imagination? For God's sake, stop worrying – it's Mum who's sick.* The whole day has clouded my mind with fear; but I remained hovering between the front room and the hall.

'Dad, you're worrying me. Are you all right in there? You're taking ages.'

'Yeah, leave me. I'm on the toilet.'

The same voice. What do I do? Shall I go in there? But my dad's on the loo, I can't do that. I waited a few moments and then called again.

'I'm all right, Gary boy,' he said.

Gary boy? It seemed an odd thing for him to call me, something he hadn't called me since I was a child.

'Dad?'

There was no reply.

'Dad?' I pushed open the door. He was slumped on the seat, trousers around his ankles, chin deep within his chest, arms hanging by his side like those of a discarded toy soldier. I tried to lift his heavy body. Behind his thick glasses his eyes were open but staring, while his mouth made occasional gasps for breath. *Oh my God, not now, Dad. Not now. Not with Mum how she is.* I pulled my mobile from my pocket and called 999. I couldn't remember my parents' postcode, and felt his life slipping away as the operator took me through the questions she needed answers to and then put me through to the correct department. After I had explained my situation again, with as much clarity as I could find, a woman's voice told me to get him down on to his back. With the mobile tucked between my shoulder and ear, I heaved him up and, twisting him in the narrow room, and brought him towards the floor. His head made a small thump as this fourteen-stone man slipped the last few inches to the ground. His eyes were staring upwards but I felt then that there was no way back. His body felt already gone, but God, was I going to fight to keep him in this world. I put my phone on speaker mode and laid it on the floor. She talked me through it all.

The indignity of those eleven minutes are what stay with me: fumbling inside his open mouth to retrieve the two plates of false teeth that had sunk backwards into his gasping throat; his – *my poor father!* –

his nakedness below his waist, exposed to me for the first time in my life; and the beating, beating, beating that I made upon his seventy-eight-year-old ribs, each push depressing his chest with such urgent violence that it would jolt his head up and down. And then, when she told me to, I placed my mouth over his. It felt prickly and hard but inside it was hollow, and my air blew into what felt like a cavernous, useless space. It wouldn't stay in there. I could hear it coming back out, rasping through his throat like an echo. The whole time my mother was on my mind. In her hospital bed, only just recovering from her own ordeal, she had no idea that the man who'd spent the last fifty-five years with her was going. 'Goodbye, sweetheart,' he'd said.

The paramedics were at the door and I leapt up to open it. Two men and a woman – she was in charge – came through like a storm. I was blown aside as they threw machines on to him and slammed a needle into his arm. He was a job to them, a night's work, but they were human beings and giving him all they had. Watching them from the doorway, I grabbed the phone and called Martin. As he answered, my father's body leapt under the electrical charge that they'd shoved through him.

'Martin. It's Dad. He's had a heart attack. It's bad. I think we've lost him.'

They'd put Dad's feet up on to the toilet seat. For some strange reason, his old beige socks that he'd put on that morning broke into my heart. I imagined him innocently putting them on, not knowing then that it was the last time he'd ever perform such an act. At that moment, they represented the whole lovely man that my father was, and his beautiful simplicity; they bizarrely focused my sadness and love for the person who was dying on the floor in front of me. I wanted to lie down and hug him, tell him how much he meant to me, but the three paramedics were still fighting to save him.

They managed to get his pulse going and were now starting to transfer him to the ambulance. 'You've kept him alive. Well done,' said the woman.

It was only right: his eldest son – he'd brought me into this world and I'd fought to keep him from leaving it. It was the correct order of things. Suddenly I felt a rekindling of hope as the siren cried above my head and we raced towards Poole General.

But in the hospital it wasn't long before they spoke to me in soft voices, their urgency gone. He'd lost too much oxygen to his brain and wasn't going to regain consciousness. They were going to put him in a room and 'make him comfortable', and he would gradually slip away.

I sat alone in a little room with some hard chairs and a discarded gossip mag and thought about my mother in hospital sixty miles away. Why hadn't I gone into the toilet sooner, when I'd first heard him speak in that strange voice? What was I thinking? Now nothing was in my control. I'd given in to the world that was buffeting against me, allowing it to drag me along at some great speed. As much as I wanted to see Lauren, I told her not to come until the next day, it being too far for her to drive in her condition. I just wanted my brother to get here fast. The whole thing was too horrific and I needed Martin desperately. There had been two of us when the evening started; now I was alone.

When Martin arrived I broke the news to him. I played the big brother and held him to me, but I was only just keeping my head above it all myself. We sat with Dad in a narrow room of muted light and waited. His shoulders were visible above the sheet and I could see they'd dressed him in a gown that had 'Hospital Property' coldly stamped all over it. His noises and shivers, gasps and flinches, were not those of my father, and, with all the love that I had for him, I wanted him to die. I prayed that Dad, as I knew him, had already left his body, and that he wasn't in there somewhere, trapped, with the terrible knowledge of what was happening.

When, eventually, we went back to the house, the evidence of what had happened a few hours earlier was spread out on the hall floor: an empty phial, the frantically ripped-open medical packaging, and among it all, my father's glasses. Tidying away, I came across his false teeth lying in a corner of the toilet; once familiar within his smiling face, now just the jetsam of a man's collapse.

The tears I cried that night were not for Dad, nor for me, but for Mum. Tomorrow I would bring horror to her. I had to take her surgeon's advice, but she would have to know. And God knows what that would do.

There is a painting by Picasso called *Weeping Woman*. The subject's face is crumpled with grief; her tears become her handkerchief become her fingers become her broken heart. But what makes the picture so unbearably sad is the little red bonnet on her head. That morning, she'd put the gay little thing on, with its pretty blue flower, hoping to brighten herself, not knowing the tragedy her day had in store. That's what makes the painting so devastatingly powerful. I've always thought the woman, with her narrow face, looked a little like my mother. That morning Mum's nurse had washed her; Mum had wiped a little lipstick around her mouth, brushed her grey hair, and waited in a bedside chair for her darling Frank to make his journey in. Instead, it was her two boys with their wives, and an arrow of news that would pierce her poor heart.

The second or third thing my mother said through her tears after she'd heard what had happened was this: 'And he was so looking forward to Spandau Ballet.' Under the circumstances, it sounds pathetic, trivial, but she knew what excited my dad most of all about the coming year. She rocked her head backwards and forwards, her paper-thin lids shutting out the light of the day, the day that had brought such horrors, and blamed herself for praying for her own survival, as though there had been some kind of heavenly exchange. Pipes rudely entered her skin where I stroked her arm, whispering as many caring words to her as I could. And then she said, 'There's no regrets. We have a beautiful family. My two boys have lovely wives. No regrets.' And she hugged us all individually, finally putting a cupped hand on Lauren's bump – her future grandchild, almost born. What did she mean? It felt oddly like a goodbye. An acceptance that her work on the earth was done. And then she returned to her mantra: 'My Frank. My Frank.'

My mother never survived the news. Four days after Dad died Martin and I were in another little room being told by a doctor that the more they were chasing after her the faster she was running away. Her breathing had deteriorated over the four days, not helped by the fact that she wouldn't do her physiotherapy. At night, lost in grief, she endlessly spoke his name. Only hospital had ever separated them. And now death.

Two days before she died, my cousin, Vivian, who'd shared that house on Rotherfield Street with us and her two sons, came to see her and gave Mum some news. Her own mother, Mum's elder sister Lil, was in a home and had been visited by a friend. Lil had no idea that her sister was even in hospital, nor what had happened to my father, but as the woman sat with her, Lil suddenly spoke.

'Innit a shame?'

'What, Lil?'

'About Frank. He died, y'know.'

What Lil's friend didn't know was that my dad had died an hour earlier. No one had even told Lil that he'd had a heart attack.

The story gave my mother great comfort. 'Ah,' she said, her tired features suddenly relaxing, 'he went to visit her,' and she sunk back into her armchair. Mum knew that her husband was only her death away, and she hurried to find him as soon as she could.

When my father died, I stood in his garage, looked up at his work tools, his model planes, the doll's-house replica of his own house that he'd made for Martin's daughter – which included a little TV with a picture of himself on it – and I sobbed great gusts of grief. But with Mum going, there were surprisingly few tears. Instead, a strange sense of elation lifted me, as though I were floating above all the horror. I never wanted my mother to die, but for them to go together was exactly what they would have wanted; they would have signed a contract for that to happen; there was something innately right about it. I drove back from Southampton that night and it felt as though my car was motionless and it was, in fact, the road racing into me. I wanted to get home and fall into the arms of my wife. It was a terrible, terrible tragedy, but – as I told myself over and over again on that dark road – it was also, for them, a beautiful love story. I just wished its denouement had been later.

At their joint funeral in Poole, the old cockneys gathered – my Uncle Percy, now eighty, being the last left to tell the story of my father's childhood, while my mother's sister Lil was too frail to even be told of Eileen's death. By the side of my parents' two coffins I stood and described them as being true working-class heroes; their generation was. As children they'd suffered the trauma of evacuation and the bombing of London, and as young adults they'd faced times of great austerity. It had given Frank and Eileen an even greater incentive to create a secure, loving home for themselves and their two boys.

My son, Finlay, finished the readings with a passage from an account my father had written about his childhood during the war. It told of the moment when he was evacuated with his brother, and ended with these words:

> When we arrived at the entrance to the station, all the parents waved and called out their goodbyes, and we all walked through the doors onto the platform where a train was waiting for us, steam gushing from the side of the engine, smelling like a load of damp washing. The two men inside the engine were shovelling coal into its belly. It was like a monster, and it was getting ready to take us into history.

And then, as we said our final farewells, we played through the small PA system of the crematorium the song they would have wanted; a love song – 'True'.

Two weeks later, I watched my new son being pulled from my wife's body. It felt like a recycling of life. My parents were in him; their coming together had helped to create him; their gift to me was still coming. We named him Kit Frank Kemp.

The guitar growls and spits in my hands, desperate to be played, straining to be unleashed. There has been birth, death, and now resurrection, all within a month, and I'm suddenly doing this for more reasons than personal satisfaction – I'm doing this for Mum and Dad. Just after they'd died, Tony told me that the news of their death had made him want to do Spandau even more. I never asked him why, I was too moved by what he'd said.

Behind me in the rehearsal room, Steve is warming up his saxophone; to my right John is settling inside his kit; at the other side of the stage Martin adjusts his bass guitar; and at the front of us all stands the formidable presence of Tony. I've been here before; a long time ago; schoolboys with grand ideas.

'What do you wanna do?' It was John, sticks spinning in hand.

'I dunno,' I said. '"I'll Fly For You"?'

A steady pace for the first foray.

'All right,' said the drummer. 'Ready?'

Of course I was ready. I'd waited long enough.

ACKNOWLEDGEMENTS

I would like to thank my literary agent, Simon Benham, who gave me the confidence to begin; all at 4th Estate who've shown such enthusiasm towards this new boy, especially my editor, John Elliott; also Steve Dagger, Brian Carr, and most of all I'd like to thank my wife, Lauren, who gave me enormous support during the consuming process of writing this book.

In memory of Frank and Eileen Kemp – 1930/32–2009

Where are the West Side Boys
fighting on the scaffold of love.

Facts are an awful
A shadow of a doubt

Heaven is a secret
It's a passion
It's a long way over
far from her arm

She'll sing a 'Wes
You could be it

Here in her
Maybe it's the

Script
Book
Film
Image
Key
Code

MEMBERSHIP
BLITZ
NAME
RESIDENCE
SIGNATURE

KEY - E   Chart No 1

Guitar riff solo + Bass | Drums, bass, congas qui

Talking over feel 8 bars

I feel the graze against my skin | Feel

I feel the

I know this feeling is a lie, I know

harmony
There's a quiet within my mind

I know this feeling is
Oh, I should question not ignore, I ou

4 bars | I don't need this pres

17/8 CHORUS 8 BARS

19 4 BAR FEEL

20/21 8 BAR BRIDGE (G F B

32 BAR FEEL (BASS DRO

26 4 BAR BRIDGE (G F B

27/8 8 BAR BRIDGE 2

29/30 16 BAR CHORUS

22 23 26 25
8 8 8 8

It's my instinction, Oh

31 32 33 34 35
8 8 8 8 8